INVENTING BLACK WOMEN

INVENTING BLACK WOMEN

African American Women Poets and Self-Representation, 1877–2000

Ajuan Maria Mance

The University of Tennessee Press / Knoxville

Copyright © 2007 by The University of Tennessee Press / Knoxville.
All Rights Reserved. Manufactured in the United States of America.
First Edition.

This book is printed on acid-free paper.

Library of Congress Cataloging-in-Publication Data

Mance, Ajuan Maria.
Inventing black women : African American women poets and self-representation,
1877–2000 / Ajuan Maria Mance. — 1st ed.
     p. cm.
Includes bibliographical references and index.
ISBN-13: 978-1-57233-492-2 (hardcover : alk. paper)
ISBN-10: 1-57233-492-4 (alk. paper)
1. American poetry—African American authors—History and criticism. 2. Women
and literature—United States—History—19th century. 3. Women and literature—
United States—History—20th century. 4. African American women—Intellectual
life—19th century. 5. African American women—Intellectual life—20th century.
6. American poetry—Women authors—History and criticism. 7. African American
women in literature. 8. African Americans in literature. 9. Race relations in literature.
10. Gender identity in literature. I. Title.

PS310.N4M36 2007
811'.509896073—dc22   2006035355

For my parents,

Kathleen and Alphonso Mance Sr.,

my first and greatest teachers

CONTENTS

ACKNOWLEDGMENTS

I gratefully acknowledge those who supported and advised me throughout the creation of this book. I would like to thank the staffs of the Harlan Hatcher Graduate Library at the University of Michigan, the Schomburg Center for Research in Black Culture in Harlem, and the Bancroft Library at the University of California, Berkeley. Special thanks to Marilyn Kallett, Virginia C. Fowler, and Vanessa Dickerson for their extensive critical reading and astute commentary. For their support of my research and their faith in my work, I owe a debt of gratitude to Patricia Yaeger, Kerry Larson, Michael Awkward, Stephen Sumida, Rei Terada, and Rebecca Zurier. Many thanks to Michele T. Berger, Michael Bennett, Juan Battle, Michelle Wright, Virginia Chang, and Ainissa Ramirez for their intellectual support, friendship, and encouragement throughout the writing of this book. To my brother, Alphonso C. Mance Jr. and my sister-in-law, Kristin Schutjer Mance, heartfelt appreciation for their constant support and for their insightful criticism. My deepest gratitude to my partner, Cassandra Falby, for her patience, inspiration, and encouragement throughout my journey from inception to completion.

I also wish to thank various rights holders for permission to reprint selections from copyrighted material:

INTRODUCTION

INVISIBLE BODIES, INVISIBLE WORK
NINETEENTH-CENTURY AMERICAN WOMANHOOD
AND THE PASTORAL OF THE AMERICAN HOMESCAPE

[Our husbands'] hearts will be at home, where their treasure
is; and they will rejoice to return to its sanctuary of rest, there
to refresh their wearied spirits, and renew their strength for
the toils and conflicts of life.

MRS. A. J. GRAVES
Woman in America

It must be borne in mind that not many ladies in this country
are permitted sufficient leisure from the cares and duties of
home to devote themselves, either from choice, or as a means
of living, to literary pursuits. Hence, the themes which have
suggested the greater part of the following poems have been
derived from the incidents and associations of every-day life.

CAROLINE MAY
Preface to *The American Female Poets*

What Soft—Cherubic Creatures—
These Gentlewomen are—
One would as soon assault a Plush
Or violate a Star—

Such Dimity Convictions—
A Horror so refined
Of freckled Human Nature—
Of Deity—ashamed—

EMILY DICKINSON
401, *Poems*

The mid-nineteenth century marked a crucial shift in the popular understanding of woman's role in American society. The rise of industrialization and a suburban middle class enhanced and exaggerated the separation between male and female labor and space and ushered in a system of widely accepted boundaries and expectations for women's behavior. Above and beyond biological sex, the label "woman" indicated a specific discursive position. Mid-nineteenth-century Americans believed that their society was divided into two distinct, gendered realms of interest and influence, discursive spaces for which the physical spaces associated with men's and women's societal functions served as a metaphor. For women, that space was the home; the adult female subject was considered a "proper" woman if she was able to confine both her movements and her interests to the space of the single-family home and its immediate surroundings. In *Doing Literary Business: American Women Writers in the Nineteenth Century* Susan Coultrap-McQuin echoes the current scholarly consensus that the isolation of woman within the middle-class family dwelling evolved as a side effect of early- to mid-nineteenth-century industrialization:[1]

> As America industrialized, adult activities were more frequently segregated by sex than they had been in earlier times. The separation between home and business meant that the control of economic resources shifted from the home to employed males in the marketplace, leaving women and children in the middle-class or affluent home, who did not have income-producing jobs, in a more subordinate and dependent position. (Coultrap-McQuin 9)

Barbara Welter, in her article of the same name, originated the term "The Cult of True Womanhood" to describe the mid-nineteenth-century preoccupation with the ideal of woman in her home. True Women were distinguished by their sweet acquiescence, pious humility, and moral virtue. These qualities were widely perceived as inherent to woman's nature, and the popular media of the period presented them simultaneously as evidence of women's predisposition toward domesticity and as an ideal to which all adult females should aspire. Further, the new American middle class embraced the ideal of the True Woman isolated within her home as a marker of financial achievement. Middle-class families highlighted their prosperity by means of the sharp contrast between working-class and poor women who labored outside the home and the middle-class True Woman isolated therein.[2] In *Home and Work: Housework, Wages, and the Ideology of Labor in the Early Republic,* Jeanne Boydston writes that

> members of the new middle class . . . confidently celebrated what they supposed to be the complete and successful withdrawal of wives and daughters to "that paradise . . . that bright and central orb," the middle-class home, where neither "strife" nor "selfishness" could enter. (Boydston 99)

Thus, even as True Woman's confinement within the space of the home placed strict limitations on the activities of the woman who aspired to that ideal, it also outlined for her a very specific role in maintaining the family's middle-class lifestyle. For the adult female within the single-family home, to adopt the behavior of the True Woman was to take on the appearance of middle-class prosperity.

Even more compelling, however, than the covert equation of True Womanhood with middle-class status was the overt presentation of True Womanhood as "normal" womanhood.[3] For all women, failure to conform to either the qualities (sweetness, submissiveness, piety, and humility) or the requirements (withdrawal of the female subject from all aspects of the public sphere into the space of the remote, single-family dwelling) of True Womanhood was perceived as rebellion against woman's fundamental nature;[4] such behavior was considered unnatural at the very least, deviant and abnormal at worst.[5] Consequently, African American and poor white (mostly immigrant) women's labor outside the home[6] and/or their occupation of tenement, multifamily, or extended-family dwellings was cast in the popular imagination as evidence of their innate inability to conduct themselves appropriately, as True Women.

In *Reconstructing Womanhood: The Emergence of the Afro-American Woman Novelist,* Hazel Carby investigates one aspect of Black women writers' response to the broad, mainstream acceptance of the True Womanhood ideal and its marginalization of African American women's experiences as abnormal or "unwomanly." Carby argues that nineteenth-century African American women novelists responded to mainstream conceptions of gender which "excluded them from the definition 'woman'" by constructing an "alternative discourse of black womanhood" that acknowledged and engaged with the interactions of race, gender, and class (Carby, *Reconstructing* 6–7). Carby focuses on Black women novelists' and their response to the specific ways in which ideal womanhood was represented in the sentimental prose of the period. However, nineteenth-century popular poets also played a significant role in disseminating the ideal of True Womanhood. And just as nineteenth-century Black women novelists wrote against those notions of womanhood that marginalized their experience, African American women poets of the period used their writings to challenge the hegemonic understanding of woman as a white, middle-class identity category.

In *The Wicked Sisters: Women Poets, Literary History, and Discord,* Betsy Erkkila suggests that American women poets have resisted hegemonic constructions of womanhood by using their poems to position themselves "at odds with and wickedly in excess of their identity as Woman" (Erkkila 4). She begins by suggesting Emily Dickinson's origination during the mid- to late nineteenth century of what amounts to a poetics of "wicked excess" in which she uses sarcasm and other techniques to call attention to her willful existence outside of the identity category of woman as conceived in the popular literature of the period: "In her poems [Dickinson] consistently mocked the 'Dimity Convictions' of the angel of the house" (Erkkila 58). I am interested in investigating the possibility of a distinct Black women's poetics of wicked excess, rooted in African American women poets' exposure of True Womanhood as a sociopolitically constructed identity category. I also wish to trace the means by which Black women poets writing since emancipation have used representations of the Black female subject's own willful occupation of and signification from spaces outside of those associated with True Womanhood to challenge and disrupt the hegemony of that mythic ideal.[7] To fully comprehend the courage and emancipatory deviance of these Black women poets' counterrepresentations of womanhood, however, we must first understand the dominant tradition against which they wrote. This introduction explores some of the specific themes, images, and techniques that white women poets of the nineteenth century used to perpetuate and disseminate the ideal of True Womanhood. When, during the earliest decades of the postbellum period, Black women poets began to write against this ideal, they would intertwine their appropriation of white women poets' forms and techniques with their inversion of the most common popular images of the Euro-American middle-class family home in order to make space for the recognition of a woman's subjectivity that is not white.

In the United States, poetry and other forms of literature have reinforced ideals of both male and female behavior through the conventions of the pastoral mode.[8] In its original, classical incarnation, pastoralism depicts the innocent—the shepherd boy—whose contentment and whose complacent, single-minded pursuit of his labors combine to represent a nostalgic look backward to the origins of those qualities considered best in classical man. In the pastoral, the setting in which the idealized subject is depicted is as important as the subject itself. The shepherd boy of the earliest pastoral writings is most often depicted in an Arcadian setting, if not in Arcadia itself. At the center of the pastoral in classical Greek literature is the understanding that the shepherd boy cannot flourish outside of the idealized setting in which he is depicted. Thus the relationship between physical setting and identity is established; the physical setting—the landscape—facilitates the development of the shepherd's persona. The pastoral of the classical world codified and then institutionalized the shepherd boy in the Arcadian landscape as that ideal persona—that figure whose qualities represented a paradigm of classical male existence—around which the collective identity of the classical male was constructed.

Just as the pastoral tradition in classical Greek literature offers up a vision of the archetypal Greek citizen, the American pastoral establishes an archetypal

U.S. citizen through the depiction of an imaginary person in an idealized setting whose attributes foster the development by that figure of a set of desirable qualities which are, in turn, normalized as paradigmatically "American." The earliest proliferation of pastoral writing in the United States occurred between about 1775 and 1840, during which time Americans struggled with the notion of an identifiable and communicable Americanness, even as they struggled to win recognition as an independent nation. Many writers of the period believed both in the American landscape as Arcadia apparent—in the Columbian landscape as vital, aesthetically unparalleled, and infinitely plentiful—and in the American colonist as ordained to partake in the agricultural plenty and physical beauty of that setting.[9] This perceived relationship between the landscape of the early republic and the personal attributes of the colonists who dwelled therein gave rise to the American pastoral through which writers and artists communicated a new and unifying ideal—a unifying myth—of Americanness. When Thomas Jefferson observes, "Those who labor in the earth are the chosen people of God, if ever He has a chosen people, whose breasts He has made his peculiar deposit for substantial and genuine virtue" (Jefferson 14), he is not merely registering his approval of the agrarian lifestyle. Rather, this passage represents Jefferson's clearest expression of the relationship between the idealization of the North American landscape and the emergence of a new ideal of personhood, as he articulates his profound faith both in the North American landscape as provider and in the newly sovereign American citizen uniquely suited to the task of extracting the abundance of those lands.[10] Jefferson's designation of the agrarian as embodiment of the American spirit exemplifies the means by which *Notes on the State of Virginia* and other canonical texts[11] written in the pastoral tradition participate in the construction of a myth of the American as the rugged, agrarian individualist by describing the setting in which that figure is located.

Lawrence Buell conceives of the American pastoral tradition as "a recurring fascination with physical nature as subject, symbol, and *theater* in which to act out rituals of maturity and purification" (Buell 430, emphasis added). I emphasize the word "theater" because it connotes the space in which a person performs a role. If the defining space in constructing a unifying ideal of European American masculinity is the agrarian landscape,[12] then the single-family dwelling is the defining space in constructing the ideal of True Womanhood. In popular poetry of the nineteenth century the woman writer perpetuates dominant contemporary constructions of normal womanhood by describing woman's setting—the middle-class, single-family home and its immediate surroundings. Consequently this poetry constitutes a distinctly female, pastoral subtradition, the *pastoral of the American homescape.* In the pastoral of the American homescape the woman poet's representation of True Womanhood is rooted in her understanding of the two relationships that exist at the center of that space. The first is the relationship between woman and home. The second is the relationship of home to other institutions, especially the institution of work.

The pastoral of the American homescape revolves around the figure of the True Woman. In "The Cult of True Womanhood: 1820–1860" Barbara Welter contends that "Woman, in the cult of True Womanhood presented by the women's magazines, gift annuals and religious literature of the nineteenth century, was the hostage in the home" (Welter 151). Welter suggests that woman and home are wholly distinct from one another, so that woman and home signify as discrete entities, the relationship between the two being that the home alienates woman from public life and labor. However, Welter's contention that women are in conflict with their everyday setting draws too heavily upon the late-twentieth-century emancipation of the subject from its locus of signification, the setting in which the subject becomes visible.[13] Those who conceive of signification in this way tend to perceive an adversarial relationship between the subject and the space from which it signifies (locus of signification, or setting), rather than a reciprocal relationship in which those ordering institutions among which the subject locates itself are, in turn, enabled to signify (given or endowed with meaning) by their orientation relative to the subject.

Welter's representation of the relationship between woman and domestic space echoes the relationship between home and woman advanced during American feminism's "second wave."[14] Writing from within that early feminist discourse, Welter perceives a tension between home and woman that corresponds to first-wave conceptions of woman as inhibited from "authentic," emancipated signification by her confinement within the single-family dwelling, the space in which she most often appears. She argues that woman's confinement within the domestic sphere prohibited nineteenth-century readers from perceiving the female subject herself; the real woman and her experiences within the private sphere were rendered invisible by her isolation in the home, with only the image of the mythic True Woman remaining as visible evidence of the nature of womanhood. However, in setting up this antagonistic relationship between woman and home, Welter overlooks the reciprocal relationship between the signifying subject and its setting.[15] She fails to take into account that the figure of the True Woman and the space of the pastoral home each determine the way that the other becomes visible.

Instead of the division between the signification of woman and home that Welter suggests, popular poetry of the mid-nineteenth century indicates that woman and her sphere were considered different aspects of the same subject. Thus the vision of womanhood constructed and disseminated through women poets of the pastoral of the American homescape is not of woman confined by or "hostage" within the home but of woman inextricable from home and from domesticity itself. Woman becomes the embodiment of home, so that she is not merely within the home but of the home. The True Woman, as she appears in poems depicting the pastoral homescape, is sustained by the domestic sphere; the homescape, as that space to which she is uniquely suited, becomes that space in which she flourishes. At the same time, the American home is maintained and sustained by woman; the home and its surroundings flourish under her care. Woman and home become reflections of each other, their relationship analogous to that which exists between mind and body. Womanhood is thus characterized by the total absorption of the female figure into the structure and function of the home.

In the pastoral of the American homescape, the representation of this absorption is characterized by woman's physical absence from most poems depicting this setting. The physical absence of woman from representations of domestic life does not, however, preclude her thematic presence. Her physical absence from midcentury women poets' representations of domestic life is, in fact, the most common response to the somewhat paradoxical task set out for such writers, that they present, to the reading public, images of the ideal, True Woman figure who, by definition, shrinks away from any public activity or accolade. In *Dickinson and the Strategies of Reticence: The Woman Writer in Nineteenth-Century America*, Joanne Dobson writes:

> For women's writing the significance of the decorum of "invisibility," which amounted to the barring of female subjectivity from the public sphere, was profound; it resulted in a conspiracy of literary discourse that pitted the "feminine"—or the societal definition of womanhood—against the "female"—or the personal experience of womanhood—in such a way that the latter was all but eliminated from women's text. (Dobson 56–57)

In fact, only through the suppression of women's personal, physical experiences does the True Woman become visible. The appointment and care of the home, its surroundings, and residents confirm that there is certainly a True Woman inside. That she will not let herself be seen demonstrates her refinement and modesty, in accordance with nineteenth-century notions of womanly comportment.

While the white female reader of *Godey's Magazine, The Ladies' Repository* or any of the other popular magazines of the period may never have encountered a detailed physical description of the woman of the house that captured the shape of her body, the curve of her neck, the curl of her lip, or the texture of her hair, and while she rarely encountered woman at the task of maintaining her home, she was often privy to the color of an infant's eyes, the surroundings and appointment of a cottage, and the warmth of the hearth. In the pastoral of the American homescape, these and other aspects of the home and household represent the qualities and characteristics of the adult female subject inside, indicating by their health, warmth, and virtue her achievement of True Womanhood, and by their depravity, illness, or death, her inadequacy. In "The Cult of True Womanhood," Barbara Welter identifies the four qualities of "purity, piety, submissiveness, and domesticity" as those "cardinal virtues" most commonly associated with the True Woman figure. It follows, then, that in the pastoral of the American homescape, those qualities most frequently displayed by the features and surroundings of woman's home correspond with one or more of these virtues. If woman is pious, so too is the space of the home itself; it appears as holy space because True Woman cannot appear as holy person. If she is pure, so too is the infant child; the child exhibits the virtue because True Woman cannot.

In "My Own Fireside" by Alice B. Neal the speaker makes no explicit reference to the True Woman within the home, but her presence is apparent in the comfort of home and hearth. The hearth takes on the role of the True Woman, providing welcome and comfort, and even lulling the speaker to rest with its song:

> The fireside sendeth us greeting—
> Why linger to glance down the street?
> The glow and the warmth both invite us
> To lounge in our favorite seat.
> How cheerily sounds its low humming.
> How ruddily flashes the flame.
> Ah! who could resist such soft pleading?
> So gently it urgeth its claim. (9–16)

Similarly, in "The Deserted Homestead" by Marguerite St. Leon Loud the absence of woman from the home that the poet describes is reflected in the chill of the hearth and the general deterioration of the home:

> There is a lonely homestead
> . . . .
> Its walls are grey and bare.
> . . . .
> Where once glad voices sounded
> Of children in their mirth,
> No whisper breaks the solitude
> By that deserted hearth.
> . . . .
> And through the broken casement-panes
> The moon at midnight shines. (1, 3, 9–12, 44–45)

In the pastoral of the American homescape, the home's immediate surroundings also function as proxy for the True Woman within. Cultivated nature—gardens, domesticated animals, ornamental trees and shrubs—indicates the presence of a functioning True Woman within the home. Wild and unruly nature, or uncultivated nature—such as a garden overgrown with weeds or a lawn gone to seed—indicates the dissolution of the family, either through the death of the True Woman of the house or through her abandonment by one or more members of the household. Loud describes the immediate surroundings of "The Deserted Homestead":

> There are many mansions round it,
> In the sunlight gleaming fair;
> But moss-grown is that ancient roof.
> . . . .
> No hand above the window
> Ties up the trailing vines. (5-7, 33–34)

Here, as in Neal's "My Own Fireside," home signifies in the same way as the woman within, serving in the same capacity as woman, exhibiting qualities correspondent to the cardinal virtues of True Womanhood, having the same relationship to manhood as does womanhood, and existing at the same proximity to or distance from the worldly sphere of men's labor and camaraderie, or, in woman's absence, reflecting the removal from the homescape of the primary agent of household maintenance and care.

At what proximity to or distance from the worldly sphere of male labor and camaraderie is True Womanhood located? And what relationship to manhood do homespace and womanhood share? Jeanne Boydston argues that the idea of separate gender-based spheres of activity is derived from the perceived relationship of each gender's activities to the predominating definition of labor during the nineteenth century:

> The language of the ideology of spheres was the language of gender, but its essential dualism was less precisely the opposition of "female" and "male" than it was the opposition of "home" and "work," an opposition founded upon the gendering concept of labor. (Boydston 159)

Nineteenth-century American notions of the distinction between public workspace and private homespace are based upon the activities of the adult male members of the household within each sphere. Because the private sphere is that sphere in which male labor does not take place, no activity undertaken within that sphere may signify as work. It follows that none of the activities associated with womanhood, including acts of service undertaken in the maintenance of home and family, are recognized as actual labor.[16] Thus the relationship between man and woman, as understood and advanced in popular women's poetry of the nineteenth century, becomes the relationship between he who does labor and she who does *not-labor.*

Yet, in popular women's poetry of the nineteenth century, all facets of the domestic sphere, including male members of the household, function as proxies for woman. In fact, aside from the home edifice itself, those elements of the woman's domestic sphere that appear most frequently as signs of womanhood are the intrafamilial relationships of mother to child (most often the male infant or boy) and husband to wife. While the husband depicted within woman's sphere in relation to his wife and family is still male, he is *not* a man. When the adult male subject appears within the domestic sphere, depicted in relation to woman or any of the elements of woman's domestic sphere (including the home itself), he is absorbed into that setting; he takes on the qualities of True Womanhood. In Edith's "The Homeward Bound," the figure of the adult male within the home (the father) appears simply as another of the domestic features that enhance the sweetness and beauty of the pastoral homescape:

> . . . the sailor-boy aloft
>> A bright and golden web of fancy weaves,
> Sees o'er the rolling billows his loved cot,
>> Hears the low rustling of the forest leaves,
> The bird's blithe song amid the summer bowers,
>> And drinks the perfume of his garden flowers.
>
> See once again the dear and household band,
>> A father's smile, a mother's blissful tears;
> And in the breeze that wafts him joyful on,
>> The sweet glad voices of his home he hears. (13–24)

In Lydia H. Sigourney's "Evening at Home: Written in Early Youth," the actions of the adult male within the home correspond with the virtues of True Womanhood. His indulgent smile recalls woman's sweetness, and his affection for "the tuneful hymn" corresponds to woman's piety ("hymn") and sweetness ("tuneful"):

> Close by my side my tender mother sits
> . . . .
>> while he, the sire,
> The faithful guide, indulgently doth smile
> At our discourse, or wake the tuneful hymn
> Which best he loves. (15, 17–20)

The children who appear in poems depicting the pastoral homescape take on not only the personality traits but also the physical characteristics of the

True Woman figure. This is particularly intriguing in light of the fact that within the subgrouping of poems that depict the relationship between woman and her infant child, the women poets focus almost exclusively upon describing the interaction between mothers and their sons. In *Sexes and Genealogies* Luce Irigaray offers a possible explanation for this representational bias:

> If we are not to be accomplices in the murder of the mother we also need to assert that there is a genealogy of women. Each of us has a female family tree: we have a mother, a maternal grandmother and great-grandmothers, we have daughters. Because we have been exiled into the house of our husbands, it is easy to forget the special quality of the female genealogy; we might even come to deny it. (Irigaray 11)

The True Woman embodies the notion of women's exile "into the house of our husbands" (Irigaray 11), a condition which Irigaray argues will eventually result in woman's denial of the female genealogy, the relationship between the female child and her mother(s). In the pastoral of the American homescape this erasure of woman's female lineage is manifest in the virtual erasure of the relationship between the True Woman and her infant daughters. Within this subcategory of pastoral representations of the home, a subgrouping which emphasizes the isolation of both woman and her children in and around the pastoral home (what Irigaray calls "house of our husbands"), infancy is equivalent to boyhood; there are relatively few exceptions.

In such poems the infant boy is presented in the context of his relationship to a loving mother. In these pastoral representations of the relationship between mother and her infant son, the mother—the True Woman within the home—is cast as speaker of the poem, and she interacts with the infant child through her descriptions and/or recollections of the child. However, even as the mother actively mediates her readers' experience of the relationships that exist within the home (the woman poet situates the mother-speaker as the "I" figure in the poem), she herself remains conspicuously absent from or passive within both the homespace she describes and the intrafamilial relationships which exist therein. The mother's conspicuous absence as physical presence, in stark contrast with the child, who is usually described in lavish and loving detail, seems to locate the infant child at the center the home, a physical and discursive position usually associated with the True Woman/mother. At the same time, however, the mother projects onto the child the physical and behavioral characteristics identified with True Woman-hood. Thus, while the female speaker humbly displaces herself from view within the pastoral home, her qualities (as True Womanly virtues) remain at its center.

Poems that use the infant child to depict the physical beauty and grace of True Woman combine images of female beauty with common symbols and themes of the pastoral home. In Jessie Atherton's "A Mother's Influence" the infant male manifests the physical qualities of the invisible woman. The True Woman in the house is scarcely visible; we are permitted only brief glimpses of "a mother's knee" (1) and "[a] mother's tender smile" (5). Instead, her physical, spiritual, emotional, and behavioral qualities are projected onto the boy child within the home setting. And it is in the poet's detailed redaction of these features—of the sweetness and love which characterize the mother's interactions with her child and of the feminized beauty and grace of the infant boy—that the True Woman herself is revealed:

> There stood beside a mother's knee
> A child of beauty rare;
> With fair and rosy cheek half hid
> In curling chestnut hair.
>
> A mother's tender smile fell on
> That sweet and loving face—
> Each lineament so strongly marked
> With beauty and with grace. (1–8)

Many poems use images of the infant child in privileged communion with God to highlight the relationship between childhood innocence and the womanly virtue of piety. Ann E. Porter's "The First Born" highlights the child's privileged relationship to God and Heaven. Despite his recent birth into earthly existence, the "first born" infant continues to enjoy access to heavenly care:

> One tiny foot from 'neath the mantle's folds
> Had strayed, all stainless from the dust of earth.
> I hushed the song that hung upon my lips,
> For voice like mine brought not such blest repose
> But music, such as cherubs chant in Heaven,
> Had lulled the slumberer in the arms of peace. (5–10)

Here the unearthly purity of the infant, "[a]ll stainless from the dust of earth" (2), corresponds with the unearthly care that he enjoys ("... music, such as cherubs chant in Heaven, / Had lulled the slumberer in the arms of peace" [9–10]).

In "Lines on an Infant Sleeping," R.H. describes the bubble of heavenly peace and light which surrounds the sleeping child:

> ... innocence displays
> Its calm of holy feeling.
> Oh! lovely, hallowed sight
> ....
> A heaven doth round thee shine (8–10, 14)

Similarly, in "To My Sleeping Babe" poet Sarah A. Weakley depicts the infant child in privileged communion with the Kingdom of Heaven, a relationship that is evident in the halo of heavenly light and peace that surrounds him:

> Thy life thus far is free from sin;
> With heaven and holy peace within:
> Angelic innocence is thine—
> Seraphic joys around thee shine. (17–20)

Just as the midcentury women poets' vivid descriptions of infant grace and beauty both preserve and underscore the humility of the True Woman/mother who modestly hides her own beauty from the public scrutiny of the reader, so too does the absence of any representation of active childcare, even from poems that describe interactions between infant and mother, preserve and highlight the True Woman's modest withdrawal from the vulgarities of labor. Representations of the True Woman/mother rarely capture her engaged in any form of care more active than wishing or prayer. In "A Mother's Pride" J.J.A.'s speaker uses the image of benign nature standing in resistance to the turbulent storm to spell out her wishes for the continued health and prosperity of her child:

> Oft we may mark some lowering envious cloud,
> Threatening, the storm, in gathering gloom arise,
> Careering darkly, night's bright Queen to shroud—
> Then, shrinking, as abashed at the Empires,
> In blushes adds new lustre to the skies.
>
> So proves the cares that may thy breast invade,
> Like rain-drops from the spring-cloud smiling come—
> Perennial joys be thine—no blighting shade
> Awake regret—or cause a thought to roam;
> All bliss be centered in thy home—sweet home. (11–20)

In "To My Sleeping Babe" Sarah Weakley's mother-speaker wishes a life of innocence for her child, as lasting purity would extend the length of his privileged communion with God:

> I would thou wast thus ever pure;
> That naught on earth would ever lure;
> That smiles of home, and joy, and love,
> Would ever glad thee from above. (21–24)

Similarly, in "The Water-Lily" by Pauline Forsyth, the mother-speaker echoes Weakley's woman narrator in her wishes for her child's continued purity and faith:

Yet ever through life's thronging hours,
Fair child, may this be given;
While in thy hand thou hold'st earth's flowers,
May thine eyes be turned to heaven. (33–36)

The conspicuous absence from such poetry of any images depicting women engaged in the duties of mothering reinforces the definition of the pastoral homescape as place of not-work, a move that both feeds and reflects the popular notion that a proper woman, as spirit of the homescape, maintains herself and her interests at a safe and respectful distance from the world of labor. In the end, such poems do, by extrapolation, perpetuate the link between womanhood and elevated or privileged economic and social standing.

The rare poem that does depict the woman engaged in some form of active care serves as a cautionary tale, no matter how benign her intentions might be. In "My Flower" poet Martha G. Withers portrays woman's attempts to provide active childcare as self-indulgent and frivolous. Her graphic images of woman's acts of loving flagrantly transgress the conventional limits imposed upon the physical representation of True Woman. In the first stanza the maternal embrace becomes an emblem of woman's attempts at (inter)active childcare:

She was a lovely, tender bud,
Nestling upon my breast,
Her little velvet cheek to mine
In fond affection prest;
She was a flower that had twined
Around my very heart
So closely that of life itself
She seemed to be a part. (1–8)

Similarly, the graphic metaphor of the infant child as flower—benign, often cultivated symbol of the family intact—"twined" completely around the speaker's "very heart" so that "of life itself / She seemed to be a part" (7–8) indicates the condition of maternal love out of control. Note as well that the child in this poem is female. This poem is a warning against woman's predisposition to exaggerated and self-indulgent acts of love, as well as the peculiar dangers posed by the formation of bonds between the woman and the infant girl. Looking back on her season of folly, the mother-speaker acknowledges the sin and vanity of her own active, self-indulgent expressions of love and care:

I watched o'er her as jealously
As misers guard their store:
And day by day her opening charms
New pleasure for me bore: .... (9–12)

She confesses that her focus upon the sensual pleasures of motherhood—the touch of her infant's skin, the sight of her beauty—compromised the clarity of her vision; symptoms of illness were overlooked, and the child eventually died:

> But on her cheek the roses burned
> Most strangely, sweetly bright—
> Yet I, in blindness, welcomed them
> With transport of delight;
> Their fatal brightness I but deemed
> The coloring of health;
> So slowly had the foe drawn near
> I had not marked his stealth. (17–24)

The fatal illness—the "stealthy foe"—that eventually kills the young infant is gendered male ("I had not marked *his* stealth" [emphasis added]). The gendering of this element in the narrative highlights the status of death and disease as worldly interloper-aggressor within woman's private sphere. Ultimately, the mother-speaker, stripped of the sensory pleasures of her role, is sustained by the belief that a heavenly kingdom awaits, marked by eternal peace and perfect beauty:

> Long rayless my crushed spirit was
> When its dear joy had fled;
> But now her mem'ry like the sweet
> That withered blossoms shed;
> For I in climes that never change,
> Where blights possess no power,
> Will see perpetually bloom
> My loved and lonely flower. (29–36)

Although the True Woman is that adult female figure who exists at the center of the American homescape, two other adult female identity categories—the young maid and the old woman—also occasionally appear in the popular poems depicting this space. The absence of any additional categories of woman from the popular poetry of the period reflects the inability and, more importantly, the unwillingness of women poets of the era to grant visibility to—and thus acknowledge the possibility of—those female identity categories which signify from spaces located outside of the domestic sphere. Note, however, that although the identity categories of young maidenhood and old womanhood each share with True Woman the setting of the pastoral home, each signifies at a discursive distance from the True Woman who exists at its center. Further, while each of the female identity categories that appear in the popular poems of this period is associated with a particular age group, it is actually the relationship of each identity category—maidenhood, True Womanhood, and old womanhood—to the home itself that distinguishes it from the others.

If, in popular women's poetry of the nineteenth century, womanhood is characterized by the adult female subject's humble commitment (formalized through the ritual of marriage) to service within the domestic sphere, then maidenhood is its antithesis. The maid enjoys some of the privileges of adult female existence but without the humility and service required of woman. Representations of the maiden are distinguished by their conspicuous emphasis upon detailed physical description, in stark contrast with the invisibility of the woman-mother. In addition, poets often identify their maiden subjects by name. The True Woman, having given up her (sur)name for that of the household (her husband's family name), need no longer be named as a subject distinct from her home. "Anna's Cottage," Leila Mortimer's detailed portrait of the young, unmarried woman named in the title, is a typical midcentury portrait of maidenhood:

> I am thinking, I am thinking
>   Of a slight and fairy form—
> Of a cheek now pale, now blushing,
>   And of lips all red and warm—
> Of a brow of pearly whiteness,
>   And of eyes of deepest blue,
> Meek and gentle as a dovelet's,
>   Starry bright, and soft and true:
>
> And of tresses brown and golden,
>   Floating out upon the air,
> Like a pile of brilliant sunbeams,
>   Bright and gloriously fair!
> Of a voice whose softest murmur
>   Is like waters creeping o'er
> Clustering flowers, whose waven leaflets
>   Bend below the grassy shore! (33–48)

Similarly detailed is Mary N. M'Donald's description of the title figure in "To Lizzie":

> There's a charm about thee, Lizzie,
>   That I cannot well define,
> And I sometimes think it lieth
>   In that soft blue eye of thine;
> And yet, though pleasant is thine eye,
>   And beautiful thy lip—
> As a rose-leaf bathed in honey dews,
>   A bee might love to sip,—

> Yet I think it is not lip, nor eye,
>   Which binds me with its spell;
> But a something dearer far than these,
>   Though undefinable. (1–12)

The period of old womanhood is characterized by the female subject's freedom from service within the household, often as a result of the maturing and departure of her children and/or the death of her husband. Having passed through the period of True Womanhood, in which woman's signification is indistinguishable from that of the home, the old woman reenters a period of visibility as subject within but distinct from that space. Thus, like depictions of the maiden, representations of the old woman place a much greater emphasis upon reporting the physical characteristics of the female subject than do representations of the True Woman. For example, we learn that the aging woman in Cornelia M. Doward's "Old" is "wrinkled and gray" (11), with a "silvered head" (3). In "The Old Arm-Chair," written by a woman known only as Mrs. Cook, the speaker recalls how her elderly mother's "eye grew dim, and her locks were gray" (18). The deterioration of old age is also a theme in "Recollections of an Aged Pastor" by Lydia H. Sigourney. The speaker in this poem describes the pastor's last visit to the bedside of her dying mother:

> I do remember him, when one I lov'd
> Lay with a ghastly whiteness on her brow,
> And a fix'd glazing eye. Her head was white
> With many winters, but her furrow'd brow
> To me was beautiful . . . (9–13)

In Caroline Gilman's "The Fortieth Wedding-Day" the elderly woman herself describes her aging features and contrasts them with the youthful beauty of her wedding day:

> Again thou'rt come, and I am here,
>   With faded eye and locks of gray;
> How changed the scenes of life appear
>   On this, my fortieth wedding day.
> . . . .
> And where are they, the young and fair
>   Who graced that day with opening bloom?
> . . . .
> I see them 'round my toilette press,
>   And fold the plait, and smooth the hair,
> And give the soothing fond caress,
>   And kiss the brow they said was fair.

'Tis gone—'tis gone—the fading dream!
My hair is blanched, my eyes are dim;
I'm floating on life's closing stream,
But, (praised be God) it leads to Him.
(1–4, 7–8, 13–16, 21–24)

Critics of the widespread use of the public-private model as a means to understand nineteenth-century womanhood correctly point out the over-simplification and inaccuracy of attempts to portray women of that period as isolated within the pristine, remote sanctuary of the private domestic sphere. Since the late 1990s key scholarly voices have come forth to argue that both the model of a private woman's sphere and the idea of the True Woman wholly withdrawn into that sphere[17] existed primarily in widely publicized myths.

In fact, it is primarily in its capacity as myth—as an unattainable but widely acknowledged ideal—that the notion of True Woman within her private sphere is relevant to this study. Identity groups are distinguished by the archetypes they uphold. The members of an identity group are joined by their aspiration to a common ideal that, in turn, reflects the values of those who strive toward it. In the case of the mid-nineteenth-century figure of the True Woman, white, middle-class women of that period were affirmed as members of the dominant American mainstream not so much by their achievement of True Womanhood as by their embrace of that ideal and the values which it implied. Embrace of the values of True Womanhood was determined by a woman's discernible effort to adopt the behaviors, roles, actions, and activities (or inaction and inactivity) attributed to the True Woman. Space played an essential role in determining woman's acceptance of this ideal, as the most visible meter of her aspirations toward fulfilling it. The sweetness and piety that a female subject brought to her interactions with members of the household were considerably more difficult to monitor than her withdrawal from all forms of remunerative labor in the public sphere (all spaces outside of her own home, including the homes of other women, so that Black woman's labor as a housekeeper or cook in another woman's home was perceived as public labor); and so the white, middle-class woman's confinement of her interests and—most importantly—her activities to the space of her home and its surroundings became the most visible and the most easily interpreted sign of the True Womanhood ideal.

Throughout the nineteenth century, the socioeconomic conditions in which most Black women existed, as chattel slaves or, in the closing decades of the nineteenth century, as tenant farmers (sharecroppers) and household servants, defined for them a relationship to the private space of the middle-class, single-family dwelling that located them well outside of the identity category of woman.

This book traces how, beginning with that handful of Black women poets who emerged during the post-Reconstruction period, communities of African American women writers have struggled to invent publicly, in their literary texts, a subject position that corresponds to the way that they experience themselves—that is, as Black *and* woman. This book investigates Black women poets' development and implementation, beginning at the close of Reconstruction and continuing throughout the twentieth century, of strategies for resisting those notions of gender and race that fail to account for the possibility of Black subjects who are women.

In it I propose that the history of African American women's poetry revolves around Black women's struggle against two marginalizing forces: the widespread association of womanhood with the figure of the middle-class white female, and the similar association of Blackness with the figure of the African American male. I argue this position by looking at the major trends in Black women's poetry during each of four critical moments in African American literary history: the decades of Reconstruction and post-Reconstruction, from 1865 to 1910; the Harlem Renaissance of the 1920s and '30s; the Black Arts Movement, from 1965 to 1975; and the late-twentieth century, from 1975 to 2000. As I explore the strategies of resistance that emerge during each period, I also discuss the sociopolitical and literary developments that shape and define Black women's writing at each of these points.

The first chapter, "A 'Sole and Earnest Endeavor': African American Women's Poetry in the Late Nineteenth Century," examines some of the strategies employed by Black women poets of the late nineteenth century as they write against the exclusivity of the True Womanhood ideal. This chapter explains how the earliest Black women poets resist the hegemony of the European American, middle-class Cult of True Womanhood, not only in their representations of the African American woman, but in their representations of the figure of the husband/father, of childhood and infancy, of the intrafamilial relationships within the home, and of the home itself. Earlier in this introduction I discussed how Euro-American writers and artists have used representations of the archetypal figure in an idealized setting to define and disseminate notions of identity in the United States. Correspondingly, African American women use representations of the Black woman and her physical setting to resist invisibility and create a discursive setting within which Black woman's subjectivity becomes possible. The women poets of the post-Reconstruction era depict the space of the African American home, and the figures located therein, to challenge the notion of distinct and gendered spheres of influence, upon which the very understanding of woman as an inherently white identity category is based.

During the Harlem Renaissance, however, the influence of modernism and the increasingly masculinist bias within the African American literary community combine to create an environment in which the African American home and the daily life of Black women are no longer perceived as viable sites of meaningful resistance. Chapter 2, "The Black Woman as Object and Symbol: African American Women Poets in the Harlem Renaissance," explores how African American women writing poetry during the 1920s and '30s use their poems to negotiate the conflict that arises, at this time, between their interest in creating realistic, dynamic portraits of the everyday lives of Black women and the real possibilities for prominence and inclusion in an African American literary community that, despite its unprecedented openness to the participation of women writers, actively resists representations of the Black woman as anything but object and symbol.

The third chapter, titled "Revolutionary Dreams: African American Women in the Black Arts Movement," reconstructs the cultural and political landscape for young Black writers of the late 1960s and early '70s as a context for the reemergence of the Black woman subject. This chapter diverges from most treatments of gender in the Black Arts Movement in that it depicts a surprising relationship between the masculinist aesthetic that defined the movement and the Black feminist aesthetic that was one of the its most important results. This chapter argues that the dynamic representations of the Black woman subject that emerged from the twilight years of the movement were precipitated by the reidentification of the everyday as a site of resistance in poems that locate political power and social transgression in the bodies of Black men.

Chapter 4, "Locating the Black Female Subject: Late-Twentieth-Century Black Women Poets and the Landscape of the Body," picks up immediately where the preceding chapter leaves off. This, the final chapter of my study, examines the condition of the Black woman subject in African American women's poetry written since the late 1970s. In it we see how the subject whose representation was employed initially as a tool to dislodge the conception of womanhood from the space of the middle-class home now appears at the center of her own sociopolitical and aesthetic landscape. Like their foremothers in the late nineteenth century, contemporary Black woman poets offer their images of African American womanhood as a challenge to the sociopolitical hierarchy which is built upon a framework that marginalizes the Black female subject within both Blackness and womanhood. Unlike their foremothers, however, whose images of Black family and homelife challenged the popular association of womanhood with the white single-family home, contemporary African American women poets disrupt the very system of meaning that originated this legacy of exclusion, creating emancipatory images of the Black female subject in a physical setting that not only makes space for the possibility of Black subjects who are women but celebrates them as well. The characteristics that contemporary African American women writers assign to both the Black woman subject and the site in which she becomes visible transgress and challenge the very system of meaning that has sought to marginalize and obscure that subject from view.

Each period that I cover in this study marks a crucial moment in the development of African American women's poetry. Beginning with the decades of post-Reconstruction, each time period that I address is characterized by the emergence onto the literary scene of a critical mass of African American women poets. The literary history of Black women's poetry—and, in fact, of Black writing in general—is characterized by dramatic fluctuations between periods of great productivity, in which relatively large numbers of women publish a great volume and variety of texts, and periods of stunning absence, in which only the smallest number of African American women manage to produce any writings at all.

The African American woman poet is an anomaly within her community. On average, Black women writers have more education, a wider variety of employment opportunities, and greater economic privilege than Black women who are not writers. Consequently, African American women's writing has flourished during those periods in which sociopolitical and economic conditions have created increased employment opportunities, financial well-being, and wider access to education for all Black people.

The African American women poets who are the focus of this study published their works during the periods of greatest productivity for Black writers. Despite this, however, their names will probably be unfamiliar to most readers. Oddly enough, the most celebrated African American women poets produced their most highly acclaimed texts not during the decades of greatest productivity but at those times when very few Black women were producing any poetry at all. Phillis Wheatley, Frances E. W. Harper, and Gwendolyn Brooks are among the most widely recognized and frequently anthologized women in all of African American poetry. Each of these women had access to education and resources that enabled them to produce and publish their work during those periods when even the most prosperous and highly educated African Americans experienced adversity and struggle. The most popular African American women poets were able to write prolifically either in spite of or in response to sociopolitical and economic adversity that, for most Black people, was so intense that the only conceivable response was silence. Indeed, Wheatley was literate and multilingual when the vast majority of African American women had no contact with reading at all; Frances E. W. Harper was born a free Black woman at a time when roughly 89 percent of African Americans were enslaved; and Gwendolyn Brooks was comfortably middle-class at a time when the bulk of Black women were working either as servants in white households or as unskilled laborers in America's factories and fields.[18]

Despite their prominence within the canon of both American and African American poetry, however, Black women poets like Brooks, Harper, and

Wheatley, who were able to write and publish texts during those periods that were least conducive to the creation of Black literature, each evolved strategies for negotiating the obstacles to African American women's poetry that were effective only in achieving the emergence of an individual Black woman's voice. In general, the works produced by such women are limited in their usefulness to any investigation of emergent subjectivities, in that they are more reflections of a single poet's line of artistic and intellectual inquiry than an indication of broader, community-wide shifts in the meaning of Blackness and womanhood. Phillis Wheatley's mastery of the elegiac voice, for example, causes a paradigm shift within the sociopolitical hierarchy that governs her surroundings, but only enough to inspire her affluent white readers to reenvision *her* specific position relative to theirs. The sole voice of African American womanhood during her lifetime, Wheatley's landmark *Poems on Various Subjects, Religious and Moral* stands alone as the *exceptional* text, a move that distances the poet from the very women for whom her work might serve as a voice. Without the strength of other, similar challenges to Black women's marginality to amplify her own, Wheatley's simultaneous occupation of the seemingly contradictory positions of Black, woman, and poet appear isolated and irregular. In the end, Wheatley's poems, like Brooks's and Harper's work, are limited in their capacity to effect significant transformations in Black women's positionality by the very uniqueness that has brought her work so much lasting attention. Wheatley's act of self-invention, like similar acts by Frances Harper and Gwendolyn Brooks, does little to alleviate the burdens on subsequent Black women poets.

Thus, rather than focus on the isolated achievements of individual Black women, I am writing to uncover those shifts in the visibility and meaning of African American womanhood that can only take place when a critical mass of Black women set out to represent themselves. I am interested in exploring the trends that emerge at such points, when significant numbers of Black women confront and write against the obstacles to Black woman's visibility and voice, using strategies evolved out of and in response to the conditions of the political, social, and historical moment that they share. It is only at such moments that the possibility exists for established relationships between subjects and institutions to shift significantly enough to permit previously hidden subjectivities to come into view.

CHAPTER 1

A "SOLE AND EARNEST ENDEAVOR"
AFRICAN AMERICAN WOMEN'S POETRY
IN THE LATE NINETEENTH CENTURY

[T]hough Afro-American cultural and literary history
commonly regards the late 19th and early 20th centuries
in terms of great men, as the Age of Washington and
DuBois, marginalizing the political contributions of black
women, these were the years of the first flowering of black
women's autonomous organizations and a period of intense
intellectual activity and productivity.

HAZEL CARBY
Reconstructing Womanhood

In presenting this little volume of poems to the public,
(mostly of which are closely associated with a proscribed
race,) the writer's sole and earnest endeavor, is to bring to
light their real life and character.

PRISCILLA JANE THOMPSON
Introduction to *Gleanings of Quiet Hours*

The end of slavery, the beginning of Reconstruction, and its subsequent abandonment produced overwhelming changes in the economic landscape of the
United States but comparatively few shifts in the designation of gender and
racial identity categories. The greatest concentration of Black women's poetry
of the nineteenth century was published between 1880 and 1910.[1] By this time,
the great heyday of white women's literary commerce had passed. All but the
most firmly established of the ladies' magazines had folded, as more and more
middle-class women turned from reading and publishing to active involvement
in volunteer service organizations, teaching, and social service careers as the

preferred means of spreading the tenderness and virtue of woman's influence.[2] This transformation was marked by a modest change in the name and concept of the female ideal, so that the "True Woman" (the lady, the angel of the house) became the "New Woman" (the angel of her home and the spirit of goodwill in both her community and her nation).[3] Despite the shift in name, however, differences between the New Woman and her predecessor were surprisingly few.

New Womanhood held in esteem many of the same values and traits as True Womanhood, including an emphasis on woman's purity, piety, and domesticity and woman's confinement to the affairs, interests, and spaces of the private sphere. While the rise of the New Woman did see the designation of a handful of education-, support-, and care-oriented occupations as appropriate employment for childless, unmarried women, this limited relaxation of gender restrictions fell far short of a full-scale opening of the labor market, and most areas of employment remained closed to female applicants; nor did the New Woman's era see a significant loosening of the expectation that married women—and mothers in particular—would privilege home and family over all other pursuits.[4] Newspapers and pundits predicted that the emergence of the New Woman would precipitate monumental changes at all levels of American life. In reality, however, this enormous transformation consisted of little more than the expansion of "woman's sphere" to accommodate middle-class women's participation in those service organizations, social movements, and occupations which undertook to influence the texture of private life not only in their own homes but in other households and communities as well (favorite causes included temperance, religious instruction, and visitation of the sick; common occupations included volunteer efforts, social service work, and education). Although New Womanhood rose to prominence against the backdrop of a very different racial landscape than its precursor (the decades of the post-Reconstruction era, as opposed to the slavery-based society of the mid-1800s), this late-nineteenth-century model of white middle-class femininity was as exclusionary as its midcentury predecessor. Women whose socioeconomic and/or ethnic status required that they labor either outside the home or outside the narrow range of professions that New Womanhood opened for young, white, middle-class women experienced this new model of female behavior as no less marginalizing than True Womanhood. Black women poets who emerged out of the aftermath of slavery and Reconstruction were denied visibility as New Women by the same race- and class-based barriers and assumptions that had hindered their midcentury foremothers; like their predecessors, African American women poets of the late nineteenth century post-Reconstruction era were penalized—socially, politically, and economically—for their perceived failure to limit their labor and interests to suitably feminine spaces and pursuits.

Consequently, while U.S. whites experienced the late-nineteenth-century shift from True Womanhood to New Womanhood as a substantial transformation in the nature and function of Euro-American female identity, their Black counterparts experienced little or no difference, either in the relative status of white womanhood or in the terms on which African American women were excluded from the privileges and protections that majority (white) women enjoyed. Thus the strategies of resistance employed by African American women poets writing during the decades that U.S. whites experienced as the era of the New Woman were, at their core, a response to Black women's continued subjugation on the basis of their failure to achieve those specific expressions of femininity most valued within the framework of True Womanhood. This chapter engages Black women's poetry of this period as a rejection of True Womanhood based on the ongoing impact of this mid-nineteenth century, antebellum understanding of woman's nature and woman's role on African American women's visibility throughout the post-Reconstruction period, into the twentieth century, and beyond.

In *Reconstructing Womanhood: The Emergence of the Afro-American Woman Novelist,* Hazel Carby describes how African American women novelists of the mid- to late nineteenth century responded to the continuing influence of the True Womanhood ideal. Carby posits Black women's slave narratives—Harriet Jacobs's *Incidents in the Life of a Slave Girl,* Mary Prince's *The History of Mary Prince,* and others—as the stylistic and thematic models for Harriet E. Wilson's *Our Nig,* Frances E. W. Harper's *Iola Leroy,* and other nineteenth-century novels by Black women.[5] Like their foremothers, the early Afro-American women novelists intertwine elements of the material reality of African American life (poverty, slavery, etc.) with the personal qualities (purity, piety, submissiveness, humility) and physical characteristics (pale skin, brown eyes, and long, dark, wavy hair) associated with ideal womanhood to create Black female protagonists who contradict some of the negative stereotypes associated with "colored" women and their families.[6] Indeed, such writers' characterizations of slave women as unfortunate "Negro ladies"—female subjects whose womanly virtue is revealed in their aspiration to the privileges and protections afforded True (white, middle-class) Women, even as their coloredness dooms them to failure—resist many of the controlling images that render acceptable some of the antebellum period's most egregious transgressions against the black female body.[7] In offering up images of Black women protagonists whose actions, outlook, and appearance (including, as often as not, their literal physical whiteness) closely resemble those qualities by which True Womanhood is measured, however, these early prose texts embrace an understanding of adult female subjectivity that affirms white supremacy and patriarchal dominance. Specifically focused on the abolition of slavery and the exposure of the racial hierarchies that were its immediate legacy, these texts understand and engage Black woman's upward mobility in the narrowest possible terms, seeking only to open a space within the dominant, heteronormative understanding of woman's place and privilege for adult females who are not white.

In *"The Changing Same,"* Deborah E. McDowell addresses the troubling issues raised by these early prose writers' unqualified embrace of the True Woman-hood ideal. Her suggestion that early Black women novelists like Harriet Wilson and Frances Harper, in attempting to present exemplary African American female characters, succeeded primarily "in offering alternative homogeniza-tion" speaks directly to the failure of the nineteenth-century Black woman's novel to create a vision of Black female subjectivity that is truly liberatory (McDowell 95).[8] If we accept McDowell's further argument that African Amer-ican women novelists' obsessive pursuit of a Black female protagonist whose qualities would dispel any or all negative stereotypes associated with that figure resulted "without exception in the creation of static disembodied, larger-than-life characters" (95), then it would follow that in writing not toward a condi-tional visibility based upon Black women's pursuit of True Womanhood but against the very notion of a single female archetype, African American women poets would create fully tangible characters of much greater depth and repre-senting a broader range of experiences than their prose-writing counterparts. Indeed such poets' audacious departures from the True Womanhood ideal, evident in their depiction of Black women subjects as far more dynamic than the genteel "Negro ladies" favored by the African American women novelists, indicates Black women poets' understanding—even amid the chaotic aftermath of war and Reconstruction—of the unique contribution that representations of irreverent, assertive, worldly Black women could make to the struggle against invisibility.[9]

Like Black women's novels of this period, African American women's poetry of the late-nineteenth century writes against the effects of the widespread acceptance of True Womanhood, both on the portrayal of Black women and on Black women's subjectivity. Unlike the early novelists, however, whose efforts to open a space for nonwhite women within the prevailing gender ideal suggest an acceptance of the racist, sexist, and classist hegemony out of and in the service of which True Womanhood emerged and functioned, Black women poets of the period challenged not only its patterns of exclusion but the very ideal itself. Their poems resist and undermine the hegemony of True Womanhood by con-testing popular beliefs surrounding the relationship between woman and her home codified in midcentury representations of the pastoral homescape. This quality of resistance—this impetus to disrupt the hegemony of white supremacist notions of female identity—constitutes an antipastoral poetics of rejection of both the ideology and the iconography of the True Womanhood ideal.

Black women's antipastoral poetry appropriates and deploys the most common symbols and emblems of True Womanhood, but in geographic and historical settings that undermine not only the status of this long-established archetype but also the links that it suggests between female propriety and a narrowly conceived grouping of race- and class-based conditions. These conditions include the presumption of a white, nonimmigrant ethnicity; the nonrepresentation of female labor; the definition of home as a middle-class, single-family dwelling; and the function of home as private sanctuary from public interests and activities. African American women poets answer white women poets' use of the icons and images of white middle-class home and family with representations of Black private and family life carefully crafted to undermine the dominance of the Euro-American ideal.

For example, Black women poets use representations of mischievous, spirited, inquisitive children, whose behavior contradicts the cardinal virtues of True Womanhood, to disrupt the authority of that model. If the midcentury pastoral of the American homescape relies on features of the home setting—for instance, the innocence and piety of the infant child—to indicate the qualities of the True Woman who is found within that setting, then the playful, disobedient children who appear in poems like African American writer Maggie Pogue Johnson's "When Daddy Cums from Wuk" introduce the possibility of alternative forms of womanhood, some of which value characteristics like mischievousness, independence, and assertiveness.

"When Daddy Cums from Wuk" pits the fierce independence of its youngest Black characters against the authority of their mother, the speaker, as she reprimands her children for interfering with the evening's dinner preparations:

> Cum here, Mandy, what's you chewin',
>   Take dat bread right out yo' mouf,
> Do you know what you'se doin'?
>   You'se de worry of dis hous'
>
> Put dat bread right on the shef dar,
>   Case 'tis much as we kin do
> To gib you bread at meal time
>   Till hard times is fru. (1–8)

This poem's challenge to ideal womanhood, however, extends beyond the alternative female subjectivities implied in the poet's depiction of a nuclear family home in which the children are playful and unruly. At the same time that Johnson's descriptions of their humorous antics challenge narrowly conceived notions of an ideal "womanly" temperament, her speaker's instructions and reprimands highlight woman's labor of child rearing and discipline:

> En Ike, you shet dat safe do'!
> Take dat spoon right out dem beans!
> 'Member well, you git no mo'!
> Ya'll de wo'st chaps eber seen! (9–12)

"When Daddy Cums from Wuk" and other similar poems not only defy widely held notions of woman's personality and character; they also challenge deeply ingrained beliefs surrounding the alienation of the adult female subject from all forms of work by writing labor back into the very intrafamilial relationships—in this case the relationship between mother and child—that appear static and sanitized when rendered in the symbolic language of the pastoral homescape. In this poem the African American mother-as-speaker and her mischievous children bring each other into view as active, embodied figures. The mother's commands and reproofs depict childhood as an active period of curious exploration, while the domestic chores she assigns to daughter Jane call attention to the nature and extent of her own household labor:

> Jane you set de table,
> And fix t'ings all in place.
> . . . .
> Jane, take de rabbit off de stove,
> De hominy en 'taters,
> En git dat smalles' chiny dish,
> For de stewed tomaters.
> . . . .
> You boys stop dat fightin'!
> Sich noise I never heahd,
> Put de stools up to de table,
> Not anodder word! (33–34, 41–44, 49–52)

In addition to exposing the actual means by which woman creates her home (the process by which she transforms her household into that space which her male partner experiences as sanctuary), the detailed specificity of the speaker's orders to daughter Jane ("set de table," "fix t'ings all in place," "take the rabbit off de stove," and "git dat smalles' chiny dish") implies that housework is a form of skilled labor, for which instruction is required. In addition, the notion that woman's domestic activities must be learned and practiced counters the popular conception that woman carries out her acts of care and maintenance instinctively and that expertise in household affairs is her birthright, endowed by nature. The suggestion, then, that household chores must be learned invests a level of value in woman's domestic work that directly contradicts prevailing beliefs that the apparent not labor of homemaking is inherent to woman's disposition, and therefore effortless. Maggie Pogue Johnson's revisionist portrayal of women's daily tasks challenges the essentialist legacy of True Womanhood, and this theme of rejection and resistance is echoed in Black women's poetry throughout the post-Reconstruction era.

Lizelia Augusta Jenkins Moorer, a contemporary of Johnson's, takes up similar questions related to woman's household labor.[10] In Moorer's "What We Teach at Claflin," household maintenance is elevated as "domestic art," an area of expertise to be taught and studied. Her ode to Claflin reflects the understanding at this and other historically Black colleges that woman's household labor comprises a series of skilled crafts and "science[s]":[11]

> Girls are taught domestic science, coupled with domestic art,
> Such will give them independence, which is far the better part;
> Cooking, sewing, millinery, needlework, and making lace,
> Garment-drafting; Thus we teach them how a busy world to face.
> (9–12)

Beyond their role in highlighting the labor and skill involved in daily household maintenance, the mischievous children who populate Black women's late-nineteenth-century verse also serve as the primary vehicle for African American women poets' depictions of Black motherhood. These representations of African American mothers engaged in acts of childcare and discipline serve a dual function, calling attention to another form of women's labor obscured by the ideal of the True Woman in her pastoral home setting, even as they undermine prevailing stereotypes alleging Black women's incapacity for maternal feelings and functions.

Like Maggie Pogue Johnson's "When Daddy Cums from Wuk," Clara Thompson's "Mrs. Johnson Objects" describes the activities of the mischievous child from the perspective of his mother. Her lengthy reprimand is both the narrative vehicle of the poem and an antipastoral representation of woman engaged in the household labor of child rearing:[12]

> Come right in this house, Will Johnson!
>   Kin I teach you dignity?
> Chasin' aft' them po' white children,
>   Jest because you wan' to play.
>
> Whut does po' white trash keer fah you?
>   Want you keep away fum them,
> Next, they'll be a-doin' meanness,
>   An' a givin' you the blame.

> Don't come mumblin' bout their playthings,
> > Yourn is good enough fah you;
> 'Twus the best that I could git you,
> > An' you've got to make them do. (1–12)

Thompson's speaker understands the value of her work, and she describes the troubling results, should she fail to meet her responsibilities as mother and protector:

> Go'n' to break you fum that habit,
> > Yes, I am! An' mighty soon,
> Next, you'll grow up like the white-folks,
> > All time whinin' fah the moon. (13–16)

To prevent her son from adopting the priorities and habits that she associates with whiteness and its privileges, she assigns a punishment:

> Jest set there, an' mind the baby
> > Till I tell you—You may go;
> An' jest let me ketch you chasin'
> > Aft' them white trash any mo.' (21–24)

In "Mrs. Johnson Objects" representations of woman's household labor (in this instance, child rearing, reprimands, and punishment) combine with the Black mother-as-speaker's equation of white childhood with "meanness" to challenge two key elements of ideal womanhood, the ideology of white supremacy and the icon of the innocent child.

As in "Mrs. Johnson Objects," the events in Clara Thompson's "Johnny's Pet Superstition" revolve around the interaction between a male child and the woman who reprimands and instructs him. In this humorous poem Johnny, a southern Black boy raised in his grandmother's traditional folk beliefs, debates the merits of superstition with his classroom instructor, a northern Black woman with a formal education. The poem begins on a lively note, with Johnny tattling on his classmate and friend:

> Teacher, Jimmie's toe is bleedin';
> > Stumped it comin' down the road;
> I just knowed that he would do it,
> > 'Cause he went an' killed a toad.
>
> Teacher, you jest ought to see it;
> > Oh, the blood's jest spurtin' out!
> You won't ketch me killin' toad-frogs,
> > When I see them hoppin' bout. (1–8)

The teacher responds with skepticism, and her standard English underscores the regional and class distinctions revealed in her rejection of this southern Black belief. Johnny's "saucy" retort underscores the gulf between teacher and student, despite their common identification as "colored" Americans:

> "Oh now, Johnny, that's all nonsense!
>   I told you sometime ago,
> That the killing of a hop-toad
>   Wouldn't make you hurt your toe.
>
> "Who told you that silly story?"
>   Grandma said that it is so;
> She's much older than you, teacher,
>   An' I guess she ought to know.
>
> "Come, now, Johnny, don't be saucy;"
>   Teacher, grandma did say so,
> An' she says: 'You No'thern cullud,
>   Don't b'lieve nothin' any mo' (9–20)

Thompson uses the contrast between Grandma's folk beliefs and the teacher's unwillingness to accept them to highlight this poem's juxtaposition of Black female authority within the public workplace against Black female authority within the home. The child's unwillingness to disregard his grandmother's teachings in favor of his teacher's is, in effect, a refusal to recognize any sort of hierarchical distinction between the public and private spheres.

Indeed, Thompson draws compelling parallels between the younger woman's public labor of teaching and the older woman's private (perceived) not-labor within the home. For Johnny's teacher, the "womanly" duties of nurturing and instruction are not linked to or predicated on her humble withdrawal from public remunerative labor. Instead, the nature of her work is closely related to child rearing activities performed by Johnny's grandmother (and revealed in his loyal defense of her beliefs), and where the sentimental portraits of the American homescape vaguely imply the shaping role of woman's influence, Thompson's poem is unambiguous. Johnny's specific references to his grandmother's words ("Grandma said that it is so" and "Teacher, grandma did say so, / An' she says: 'You No'thern cullud, / Don't b'lieve nothin' any mo'") make explicit the nature of her role within the home; like the young northern teacher, she is an educator and a nurturer, exerting her "female" influence willfully and strategically, through active care and instruction. Regardless of the setting (public or private), woman's interactions with those children placed under her care are defined by conscious and active labor, not by passive influence.

Like her older sister Clara, Priscilla Thompson created poems that combine descriptions of childhood mischief with images and accounts of woman's household labor.[13] In the same humorous spirit as older sister Clara's "Mrs. Johnson Objects," Priscilla Thompson's "Insulted" combines descriptions of childhood mischief with images of and references to childcare and other domestic responsibilities. The speaker in this poem, however, is not the reprimanding mother, but the scolded child. Like the schoolboy in "Johnny's Pet Superstition," the child's irreverent remarks constitute an act of mischievous transgression in and of themselves, not only against the adult female authority figure (the mother in this poem, or the teacher in "Johnny's Pet Superstition") but also against the ideal of True Womanhood and the iconography—especially the iconography of innocent childhood—on which it depends. Thompson's young speaker describes her own offenses in a lisping, toddler's version of Black, post-Reconstruction vernacular:

> My Mamma is a mean old sing,
>   An' toss as she tan be;
> I'm doeing to pack my doll trunt,
>   An' doe to Ga'n'ma Lee.
>
> My Mamma baked a dinger tate,
>   Den panked me shameful hard,
> Dust 'tause I stuck my finder in,
>   An 'filled de holes wiz lard.
> . . . .
> But Mamma, fus, she slapped my ear,
>   Den jerked me fum de chair,
> And panked and flung me on de lounge,
>   An' said, "You dus' lay dere!" (1–8, 17–20)

The nineteenth-century myth of woman's passive influence and the corresponding absence of labor from depictions of her home are undermined in this poem by detailed descriptions of both the child speaker's humorous transgressions and her mother's swift and sure response. The gracious domesticity suggested by the image of the baked "dinger tate" is offset by the mother's violent temper ("But Mamma, fus, she slapped my ear, / Den jerked me fum de chair, / And panked and flung me on de lounge").

In "Insulted" and similar poems, Black women writers' images of the mischievous child suggest the possibility of an adult female subjectivity that values or incorporates qualities beyond the virtues of True Womanhood, among them the possibility of mischievous womanhood. Such poems also counter the pastoral conflation of woman and home. In Black women poets' post-Reconstruction portraits of African American homelife, woman does not comfort and nurture her charges passively, by means of her loving presence, and household maintenance does not happen by osmosis. When "Insulted," "Johnny's Pet Superstition," "When Daddy Cums from Wuk," and similar works boldly depict Black women engaged in or describing acts of food preparation, housekeeping, and childcare, they take an important step toward establishing woman as subject distinct from her domestic surroundings, laboring within—but distinguishable from—her home and family. In turn, the notion that woman achieves subjectivity independent from both her household and the duties that sustain it is a crucial step in wresting the broader identity category of woman from its powerful association with—and confinement within—the space of the white, middle-class, single-family home. Significantly, however, and despite the transgressive value of such works (in terms of Black women's visibility and the challenge to ideal womanhood), the emergence of the Black woman figure takes place indirectly, inasmuch as it is reflected in the actions and words of her children, who are the primary focus of the narrative in each work. But Black women poets' revisions of the most common symbols of True Womanhood are not confined to representations of childhood. There are a number of poems in which the Black woman herself is the central focus.

Betsy Erkkila uses the term "wicked excess" to describe the means by which female poets in America have resisted and challenged hegemonic norms that would limit recognition and visibility as women to those female subjects who confine their activities and interests to the care and maintenance of the white middle-class home. For Erkkila, the paradigmatic "wicked excess" of the poems of Emily Dickinson is evident in her frequent reliance on speaking subjects willfully located outside the space of the home, oriented such that their interests and activities extend beyond or *exceed* the boundaries of the domestic realm. Like her representations of the mischievous child, Clara Thompson's "A Lullaby" uses the idiom and anecdotes of African American folklore to depict the Black woman wickedly in excess of the boundaries that circumscribe true, pastoral womanhood. In poems like "When Daddy Cums from Wuk" the mother-speaker becomes the backdrop against whose punishments and instructions we see the actions of her lively brood. The children's actions, in turn, reveal her transgressive position. In "A Lullaby" the child takes over that function, becoming the static figure whose sole function is to highlight his mother's performance of transgressive Black womanhood.

In the opening passage the speaker uses the conflict between her childcare responsibilities (which are, for this speaker, more pleasure than labor) and the awaiting household chores to suggest the burden and rigor of domestic labor, this in stark contrast to the pastoral representations of the homescape in which no labor is acknowledged to have occurred:

> Hush ye, hush ye! honey, darlin',
> > Hush ye, now, an' go to sleep:
> Mammy's got to wash them dishes,
> > An' she's got this floor to sweep. (1–4)

The next stanza addresses the influence of class and race in determining the shape and texture of woman's activities and duties within her own home. The speaker uses the term "lady," synonymous during this period with white middle-class womanhood, to link representations of the True Woman's leisurely contemplation of her infant's countenance—a staple in poems depicting the pastoral homescape—with the race and class privilege that figure enjoys:[14]

> You must think I'm made uv money,
> > An's got nothin' else to do,
> But to set here, in this rocker,
> > Like a lady, holdin' you. (5–8)

Thompson's mother-speaker takes the popular image of the True Woman at face value, reading the invisibility of woman's work in depictions of the white middle-class or pastoral homescape as the absence of woman's labor within that space. Unlike the figure of the "lady," this speaker, because she is a Black mother in a Black home, must balance the competing responsibilities of household maintenance and childcare:

> Now you's gone to laughin' at me;
> > Little rascal! Hush! I say,
> Mammy's got to wash them dishes,
> > She ain't got not time to play. (9–12)

The Thompson sisters cloak the transgressive in the folk. In poems like "A Lullaby," "Insulted," and "Johnny's Pet Superstition" they suggest the counter-existence of a transgressive African American womanhood even as they distract readers from conscious engagement with this radical suggestion by charming them with the lyrical simplicity of their dialect and the quaintness of their portraits of Black life.[15] At the opposite end of the spectrum are poems like "Mother" by Josephine Henderson Heard.[16] The sentimental language and shameless melodrama of this poem link it to mid-nineteenth-century representations of True Womanhood, even as the explicit references to woman's household work compromise that link. Whereas the popular poems produced at midcentury, during the heyday of women's literary commerce, celebrate the atmosphere of comfort and refreshment that reigns within mother's home, Heard's speaker casts woman herself as the active provider of the solace, care, and instruction associated with that space:

Who was it who held me on her knee?
When I was helpless as could be,
And hoped such noble things of me?
   My Mother.

Who taught my infant lips to prat,
And understood my childish chat,
And who in patience calmly sat?
   My Mother.

Who watched me grow from day to day,
Taught me "Our Father's prayer" to say,
And kept me out of evil's way.
   My Mother. (1–12)

The sentimental language and tone that dominate this poem reveal the influence of mid-nineteenth-century popular verse on Heard's style and diction. At the same time, however, the poem seems to proceed from the assumption that woman's care consists of actions (teaching, protecting, advising), undertaken deliberately, an idea that places Heard's vision of motherhood at odds with the very poems whose style is so influential in her work. Heard and the other African American women poets of the post-Reconstruction era make clear that while the idea of home enjoys a broad symbolic association with comfort and repose, the actual experience of comfort and respite—of home as sanctuary—results from real household labor—women's labor—within that space. And, according to Mrs. Henry Linden, this labor requires diligence, conviction, and mettle, qualities most often associated with men's remunerative work outside of the home. In "I Am as Happy as a Queen on Her Throne" Mrs. Linden describes the professional attitude that she brings to her daily household tasks.[17]

With pluck and ambition I have great success.
I make a strong effort and God does the rest,
I work for the future and think for the best. (10–12)

"What's Mo' Temptin' to the Palate" by Maggie Pogue Johnson goes one step further than Mrs. Linden's industrious piety, as she takes on popular notions of the relationship between gender, labor, and space. This poem cleverly uses the male narrator, home after a day of hard labor outside of the home, to conduct readers through a detailed audit of both the duties and products of woman's domestic work. The effectiveness of the poem hinges upon the reader's appreciation of the irony of a male speaker whose own understanding of work is as remunerative activity based outside of the home (which he experiences as a place of sanctuary and respite), but whose observations clearly illustrate that labor takes place within the home as well. For the male speaker, dinner in the peaceful refuge of his home is the perfect antidote to a grueling day of hard work in the public sphere:

> What's mo' temptin' to de palate,
>> When you's wuked so hard all day,
>
> En cum in home at ebentime
>> Widout a wud to say,—
>
> En see a stewin' in de stove
>> A possum crisp en brown,
>
> Wid great big sweet potaters,
>> A layin' all aroun'. (1–8)

More than a meal, the home-cooked dinner functions as that ritual which completes his transition from the rigor of outside work to the relaxation of home. The same products (stewed possum, sweet potatoes, hot coffee) and activities (the preparation and serving of the evening meal) that mark the home as sanctuary for the male speaker, however, establish the home as workplace for his wife, the "ol 'oman" of the house.

> What' mo' temptin' to de palate,
>> When you cum from wuk at night,
>
> To set down to de fiah,
>> A shining' jis so bright,
>
> De ol' 'oman walks in,—
>> Wid supper brilin' hot,
>
> En a good ol' cup ob coffee,
>> Jis steamin' out de pot. (49–56)

Johnson and her contemporaries write against a vision of female identity that, like the popular midcentury verse through which it was first disseminated, recognizes only three figures within adult womanhood: the young maid, the True Woman, and the old woman. In such poems the category of woman is thus limited to those adult females who are either anticipating (the maiden) or participating in (the old woman and the True Woman) marriage. The wider range of female subjects who appear in Black post-Reconstruction, antipastoral verse, however, suggests the possibility of mature adult womanhood outside of marriage.

Like those poems that highlight Black woman's household labor, Maggie Pogue Johnson's "The Old Maid's Soliloquy" and Effie Waller Smith's "The 'Bachelor Girl'" establish the Black female as subject discrete from her surroundings.[18] But while poems like "What's Mo' Temptin' to the Palate" and "When Daddy Cums from Wuk" accomplish this by picturing the African American woman at work within her home, "The Bachelor Girl" and "The Old Maid's Soliloquy" take a more audacious approach, with each poem offering a vision of the adult female subject willfully outside of those roles of wife and mother that would constitute the basis of her attachment to and confinement within the domestic sphere.

Maggie Pogue Johnson's "Old Maid's Soliloquy" resists the constraints of True Womanhood by inverting and exploiting the association between nature imagery and domestic stability established in the poetry of the American homescape. Johnson uses images of thriving produce to create the "Old Maid's Soliloquy," her spirited portrait of a woman living at odds with the popular understanding of the function and limitations of the female role:

> I'se been upon de karpet,
> Fo' lo, dese many days;
> De men folks seem to sneer me,
> In der kin' ob way.
>
> But I don't min' der foolin,'
> Case I sho' is jis as fine
> As any Kershaw pumpkin
> A hangin on the vine.
> . . . .
> Dey sho' do t'ink dey's so much,
> But I sho' is jis as fine
> As eny sweet potato
> Dat's growd up from de vine. (1–8, 13–16)

In the same way that the sentimental poetry of the American homescape uses gently rustling trees and lovingly tended flower beds to symbolize the family intact, Johnson's speaker uses benign images of garden vegetables to indicate the self intact. In the pastoral of the American homescape, cultivated nature signifies the wholeness and health of the family. In Johnson's "Old Maid's Soliloquy" the "fine" color and shape of the "Kershaw pumpkin" and the "sweet potato" indicate the wholeness and health of the title character, although she has rejected the traditional female roles of wife and mother. The "Old Maid" incorporates additional images of healthy produce as she explains the impetus behind her unusual choice:

> I looks at dem [men] sometimes,
> But hol's my head up high,
> Case I is fer above dem
> As de moon is in de sky.
> . . . .
> Dey needn't t'ink I's liken dem,
> Case my match am hard to fin,'

En I don't want de watermillion
Dat's lef' upon de vine.

Case I ain't no spring chicken,
Dis am solid talk,
En I don't want anything
Dat's foun' upon de walk. (9–12, 17–24)

In mid-nineteenth-century portraits of the Euro-American homescape, woman's contentment is, without exception, linked to her place within a middle-class, single-family dwelling. Such is not the case for Johnson's spinster, whose self-esteem is unrelated to her economic status:

I'd rader be a single maid,
A wanderin' bout de town,
Wid skercely way to earn my bread,
En face all made ob frowns,—

Den hitched up to some numbskull,
Wid skercely sense to die,
En I know I cud'n kill him,
Dar'd be no use to try. (29–36)

The closing image of the "Old Maid's Soliloquy" highlights the central theme of female self-worth and contentment outside of the confines of the traditional home:

I specs to hol' my head up high
En always feel as free
As any orange blossom
A hangin' on de tree. (41–44)

While Johnson's Old Maid adopts and transforms the nature-based iconography of ideal (true) womanhood, redeploying it as a tool for resisting popular notions of female nature and woman's role, the title figure in Effie Waller Smith's "The Bachelor Girl" engages the symbolism and language of domesticity and the pastoral home, not only in order to position herself outside of the boundaries that define "woman's sphere" but also to reject its vision and values. In the opening lines of the poem, Smith's speaker dismisses the derogatory term "old maid" and in so doing challenges the system of meaning that it reinforces (in which marriage and motherhood serve as the dominant identity against which other female subjectivities must be viewed and interpreted). At the same time, she embraces the title of "boss," a bold turn that challenges its conventional association with male agency:

> She's no "old maid," she's not afraid
> To let you know she's her own "boss,"
> She's easy pleased, she's not diseased,
> She is not nervous, is not cross. (1–4)

In linking the Bachelor Girl's embrace of the autonomy and privilege implicit in the term "boss" with her rejection of the stigmatization of female singlehood implied in the term "old maid," Smith's speaker moves toward establishing a new discourse with which to articulate (and through which to understand) the subjectivity of the adult woman who experiences singlehood as a lived expression of female power and self-determination:

> She's no desire whatever for
> Mrs. to precede her name,
> The blessedness of singleness
> She all her life will proudly claim. (5–8)

Whereas "Old Maid's Soliloquy" depicts the unmarried status of the speaker as a willful response to the unavailability of suitable mates ("I'll fin' a match some day, / Or else I'll sho' 'main single" [38–39]), "The Bachelor Girl," portrays female singlehood as a deliberate and proactive choice, independent of a woman's marriage prospects. Indeed, the retention by Johnson's speaker of the label "Old Maid" ("So don't let ol' maids boder you, / I'll fin' a match . . ." [37–38]) indicates her understanding of the wife and mother as the standard against which all other adult female subjectivities must be measured.

Conversely, neither the words nor the images associated with the pastoral homescape and True Womanhood hold any meaning for the Bachelor Girl. The discursive systems that recognize cultivated or benign nature, the glowing hearth, and the interaction between mother and child as symbols of female domesticity and the household intact fail to acknowledge the possibility of adult women subjects who willfully locate themselves outside of and/or in opposition to the interests and activities of that setting. The Bachelor Girl's rejection of specific domestic pastimes and the associated images and symbols amounts to a refusal to embrace the literal and iconographic language of a social order that leaves no space for the adult female subject who is unmarried by choice. The following passage describes the Bachelor Girl's distaste for traditional feminine pursuits, even as it isolates the objects associated with those activities on the second and fourth lines—the two rhyming lines—of the stanza:

> She does not sit around and knit
> On baby caps and mittens,
> She does not play her time away
> With puggy dogs and kittens. (9–12)

While the first and third lines of this stanza focus on the Bachelor Girl's disinterest in the traditional pastimes of knitting and doting on the family pets, the alternate lines of the stanza offer images ("baby caps and mittens," or "puggy dogs and kittens") that, in another context, would indicate the adult female subject's adherence to the limitations and requirements associated with the pursuit of the True Womanhood ideal.

The Bachelor Girl's distaste for traditional domestic pursuits and womanly pastimes is counterbalanced by her strong affinity for the affairs of the worldly sphere:

> The latest news she always knows,
> She scans the daily papers o'er.
>
> Of politics and all the tricks
> And schemes that politicians use,
> She knows full well and she call tell
> With eloquence of them her views. (27–32)

Yet even as the Bachelor Girl's knowledge of public affairs suggests her embrace of worldly concerns, her similar interest in spreading joy and perpetuating morality, compassion, and kindness suggests a relaxation of the hard-and-fast boundary between male and female spheres of influence and concern. For the Bachelor Girl, the distinction between public and private realms of activity and influence is a false one, and her knowledge of politics and public affairs does not preclude her manifestation of qualities and commitment to issues more closely associated with traditional womanhood, when she chooses:

> Her heart is kind and you will find
> Her often scattering sunshine bright
> Among the poor, and she is sure
> To always advocate the right. (45–48)

"Old Maid's Soliloquy" and "The Bachelor Girl" are antipastoral in that they depict women whose alienation (voluntary or otherwise) from marriage and traditional homelife positions them in excess of the boundaries that limit and define established female roles.[19] Many African American women poets of the same period, however, create depictions of the Black female subject that defy popular expectations for adult womanhood, not because their women speakers have rejected or been separated from the nuclear family home but because they introduce *into* the space of the home extrafamilial relationships, emotions, or interests that challenge established norms for women's conduct in that setting.

In Priscilla Jane Thompson's "Insulted"—and, to a lesser degree, Maggie Pogue Johnson's "When Daddy Cums from Wuk" and Clara Thompson's "Mrs.

Johnson Objects"—the parent-child relationships depicted complicate the model of home as peaceful refuge by introducing woman's anger as a shaping influence within that space. Similarly, representations of friendship between Black women introduce the possibility of woman's self-interest into the very setting that, in the popular imagination, both symbolizes and is sustained by woman's selfless humility. "An Afternoon Gossip" by Priscilla Jane Thompson compounds the challenge to mainstream gender norms inherent in its depictions of friendship between Black women by using the nonfamilial relationship at the poem's center as an opening for exploring the possibility of women whose interests within the home extend beyond humble service to their families.[20] "An Afternoon Gossip" uses a spirited first-person narrative of an encounter between Black women friends (an indulgence rarely granted the white women of popular verse) to challenge widely held expectations for women's conduct and temperament. From the start, Thompson uses the actions and words of her speaker to portray a female subject whose pragmatic refusal to observe the boundaries between public affairs (including business affairs) and private affairs counters the related notions of home as sacred space and of woman ordained by God as its sustainer. The speaker welcomes "sistah Harris," a guest in her private home, with news of her own public concerns, manifest in her ongoing dispute with the local landlord. Thus she defies the popular taboo against introducing worldly interests into the domestic realm:

> Is that you sistah Harris?
>   I knowed you when you knocked;
> Jest keep right on a-pushing,
>   The ole door isn't locked!
>
> Ole white man's been forgetting,
>   Each day since first I sent;
> He's got a pow'ful mem'ry
>   When comes time for the rent. (1–8)

The speaker's lively gossip is the vehicle that enables Thompson to construct a vision of woman's relationship to domesticity quite distinct from the popular conflation of woman's interests with the interests of her household. In particular, the speaker's witty, irreverent observations on homelife and household maintenance underscore her position—and the degree to which she locates herself— as mother and wife within but distinct from the home and family whose needs form the shape of her household duties. For example, despite the hazard that it presents to both her husband and her children, Thompson's speaker shrugs off the landlord's failure to repair her broken steps, instead using his negligence as an opportunity to signify:[21]

> Fell down them ole back do' steps!
> > She told me they wus broke;
> > Ole Smith put off the fixing:
> > > I'd make that white man smoke! (53–56)

Thompson's speaker welcomes the opportunity to put household chores aside and chastises sistah Harris for her reluctance to do the same:

> Now, sit down; Whut's your hurry?
> > You have no work to do;
> > I'm mos' done with my i'ning;
> > > You always beats me through. (9–12)

Childcare is but another responsibility that Thompson's speaker willingly sets aside at the prospect of a good bit of gossip, and, once again, she encourages her guest to follow suit:

> You ain't no bother to me!
> > Jest sit here where its cool;
> > Hush fretting 'bout them child'en!
> > > You know they're safe in school. (13–16)

The speaker's mocking appraisal of a recent local marriage underscores the theme of woman as subject distinct from the institutions and settings with which she is most often associated. In the pastoral of the American homescape the elevated status of the True Woman is predicated on the sacredness of marriage, the institution which confers on the adult female subject both visibility and propriety. Thompson's speaker, however, offers an assessment of marriage that is more cynical than sentimental:

> Well people! Don't that beat you?
> > [Flo Ann] done married Lou fo' spite;
> > The Lo'd have mussy on her!
> > > She's trapped herse'f for life. (29–32)

The poem ends when the speaker's children arrive home from school, an event that she greets with ambivalence. Her preference for conversation, however, is quite clear, and she expresses disappointment that her afternoon gossip has come to a close:

> Laws, honey! here's the child'en,
> > School caint be out so soon;
> > Ef ever time went flyin',
> > > It did this afternoon. (117–20)

One of late-nineteenth-century Black women poets' most surprising anti-pastoral inversions occurs in Clara Thompson's portrayal of the interaction between an African American housekeeper and her white female employer. In "The Easter Bonnet" Thompson uses the interaction between Jennie, the African American woman speaker of the poem, and "Mis' Nelson," her boss, to investigate the ways that Black and white women's opposing experiences of the common setting of the Euro-American home serve as the foundation for dramatically different assessments of white womanhood. That the Black female speaker experiences Mis' Nelson's private sphere as her own public workplace challenges the popular nineteenth-century perception that the distinction between public and private space is absolute by calling attention to the possibility that African American and white women might experience the common space of the Euro-American (pastoral) homescape in dramatically different ways. In this poem Jennie's experience of Black womanhood is differentiated from Mis' Nelson's experience of white womanhood by her experience of the Euro-American home not as sanctuary, but as place of work.

A home and sanctuary for her white employer, the Euro-American household is a public space from which the Black speaker gratefully retreats at the end of her workday. This is the point at which the poem begins. Having returned home from her workplace, the private residence of her employer, the speaker regales her husband with an account of her workday that underscores the divide between the two women's very different experiences of the white woman figure so often idealized in depictions of the white middle-class home:

> John, look what Mis' Nelson give me,
>> When I cleaned for her today;
> Mean, close-fisted, old white woman!
>> 'Clare, I'll throw the thing away!
>
> You may just say I've gone crazy,
>> When I wear a thing like that;
> Just look at that 'bomination!
>> Who would call that thing a hat? (1–8)

Jennie's unsympathetic description of her employer (a "Mean, close-fisted, old white woman") and of the outmoded bonnet ("that 'bomination") reveals a vision of Euro-American womanhood that contrasts sharply with Mis' Nelson's own self-perception as kindhearted and generous. Mis' Nelson's lighthearted self-satisfaction is highlighted as the speaker continues her account:

> Then she went upstairs a-prancing,
>> And I looked for something grand:

> Next I knew, she come down, grinning,
> With this fool thing in her hand. (13–16)

The juxtaposition of Mis' Nelson's cheerful mood (she leaves "a-prancing" and returns "grinning") against Jenny's open resentment throws into relief the distinction between the ways that the two women—separated by race, class, and position—each experience the notion of white ladyhood. Despite the appearance of selfless altruism, Jennie recognizes in Mis' Nelson's donation the effort to reinforce the hierarchy of white womanhood over Black. Although she has "hats in her closet, / That she only bought last year, / An' says now they're out of fashion," Jennie explains, "she would'nt [*sic*] give them to me," because she's "'Fraid I'd hold my head too high" (21–23, 25, 26). When Jennie shares her disappointment with her husband, his response, that "old Mrs. Nelson" has been "an old fool all her life" affirms her counterhegemonic understanding of white womanhood, not as an enviable paradigm, but as a contemptible annoyance.

Clara Thompson's "The Easter Bonnet" and similar poems use snapshots from the everyday lives of Black families rebuilding in the aftermath of slavery and Reconstruction to offer alternative perspectives on several of the most widely recognized symbols of True Womanhood and the pastoral home. Thompson and other Black women poets writing in the late nineteenth century created scenes of African American homelife that challenge the iconography of ideal womanhood piecemeal, each poem taking on certain of its symbols and settings. When the same poets turned their gaze backward, to reopen the question of Black family life under slavery, they shifted their emphasis from the symbols of ideal womanhood to the broader ideological framework—the separation of (men's) public and (women's) private spheres—which those symbols serve and represent.

In African American female poets' antipastoral portraits of Black family life under slavery, the enslaved wives and mothers depicted breach the limitations that define traditional womanhood because the boundaries between their private, domestic concerns and the worldly interests of the public realm (that is, the political and economic interests of the white majority) are collapsed. A common theme in Black women's poetry of the post-Reconstruction era, this collapse is most often dramatized in short scenes depicting moments when the public commerce of the slave trade comes to bear upon the familial bonds that define private family life (those same bonds between mother and child and husband and wife featured in the pastoral poetry of the American homescape).

In Priscilla Thompson's "The Favorite Slave's Story," the male speaker recalls an incident from the period before emancipation that illustrates how the public affairs of "Old Mause" disrupted the relationships that constituted what he and other slaves experienced as private domestic life. The elderly speaker describes the conditions under which his master's involvement in the public commerce of the slave trade came eventually to bear on the families and homes of his slaves:

> Old Mause an' Fairfax wus fast friends;
>   A pa' uv roscals dey;
> In gamblin', cheatin', an' de like,
>   Dey bofe had heap to say.
>
> So bofe got mixed up in a scrape,
>   Wid Richmond's bank, an' den,
> Dey bofe sold ev'ry slave dey had,
>   To keep out uv de pen. (131–38)

The "favorite slave" and his family experience the deterioration of Old Mause's public affairs as the critical disruption of their private concerns:

> An' so, at last, de day rolled 'round,
>   When all, exceptin' I,
> Wus put upon de block an' sold,
>   To any one who'd buy.
>
> Oh son! You don't know whut it is,
>   To see yo' loved ones sold,
> An' hear de groans, an' see de tears,
>   Uv young, as well as ole. (161–68)

"The Favorite Slave's Story" and other poems that describe the intervention of the commerce of the slave trade into the homelife of the slave challenge the popular nineteenth-century concepts of public man and private woman. Such poems expose the politics of positionality that govern whether or not the subject experiences home as sanctuary. In the pastoral of the American homescape the subject's relationship to womanhood determines her experience of home; adult females whose activities violate the cardinal virtues of American womanhood necessarily exclude themselves from the experience of home as earthly respite. However, antipastoral poems that describe the collapse of public-private distinctions in the Black woman's home suggest that it is not her relationship to womanhood but, instead, her relationship to whiteness, that bars the African American female subject from the experience of home as sanctuary. For the white plantation owner, the kinship bonds that define the private family life of the African American slave are simply minor variations in those changeable assets that determine his movements and status in the public sphere.

Nowhere is the antipastoral suggestion of this division between Black and white subjects' experience of a common setting more explicit than in Priscilla Thompson's "The Old Freedman." At the beginning of the poem an elderly former bondsman describes the first time that his master's financial interests as public landholder intruded into the private domestic lives of his slaves. As in "The Favorite Slave's Story," the intervention of public commerce into private homelife is epitomized in the separation of the slave mother from her child:

> He hears the fierce screams of his mother, wild,
> Anguished and startling, and loud as of old;
> While haplessly he, her remaining child,
> Is hurried "down the river," and sold. (17–20)

It is not until the elderly freedman recounts the developing relationship between him and his wife, however, that the gulf between the African American experience of slave marriage—as the foundation of private family life—and the slave master's experience of that very same union—as a financial development in his public affairs—becomes explicit. Thompson makes no reference to the physical space of the family home. Her detailed account of the interaction between the elderly freedman and his wife does, however, reveal in their marital bond the same qualities of sanctuary and domesticity that, in the nineteenth century, were identified exclusively with white, middle-class family life. The protection that the gentleman slave offers his young wife in the field of labor, even at the risk of his own safety, echoes rather poignantly the popular characterizations of male space as the space in which labor takes place and of woman's activities as isolated from the dangers and demands of the workaday world:

> He is hoeing cane, with a stalwart pace,
> And with him, a girl, the joy of his life;
> With her graceful figure and dark brown face,
> And her sunny smile—his own fair wife.
> When e'er the overseer's back is turned,
> He lends a strong hand to her lagging rows;
> That her exacting task may be earned,
> To ward from her back the brutal blow. (25–32)

Similarly, that the young woman brings joy into her husband's days, "Despite the appalling crosses of [his] life," corresponds with the links, made by popular midcentury poets, between woman's domestic space and the idea of respite from worldly concerns:

> Despite the appalling crosses of life,
> He deems himself, e'en a happy man;
> Just to have her near and to call her "wife,"
> And to hurriedly press her little worn hand. (33–36)

That each interaction between the old slave and his wife corresponds to one or more of the attributes of the pastoral home (and the ideal woman within) establishes, implicitly, that the bond between an African American husband and his wife—even under rule of slavery—constitutes the formation of a household. Having firmly established the existence of matrimonial bonds within the slave community, Thompson contrasts the perspective of the plantation owner, recounting, in the following passage, the moment when his fiscal concerns as landowner abruptly dissolve the familial attachments established by his slaves:

> His Lucy [approaches] with eyes filled with tears;
> "Oh Ruben," she's crying, "why I'm to be sold!"
> The words fall like doom upon his shocked ears. (38–40)

In this passage Thompson's focus on the emotions of the young slave and his wife (she describes Lucy's crying, her husband's shock) highlights their experience of marriage as the defining component in their private, domestic life. It also accentuates the conflict between the slave owner's economic interest in selling the young bride and the couple's personal interest in maintaining the marriage and family bonds that form the basis of their household.

Finally, in an antipastoral move that emphasizes the Black slave's experience of the collapse of divisions between public and private concerns, Thompson juxtaposes the Old Freedman's attempt to assert kinship on the basis of the matrimonial bond against his master's counterclaim of ownership based on his right to hold property:

> He [the Old Freedman] drops his hoe, with a desperate groan;
> He'll make the rude trader take back his foul pelf,
> He'll claim his wife, for she is his own.
>
> Oh, futile struggle! he sees his fair love,
> Borne off by the rude, evil, trader who spoils,
> While he helplessly, calls on his Father above,
> And is fiercely, brutally, lashed for his toils. (46–52)

Although it opens against the same backdrop of family dissolution that she depicts in "The Old Freedman," Priscilla Thompson's shorter and less harrowing "The Husband's Return" appends a rewarding, postbellum conclusion to the now familiar separation narrative. This poem dramatizes not the parting, but the reunion of husband and wife. The poem opens with a description of the events that precede the newly freed bondsman's return to reclaim his absent wife:

> He, an emancipated slave,
> From Rappahanock's side;

Assured by Lincoln's strong decree,
Had journeyed southward, bold and free,
To claim his stolen bride. (11–15)

Even as the intrusion of the slave master's economic interests into the private, domestic affairs of his slaves leads to the young freedman's initial separation from his wife, the intervention into his life of the public spectacle of the Civil War hastens their reunification:

From many a camp of Union men,
He'd found his rations free;
And by their kindly guiding hand,
He now located the plundered land,
Where his young wife must be. (16–20)

When he finally reaches the plantation to which his wife was sold, "Young Stephen" confronts the slave master with news of the *public* events that substantiate his claim to the right of self-determination in his *private* family life:

Young Stephen, to keep down his wrath,
His strongest will employs;
He simply says, "All slaves are free,
The news is heard where e'er I be;
I want my wife and boy." (41–45)

In highlighting African Americans' experience of the collapse of the separation between public and private realms and concerns, "The Husband's Return" and similar poems utilize one particular tool of antipastoral resistance more potent than any other. A recurring theme in nineteenth-century antipastoral poetry is the irony of Black women's experience of cruelty (or, less dramatically, of condescension and disregard, as in "The Easter Bonnet") at the hands of her white middle- or upper-class female employer. Poems that depict images of white female cruelty highlight the dual subjectivity of that figure; only the subject whose racial and economic position enables him or her to experience the white, middle-class dwelling as pastoral retreat experiences the white woman as True Woman, compassionate, pious, humble, and submissive. Such figures share her whiteness and her class privilege. For others, white womanhood is characterized by traits and behaviors quite starkly opposed to the virtues exalted in those poems depicting the feminine ideal. These "others" experience her home as a site of labor, subjugation, and disempowerment; their experience of white woman herself is defined by the dispassionate and often cruel self-interest that the economically privileged Euro-American woman reveals in her interactions with poor (often nonwhite) people and communities. "The Husband's Return" employs a variation on this

A "SOLE AND EARNEST ENDEAVOR"

counterrepresentation of the white middle- or upper-class woman, in which the very home by whose peaceful sanctuary her womanliness would be measured appears simultaneously as sanctuary for the white family of the slave master and torment for his Black servants. To highlight the stark difference between ideal womanhood and its inversion, the speaker offers this dramatic passage in which the two contrary functions of the plantation home are juxtaposed: "flowers adorn [the] mansion great / The Prison of his wife" (24–25).

Clara Thompson's "The Favorite Slave's Story" addresses the question of white female cruelty more directly. In this poem "Miss Nancy," the master's wife, brings the same cruelty and commodification to her interactions with the slaves as her husband, their owner. Thus she functions simultaneously as "lady" of the home for her guests and mistress to and tormenter of his slaves. Like the "Ole Mause" who would "whoop us soon as not" (25), Miss Nancy uses the threat of the lash as a tool of control, as the speaker recalls in this passage:

> One Mawning', jest to pick a fuss,
>   [Miss Nancy] said she missed a pie;
> When Mammy said dey all wus tha,
>   She said, she told a lie.
>
> 'Dat pie wus in her cabin, hid;
>   She wus a vixen, bold;
> An' ef she didn't bring it back,
>   She'd have her whooped an' sold.' (147–54)

Clara Thompson and other Black women's exposure of the dual and conditional signification of white womanhood and the pastoral home complicate their readers' understanding of this complex figure, offering a challenge to the seamless hegemony of this ideal, without which such poets' inversions and excesses might simply appear to reinforce prevailing stereotypes about African American women. Black women poets' exposure and inversion of the True Woman icon discredits and unravels the myth of ideal womanhood, calling attention to the assumptions and beliefs that supported the ascendancy of this symbolic figure and opening up a space to explore new forms of adult female subjectivity that respond to interests other than the maintenance of strict race and gender hierarchies.

Black feminist historical analysis offers a vision of nineteenth-century African American life before and after emancipation that corresponds with post-Reconstruction poets' representations of Black life.[22] Angela Y. Davis and Jacqueline Jones Royster identify the collapse of public-private distinctions in the lives of African American women as the basis for the alienation of the Black female subject from all aspects of mainstream femininity. Davis observes:

> Since [Black] women, no less than men, were viewed as profitable labor-units,
> they might as well have been genderless as far as the slaveholders were concerned.
> In the words of one scholar, "the [Black] woman was first a full-time worker for
> [the landowner], and only incidentally a wife, mother and homemaker." Judged
> by the evolving nineteenth-century ideology of femininity, which emphasizes
> women's roles as nurturing mothers and gentle companions and housekeepers
> for their husbands, Black women were practically anomalies. (Davis 5)

The white owner-employer privileged the Black woman's function in maintaining his status as landowner over any role that she might play within her own
household. In addition, his perception that Black women and men had an equal
capacity for hard labor—and thus were equally valuable as economic assets—
undercut any attempts by African American workers to transfer any gender
distinctions observed within their homes and communities out into the public
workplace. For example, Davis explains that "since Black women as workers
could not be treated as the 'weaker sex' or the 'housewife', Black men could
not be candidates for the figure of 'family head' and certainly not for 'family
provider'" (Davis 8). Writing of the period after emancipation, Jacqueline Jones
Royster points out that this equal valuation of Black women as laborers was not
a result of the progressive gender politics of white landowners. Instead, this
limited form of gender parity was a side effect of the sociopolitical oppression
and economic exploitation of Black workers in the decades following the end of
Reconstruction. She explains how African Americans working during the late
nineteenth century were uniformly subject to the dominant interests of white
landowners so that, much like their forbears who worked under slavery, "black
males and females were equal in the sense that neither sex wielded economic
power over the other" (Royster 13).

Similarly, white landowners—whose principal interest in the Black family
(and the African American home) was as an economic resource—saw even the
African American woman's duties and relationships within her own household as
profitable labor in the service of their own commercial interests. Royster writes:

> To slaveholders and later to white employers, the black family offered a steady
> and reliable source of new laborers; black women reproduced the supply of cheap
> labor at the same time that they preserved their own kin groups. (Royster 4)

Her discussion, in the following passage, of the relationship between Black
woman's service within her own home and the economic interests of the white
Southern landowner is equally applicable to both the antebellum and postbellum periods:

> If work is any activity that leads either directly or indirectly to the production of
> marketable goods, then slave women did nothing but work. Even their efforts to

care for themselves and their families helped to maintain the owner's work force and to enhance its overall productivity. (Royster 14)

The emphasis in both contemporary Black feminist history and post-Reconstruction verse upon the collapse in Black family life of any separation between public and private concerns raises one final question. If late-nineteenth-century Black women poets resist, in their antipastoral verse, the notion of home as sanctuary because it does not accurately reflect the reality of most African American lives, then what spaces do function in that capacity?

African American women's poetry of the post-Reconstruction period reveals the simultaneous influences of a Christian belief in the afterlife, first expressed in traditional poetic forms like the spiritual; widespread social and economic persecution; and the related intrusion of Euro-American political and financial concerns into Afro-American homelife. The anonymous composers of the antebellum spirituals share with their postbellum descendants the belief that African Americans find refuge from the compounded burdens of economic exploitation, sexual subjugation, and persistent racism only in death.

Mary Weston Fordham's "The Dying Girl," for example, a poem similar in tone and subject matter to the antebellum spiritual "City Called Heaven,"[23] depicts a Black woman speaker weary from the struggles of earthly existence and looking forward to her passage into the sanctuary of the next world, her "happy home above" (16).[24]

Turning away from the Calvinist understanding of Heaven as reward for earthly righteousness, Fordham's speaker instead conceives Heaven as joyful respite from earthly troubles and worldly cares. Unlike the pious mother-speaker in popular midcentury Euro-American verse (who aspires, with hopeful uncertainty, toward a place in the Kingdom of God), Fordham's speaker is sure of her place in Heaven, and looks forward to her eternal life there:

> . . . and now I'm going to join that spirit band,
> With their never-ceasing music, making glad that starry land;
> And I'm glad too, for I'm weary, and would rest me from my woe—
> Fain would land my stricken spirit on the banks of "Evermore." (17–20)

In Fordham's "The Dying Girl," the speaker submits that the grave, in its capacity as the gateway to a blissful afterlife, is the only true sanctuary that she has access to; the one true domicile is the heavenly domicile; and for this dying speaker, the beauty of the landscape that surrounds her family home inspires not a revelry in the sanctity of home and family life (as in midcentury portraits of the pastoral homescape) but rather a recognition of the challenges and difficulties of earthly existence:

See the crimson clouds are hov'ring round the glorious orb of day,
And the far-off hills are basking in its golden, garnished ray;
Listen to yon forest warbler hymning sweet and joyous lay,
Chanting forth its evening vespers to the sinking god of day.

But sister, time is waning, after all it doth but seem
That life is but a toilsome march, a weariness, a dream . . . . (53–54)

Viewed in the context of her exhaustion with the struggles of daily life, the speaker's quiet anticipation of a happy and restful future in her heavenly home carries with it an implied rejection of the popular Euro-American conception of home as the earthly retreat; and it is, in the end, only one of the diverse methods that African American women poets of the post-Reconstruction era use to liberate woman's subjectivity from the space of the white middle-class, single-family home. Conspicuously absent from Fordham's poems or the poems of her contemporaries, however, is any concrete suggestion of a new setting or symbol for a less exclusionary vision of female identity, one that leaves space for the possibility of women subjects who are not white. In fact, it would be nearly one hundred years before Black women poets' campaign against invisibility developed into a movement that had as its goals both reconstruction and resistance. In an essay called "'On the Threshold of Woman's Era'" Hazel Carby writes:

A desire for the possibilities of the uncolonized black female body occupies a utopian space. . . . Black feminists understood that the struggle would have to take place on the terrain of the previously colonized: the struggle was to be characterized by redemption, retrieval, and reclamation. (Carby, "'Threshold'" 332)

As early as the late nineteenth century, African American women writers understood the importance of dominion over the "previously colonized" space of the Black female body as essential to the achievement of emancipated Black womanhood, even though at this time such empowerment and self-determination seemed a distant hope. Indeed, for most African American women of the late nineteenth century, their enthusiasm for the possibility of self-determination and dominion over all aspects of their daily existence was not unlike their faith in the promise of peace, prosperity, and freedom; virtually all Black women looked forward to the eventual empowerment of their race and gender, but few believed it would happen during their lifetimes.

CHAPTER 2

THE BLACK WOMAN AS OBJECT AND SYMBOL
AFRICAN AMERICAN WOMEN POETS IN THE HARLEM RENAISSANCE

> If there is a single distinguishing feature of the literature
> of black women—and this accounts for their lack of
> recognition—it is this: their literature is about black women;
> it takes the trouble to record the thoughts, words, feelings,
> and deeds of black women . . . .
>
> MARY HELEN WASHINGTON,
> "The Darkened Eye Restored"

> The heart of a woman goes forth with the dawn,
> As a lone bird, soft winging, so restlessly on,
> Afar o'er life's turrets and vales does it roam
> In the wake of those echoes the heart calls home.
>
> The heart of a woman falls back with the night,
> And enters some alien cage in its plight,
> And tries to forget it has dreams of the stars
> While it breaks, breaks, breaks on the sheltering bars.
>
> GEORGIA DOUGLAS JOHNSON
> "The Heart of a Woman"

Georgia Douglas Johnson, one of the most prolific women poets of the 1920s "New Negro Renaissance," did not write "The Heart of a Woman" as a comment on the relationship between her work and that of the Black women poets who preceded her.[1] Like most of her African American contemporaries, Johnson probably had only limited exposure to earlier generations of Black women writers. And yet the juxtaposition between the two stanzas of this short poem mirrors so poignantly and with such precision the contrast between Black women poets' self-representations in the post-Reconstruction era and Black women's self-representations in Johnson's age, the so-called Renaissance that followed. "The Heart of a Woman" opens with the image of a woman, brave-hearted and self-assured, moving boldly forward into the unknown challenges of a new day. Whether the opening line of this, the title poem in her signature volume, refers to the beginning of a new age or simply to the dawn of the coming day, Georgia Douglas Johnson sees in the heart of a woman the restless desire to explore beyond the boundaries that define woman's safest and most familiar settings ("those echoes the heart calls home" [4]). Johnson's use of the image of the "lone bird" (2) to represent the experiences of the adventurous female heart suggests that the bold woman's path is a solitary one, but her willful departure from the heart's most recognizable and beloved settings—hearth, home, and its familiar comforts and obligations (family, domesticity, humility)—brings its own rewards. The image of the bold-hearted woman stretching her mind and her spirit "Afar o'er life's turrets and vales" suggest that one such reward is freedom.

In the second stanza, however, we see a forced retreat from the audacious self-determination of the first. Only moments after calling attention to the freedom of the woman whose longings and aspirations know no boundaries, Johnson depicts the same woman in sad defeat as her heart "falls back with the night" (5), literally retreating from the spirit of freedom and progress with which it earlier greeted the dawn. Paired with Johnson's portrayal of "The heart of a woman" as it "tries to forget it has dreamed of the stars" (7), this retreat from autonomy points to the familiar historical pattern in which periods of social progress for women alternate with periods of backlash and retreat, often connected to shifts in the sociopolitical climate and the economic conditions of their communities. Johnson's model of bold optimism and audacious forward movement juxtaposed against a dramatic and enforced withdrawal captures the curious contrast between the unprecedented focus on the daily lives of Black women by the first African American women poets to emerge after the end of Reconstruction and the conspicuous retreat from that topic by their Jazz Age successors. Black women of the post-Reconstruction era were among the earliest writers of any ethnicity or gender to explore the social construction of gender and race. Confronting head-on the racist, essentialist gender ideals of the nineteenth century, they set the stage for subsequent generations to undertake even bolder explorations of the intersections between ethnicity, class, and the idea of womanhood.

Nevertheless, although only ten years separate the end of the post-Reconstruction era and the beginning of the Harlem Renaissance, it would be more than fifty years before Black women writers would, as a group, revisit the representation of African American women subjects.[2] This chapter explores how the male-dominated Black literary establishment of the 1920s placed restrictions on African American women poets' representations of female subjects that inhibited their continued engagement with those issues of gender, race, and visibility first raised by their late-nineteenth-century predecessors. This chapter will also provide an overview of the poetry that resulted from the peculiar convergence of ideologies and circumstances that brought about this dramatic shift in Black women poets' approach to self-representation.

Many of the elements that distinguish African American literature of different periods can be understood by taking into account changes in writers' perceptions of the intended reading audience. For example, the differences that separate the characterization of slave owners in Harriet Jacobs's *Incidents in the Life of a Slave Girl* from the characterization of slave owners and their families in Booker T. Washington's *Up from Slavery* are, at least to a certain extent, due to the relationship of each writer and his or her text to the institution of slavery.[3] At the same time, however, the discrepancy between the ways that these two autobiographies depict the white antebellum slaveholder is also related to differences in tastes and expectations between Jacobs's intended audience of white northern liberals and Washington's intended audience of northern white philanthropists and southern white partisans.[4] Even the most dramatic shift in African American literature, from the protest writings of the postwar era to the radical nationalist texts of the 1960s, was largely due to the deliberate choice by the young urban intellectuals of the latter period to privilege what they understood as the interests and needs of their intended audience of African American readers.

Because they sought only to reach a small "parlor audience," African American women poets of the post-Reconstruction era were free from both the demands of the Black literary establishment and the inflexible expectations of a racially conservative white reading audience.[5] The complexity of African American female figures in Black women's late-nineteenth-century poetry (subjects who are depicted simultaneously as Black, female, and often poor) reflects the many different contexts in which individual members of the parlor audience—the reading community as subset of the intellectual, familial, and civic community in which the poet lived—experienced the writer in their day-to-day encounters with her. In short, the complexity of the African American woman figures that we see in the post-Reconstruction poems reflects the complexity of each poet's role in the community from which her original readers were drawn. African American female poets of the post-Reconstruction era could write simultaneously as women and as Black people because their intended audience consisted of readers who experienced them as both.

For African American women poets of the Harlem Renaissance period, there was little overlap between a Black woman writer's local community and her reading audience. The potential reading audience for African American poetry—comprised of working-, middle-, and upper-class northern Blacks and northern white intellectuals, bohemians, and philanthropists—was far too broad to facilitate the type of daily intimacy that characterized the post-Reconstruction poet's relationship to her likely readers. Thus the Harlem Renaissance woman poet was considerably more likely to seek and find publication channels and readers among people whose communities were far removed from her own and who would likely experience her as an outsider or an anomaly.[6] So while the socially complex woman figures who appear in African American women's post-Reconstruction verse reflect the parlor audience's intimate encounters with the dual identities of the writer who is both woman and Black, African American women's poems of the Harlem Renaissance period offer representations of womanhood that respond to the demands of a male-dominated Black literary establishment preoccupied with the capacity of Negro poetry and prose to influence that majority of white readers whose beliefs about the oppositional relationship of Blackness to womanhood would never be challenged by a physical encounter with the writer who experienced her Blackness and womanhood simultaneously.[7]

Ironically, the very same post-Reconstruction decades that witnessed the rise of bold, transgressive female images in African American women's verse revealed a marked ambivalence on the part of African American men about the role of Black women writers and about their depictions of Black women's lives. Black male artists and intellectuals of the period were deeply influenced in their decisions about the shape and extent of Black women's participation in the emerging literary community by the very gender restrictions—based in the Euro-American ideology of "separate spheres"—that African American women were writing against. In identifying the "proper" place for Black women in the literary and artistic movements within the civil rights establishment, African American male leaders were especially responsive to the dominant culture's designation of women's domestic work (child rearing, household maintenance, etc.) as "private" life and thus peripheral to whites' political, commercial, judicial, legislative, and other "public" interests, including the subjugation of Black people in each of these areas. Inasmuch as white dominance in those areas where Blacks experienced the most visible forms of racial prejudice—judicial, legislative, commercial, political—manifested itself in whites' dominance of the male "public" sphere, African Americans' struggle was conceptualized as a gendered offensive to make a place for Black manhood within a social order that sought to limit the exercise of male power—especially male power within the public sphere—to those men who were white. As a result, Black struggle came to be understood as Black male struggle, with the larger interests of the race depending on (and perceived by many to be interchangeable with) the African

American male's attainment of access to manly privilege within public spaces and institutions.

During the last decades of the nineteenth century, the perception by Alexander Crummell and other Black male artists and intellectuals that poetry by Black women, depicting the events and conditions of Black women's lives, either undermined or was irrelevant to the larger struggle for racial justice became the basis for restricting female writers' participation in the organizations and publications of the growing Black artistic and intellectual community. This thinking continued to prohibit women's meaningful participation in Black artistic circles throughout the first two decades of the twentieth century.[8] In the 1920s, however, the widespread relaxation of gender roles, especially in urban arts communities, resulted in an unprecedented openness of the Black literary establishment to the contributions of African American women and others who had previously been either marginal to or unacknowledged within the community of Black artists and writers.[9] The dramatic increase in the number of women poets recognized as members and participants in the New Negro (Harlem) Renaissance of the 1920s and 1930s is clear in a comparison of the two most important anthologies of Black poetry produced during that period. *The Book of American Negro Poetry*, edited by James Weldon Johnson, represents the late-nineteenth- and early-twentieth-century practice of limiting women's participation in Black literary and artistic communities. One of the original members of the conservative and predominately male American Negro Academy, described by Mary Helen Washington as "an organization of Colored authors, scholars, and artists, with the expressed intent of raising the standard of intellectual endeavor among American Negroes" (Washington, Introduction 33), Johnson considers very few female writers worthy of inclusion in what otherwise appears to be a fairly exhaustive overview of Negro literature.[10] Of that handful of women whom Johnson deems worthy of recognition, only one is perceived to be of sufficient historical and artistic merit to warrant the inclusion of more than one or two of her poems. Of the thirty-seven poets featured in this volume, only three are women. Overall, seven of the poems in this book were written by women, the greatest number (four) by Phillis Wheatley. Perched at the opposite end of the spectrum is the other major anthology of the period, *Caroling Dusk: An Anthology of Verse by Black Poets of the Twenties*. This volume represents editor and poet Countee Cullen's attempt to capture all of the innovation of the New Negro Movement, including its gender inclusivity. The anthology has as its stated mission the representation of the new movement in Black literature.[11] In fact, *Caroling Dusk* is intended both to chronicle and to incite young poets' movement away from the subjects, themes, and perspectives of the past. In this anthology, 13 of the 38 poets featured are women, and 37 of the 219 poems in the volume were written by women.[12]

Cullen's anthology is intended to represent the newest developments in Black literature, and thus it reflects the shift during this period in favor of a gender-inclusive African American literary community.[13] But while the demographics of the artistic movement now known as the Harlem Renaissance look quite different from the demographics of prior Black artistic movements and organizations, the underlying basis for evaluating the aesthetic merit of a piece of writing retained the previous century's biases and limitations, if not on the issue of women's participation, then certainly on questions surrounding the representation of women's lives. The survival well into the 1930s of several of the earliest pioneers in the creation of a Black aesthetic that combined artistic innovation with political expediency resulted in the persistence, throughout the more gender-inclusive Harlem Renaissance period, of some of the very same attitudes surrounding the interaction of politics, art, and representation that led to women's exclusion from African American artistic communities in prior decades.[14] A cornerstone of the artistic vision advocated by this older generation of Black intellectuals (Du Bois, Johnson, and others) was the rejection of "pure" artistic expression (what we might call "art for art's sake") in favor of art created for the purpose of racial uplift; Black art was art that struggled toward the greater goal of African American sociopolitical freedom. As Barbara Christian in *Black Feminist Criticism* explains, "many black ideologues" of the Renaissance Era "saw art as a means of proving the worth of the race" (Christian 122). This understanding of the mission of African American arts and literature reflects the values and hopes of many Black thinkers of the late nineteenth and early twentieth centuries, including the members of the American Negro Academy.[15] Their vision of art as vehicle for racial uplift is perhaps best exemplified in the words of advice from academy member James Weldon Johnson to the New Negro writers, "whom he charged with the serious task of re-educating white opinion" (Birch 34):

> But these younger writers must not be mere dilettantes; they have serious work to do. They can bring to bear a tremendous force for breaking down and wearing away the stereotyped ideas about the Negro, and for creating a higher and more enlightened opinion about the race. (qtd. in Birch 34–35)

In *Black American Women's Writing: A Quilt of Many Colors* Eva Lennox Birch cites one writer's observations of the uneasy relationship between artistic freedom and the notion of literature as a tool for racial uplift:

> In his article on "The Negro Artist and the Racial Mountain" in *The Nation* in 1926, Langston Hughes . . . identified the double bind in which the Harlem writers found themselves. They were constrained by political pressures from black leaders, and by their financial dependence upon white patrons. (Birch 36–37)

THE BLACK WOMAN AS OBJECT AND SYMBOL

If young African American male writers of this period found themselves locked in a double bind, as Langston Hughes contends, then Black women writing at this time were caught in a triple bind, the third and most perplexing aspect of which was that to write against racism—to take on the "serious work" with which James Weldon Johnson and others charged young Black artists—was to privilege the African American male's experience of racially motivated oppression. In this passage from *The Sexual Mountain and Black Women Writers* Calvin Hernton addresses the origins of this trend that obliged African American women to frame their treatments of racial struggle in terms of the interests and aspirations of Black men:

> Historically the battle line of the racial struggle in the United States has been drawn exclusively as a struggle between the men of the races. Everything having to do with race has been defined and counter-defined by men as a question of whether black people were or were not a race of Men. The central concept and the universal metaphor around which all aspects of the racial situation revolve is "Manhood." Whatever whites have done to blacks, it is viewed, by the men, not as the wrongdoing on an entire people, males and females. Rather, it is viewed solely in terms of the denial of the MANHOOD of a people. (Hernton 38)

In order for their antiracist works to achieve recognition within the African American artistic and intellectual establishment, Black women writers had to capitulate to the prevailing construction of Blackness as a male identity category. In the poetry of the Harlem Renaissance African American women's capitulation to this demand is manifest in their almost universal retreat from depicting the actions or experiences of Black subjects who are women. Instead, we see that, with few exceptions, the women poets of the New Negro era responded to the popular understanding of Blackness as a male identity category by writing either as Black people or as women, but never as both.

Racist institutions and individuals seek to limit African Americans to a state of objecthood. African Americans become devices to be manipulated by institutions like the justice system, or institutionalized practices like segregation, as a means of building and maintaining the ideological and economic framework of white supremacy; or else Black people function as objects on which racist individuals perform acts like lynching and rape, whose practical and symbolic function is to maintain the hierarchy of white people over Black people.[16] The objectification of the Black individual is, then, both a goal and a means of expressing white racism against Black people. When African Americans retaliate against those institutions and individuals whose actions support white supremacy, however, they resist that very object status that is so essential to white racial dominance, thus reclaiming their status as subjects. Poems that portray, suggest, or promote such actions dislodge the Black figures they depict from the status of objects who are acted upon and thrust them into the status of subjects who act. Inasmuch as antiracist resistance implies the pursuit of subjectivity, Black women poets' scrupulous avoidance throughout the Harlem Renaissance of any direct representation of African American women's experience of, response to, or (re)action against U.S. racism amounts to an abandonment of the cause of Black female subjectivity. Such poems retreat from the boldly articulated struggles of African American women's everyday lives favored by many Black female poets of the post-Reconstruction era, relying instead upon delicately crafted verses that either privilege the African American male experience of racism or avoid any reference to gender at all.

In the humbly titled "A Poem," for example, Gladys Casely Hayford creates a meditation on the nature of Black responses to racism that is cleverly structured to evade the question of gender. Given the gender-conscious environment of Jazz Age Harlem, it is impossible to dismiss as coincidence the complete absence of gender references from this short work:[17]

> Let my song burst forth on a major note,
> Check the minor lilt in the Negro's throat.
>
> But how can the Negroes play their harps,
> With sorrow for intervals pain for sharps?
>
> With a knife in the wound, and tears on the face
> Should the song be quavered in treble or bass?
>
> Though the tempo is kept by the shining stars,
> Notation is writ on prejudice bars.
>
> When God gives no sign when we reach the refrain,
> Have we the courage to start again?
>
> With conflicting fuges [sic] and odd times to keep,
> It's a wonder we laugh as well as weep.
>
> It is a most marvellous [sic] wonderful thing
> That inspite [sic] of all this, the Negro can sing. (1–14)

Equal parts homage to and exploration of African Americans' persistence in the face of prejudice, Hayford's Blacks are neither the outspoken mothers and wives who populate women's post-Reconstruction verse nor the heroic "Colored" gentlemen who personify racial uplift throughout the Harlem Renaissance era. They are, instead, gender-neutral "Negroes" set in neither the home nor the workplace, settings whose associations with womanhood and manhood, respectively, would effectively sex any figures located therein. Hayford rejects these physical settings for the rigidity of their gender associations,

instead choosing an abstract notion as her backdrop—the Negro folk tradition in song—whose broad associations with the lives of both women and men
make it an ideal stage for a gender-neutral (or gender-inclusive) exploration of
race. This poem aligns both the "major note" of the poet's own song (the poem
itself, representing the growing Afro-American literary community) and the
"minor lilt in the Negro's throat" (a reference to the African American spiritual)
with the survival technique, long practiced in U.S. Black communities, of easing
the pain of racism with the eloquent grace of rhyme and song.[18]

Her open wonder at the seeming contradiction between the "marvellous wonderful" tradition of African American song and the daily humiliations endured
by those Blacks who created and, in the present day, sustain it aligns Hayford's
concerns with those of her most prominent male contemporaries. First published in 1908, James Weldon Johnson's famous "O Black and Unknown Bards"
is one of the earliest poems to call attention to the unlikely artistry of the African
American spirituals. Johnson, however, stops short of suggesting the miraculous-
ness of his own existence as a Negro poet. Subsequent poets, Hayford included,
were more willing to frame the literature of their generation in the same positive
light as the oral tradition of their predecessors, applying the theme of what June
Jordan labeled "The Difficult Miracle of Black Poetry in America" equally to the
oral tradition of the antebellum years and the literary poets of their own communities. In fact, Hayford's closing lines on the subject ("It is a most marvellous
[*sic*] wonderful thing / That in spite of all this, the Negro can sing") echo the same
sentiments as—and were likely inspired by—the closing lines of Countee Cullen's
similarly themed "Yet Do I Marvel" ("Yet do I marvel at this curious thing, / To
make a poet black and bid him sing" [13–14]). By locating the voice of her Black
speaker within a larger tradition of Negro poetic expression, Hayford replaces
the gendering impulse in Harlem Renaissance literature with a historicizing one,
a move whose ambiguity, by refusing to name either men or women as the object
of her accolades, implies the inclusion of women among those Negroes whose
"marvellous wonderful" capacity for song is worthy of praise.

Despite its effectiveness as an artful negotiation of the taboo against incorporating explicit references to Black womanhood into poems that address racism, however, Hayford's "A Poem" is, in fact, an anomaly. Unlike Hayford, whose
gender-neutral references to "the Negro" do not exclude Black women from the
racial discourse of her period, most African American women poets of the Harlem Renaissance did, at least in their engagement with questions of racial uplift
and resistance, use specific references to a Black male subject whose representation, while marginalizing to the interests and experiences of African American women, also facilitated the construction of poems that are more outspoken
on issues of race and inequality than Hayford's approach would permit.

The delicate blend of sentimental wonderment and grief in Hayford's poem contrasts sharply with the bold call to arms that is Georgia Douglas Johnson's "Question." Hayford's contemplation of the "knife in the wound, and tears on the face" of her gender-neutral Negro seems restrained alongside the defiant resolve of Johnson's passionate call for strong male soldiers to rise up against the forces of prejudice:

> Where are the brave men, where are the strong men?
> Pygmies rise
> And spawn the earth.
> Weak-kneed, weak-hearted, and afraid,
> Afraid to face the counsel of their timid hearts,
> Afraid to look men squarely,
> Down they gaze—
> With fatal fascination
> Down, down—
> Into the whirling maggot sands
> Of prejudice. (1–11)

Likewise, the highly metaphorical inquiries in Hayford's piece ("But how can the Negroes play their harps, / With sorrow for intervals pain for sharps?" or "When God gives no sign when we reach the refrain, / Have we the courage to start again?") seem timid alongside the terse and unembellished inquiry that is "Query" by Virginia Houston.

> In what coinage, America
>   Will you repay your darker children
>   For lost illusions,
>   Embittered youth,
>   Redeem the blood of our fathers?
> With what coin, O my country? (1–6)

Equally insistent is the speaker's candid warning in Angelina Weld Grimké's "Beware Lest He Awakes":

> You are a nobler man
> Because you have no tan,
> And he a very brute
> Because of nature's soot;
> But though he virtue lack,
> And though his skin be black,
> Beware lest he awakes!
> When called he follows you
> With arm as strong and true

As though you were his friend,
And fights unto the end,
That you may safely live;
Then surely you must give
The laurel branch and crown,
And gifts of just renown;
At least you must and can
Call him your brother man!

Ah, no! The cruel jeer
The ready curse and sneer
Are all that he may have—
A little less than slave,
He's spurned by your scorn,
And bound, both night and morn,
In chains of living death;
And if with longing breath
He breathes your air so free,
You hang him to a tree,
You hound of deviltry.
You burn him if he speak,
Until your freelands reek
From gory peak to peak,
With bloody, bloody sod,
And still there lives a God.
But mark! there may draw near
A day of endless fear;
Beware, lest he awakes! (20–55)

The common denominator that links these three poems to each other and distinguishes them from Hayford's example is their outspoken rage. In each work anger spawns confrontation: Johnson ridicules the prejudice of her enemies, calling them "pygmies" who are "Weak-kneed, weak-hearted, and afraid"; and Houston insists on redress for the losses of slavery, demanding "In what coinage, America, / Will you repay your darker children"; while Grimké taunts the perpetrators of white racial violence ("You hang him to a tree, / You hound of deviltry"), and threatens revenge ("But mark! there may draw near / A day of endless fear"). On the surface, these bold statements seem to contradict any suggestion that Black women's expression was limited during the Harlem Renaissance. There is, however, a direct relationship between each speaker's rageful audacity and the corresponding location, in each poem, both of Black masculinity as the sole identity category around and through which African American anger can be expressed, and of the Black male as the sole figure through whose direct actions racial uplift may be achieved. Johnson's "Question" imagines a battle among men, pitting courageous Black freedom fighters against the cowardly champions of prejudice; Houston's "Query," casts any efforts to compensate America's "darker children" as the redemption of "the blood of our *fathers*" (emphasis added); and Grimké's ominous refrain ("Beware, lest *he awakes*"[emphasis added]) uses androcentric language to frame the discussion around the potential for a U.S. Black people's uprising as a reflection on the prospect of a rebellion by U.S. Black men.

In each of these poems African American manhood is the vehicle through which the woman writer is able to articulate a level of outrage and dissent far in excess of the acceptable (and publishable) range of expressions for Black female poets writing about Black women's lives. Indeed, the literary establishment of the Harlem Renaissance embraced a much broader range of images, emotions, and themes in poems that engaged the question of race through the figure of the Black male than it accepted in poems like Hayford's, which engaged the question of a gender for Blackness with more ambiguity. Through their capitulation to a male-centered discourse on racism, Johnson, Houston, and Grimké even gain access to the rhetorical power of being able to speak of Black subjects. The aggressive acts described in each of these poems either encourage (in Johnson and Grimké) or allude to (in Houston) rebellious acts that might potentially transform African Americans from acted-upon objects within the white-over-black racial hierarchy to acting subjects. Johnson, Grimké, and Houston are free to speak of Black subjects, to express anger and indignation, to be outspoken and audacious, and even to issue threats, not simply because they are privileging the Black male experience of racism in their works but because the male figure at the center of each poem—in whatever capacity he is depicted—functions as a mask behind which the African American woman poet is able, momentarily, to shrug off the limitations of genteel ladyhood.[19] Hayford's speaker, in eschewing the specifics of gender wholesale, has no such mask. Although her speaker's awed appreciation for the unlikely coexistence of African American song and African American suffering challenges prevailing conceptions of Blackness and art that would diminish the significance of Negro achievement in music, the musing tone of "A Poem" positions the speaker as a passive observer, thereby diminishing the impact of her words. Indeed, the tone itself is a side effect of the absence of a male figure through which Hayford could issue forth a more decisive or direct voice.

When Black women poets turn from more generalized demands for resistance and redress, as in the previous poems by Houston, Johnson, and Grimké, to address the specific impact of racism upon Black communities and individuals, their reliance on examples culled exclusively from the experiences of

African American males creates a space not only for their articulation of what would otherwise seem an unwomanly level of outrage but for a limited exploration of the influence of male resistance on woman's domestic sphere. Esther Popel's lynching poems and Georgia Douglas Johnson's parent-to-son poems both utilize the male figure at the center of the poem to write past the limitations placed on female expression in the New Negro literary scene. Moving beyond the simple appropriation of what at the time was perceived as male anger, however, Popel and Johnson complicate their explorations of Black men's struggle against racism with suggestions of either the impact of that struggle on African American home and community life or the role of the domestic sphere in shaping Black men's fate.

In "Flag Salute" and "Blasphemy—American Style," Esther Popel uses the Black male lynching victim at the center of each poem as the basis for interrogating the origins and extent of white southerners' investment in this violent ritual. Popel's true interest in these poems is in creating a vision of lynching that will cast the net of blame and accountability for this practice wide enough to include the white women and children whose approval of and participation in the violence of the lynch mob is often obscured by the high visibility of the adult Euro-American males who actually perpetrate this crime. In both "Flag Salute" and "Blasphemy" Popel's willing placement of the interests of African American men at the poem's *center* allows her to pursue at the poem's *periphery* questions vaguely associated with home and private life. In particular, the poem's emphasis on a practice that pits white male supremacy against Black men's right to due process enables her to explore the complicity—in lynching and other forms of racial violence—of those figures within white America who are most commonly associated with the pious serenity of the household.[20]

"Flag Salute," a poem that first appeared in August of 1934, begins with a brief introduction in prose. In it Popel describes an event whose details underscore the vulnerability of Black male youth in the racial climate of her day: "In a classroom in a Negro school a pupil gave as his news topic during the opening exercises of the morning, a report of the Princess Anne lynching of October 18, 1933."[21] This opening statement, with its image of the young Black schoolboy combines with the overall focus of the poem on the fate of Princess Anne's "feeble-minded" male victim to establish Popel's belief in the centrality of the Black male experience of racism to the struggle for equal rights. It also affords her a bit of latitude in terms of the aspects of white racism that she is able to explore. Any attempt to insert a reference to the specific impact of racism on the lives of African American women would be perceived as detracting from a focus on the injustices perpetrated against Black men, and accordingly Popel offers neither grieving mother nor stricken female siblings to complicate the broadly accepted vision of lynching as the physical suffering of an individual African American male. Popel is not, however, bound by the same system of taboos when it comes to the representation of women who are white; and while the placement of the white female figure in a context that might suggest the existence of two parallel battles for racial equality—one based on Black men's pursuit of male power and the other based on a conflict between Black and white women over the influence of middle-class domestic life on female visibility— Popel's emphasis on the suffering of African American men offsets any challenge that her implication of white private life (in the cultivation of mob rule) might initially pose to the New Negro Movement's emphasis upon the image of the Black male engaged in a public struggle for his own freedom and dignity.

Popel foregrounds her representation of the Princess Anne lynch mob by asserting the innocence of the Black male victim:

> They dragged him naked
> Through the muddy streets,
> A feeble-minded black boy! (2–4)

Because the Princess Anne victim is a "feeble-minded" youth rather than a worldly and sophisticated man, his nakedness signals childlike honesty and tragic vulnerability, in poignant contrast to the "muddy streets," a reference to the impurity of the adult world where he meets his demise. This premise, that the Black victim of the Princess Anne lynching—and by extrapolation, the Black victim of any lynching—is an innocent, becomes the backdrop against which Popel sets up a compelling inversion, which itself becomes her vehicle for implicating white women, the whole white southern family structure, and its institutions (southern womanhood, in particular) in creating and maintaining an atmosphere that encourages this practice of so-called lynch law.[22] While the ideological justification for the lynching of African American men emphasizes the protection of white women and children—considered Euro-America's most vulnerable citizens—from the perceived threat of Black male sexual aggression, Popel presents us with an opposing perspective on the practice, in which the vulnerable Black male innocent is victimized by both the predatory aggression of Euro-American men and the dispassionate cruelty of white southern women and children. Far from the stewards and protectors of childhood innocence and vulnerability, the white women of "Flag Salute" are collaborators in their undoing, both in the life of the lynched Black boy and in their own households. The claims of the elderly white female accuser ("And the charge? Supposed assault / Upon an aged woman!"[5–6]) bring a swift and violent end to any youthful illusions held by the accused Black boy, but Popel's southern ladies are not simply instigators of Black children's victimization. "Flag Salute" goes on to portray

white women as active participants in the undoing of their own children's innocence as well. The following lines reinforce this vision of the Euro-American
mother as corrupter of the sanctity of her own household, as we hear the

> . . . brutish, raucous howls
> Of men, and boys, and women with their babes,
> Brought out to see the bloody spectacle
> Of murder in the style of '33! (18–21)

While the association of white womanhood with the brute cries (the "brut-
ish, raucous howls") of the lynch mob boldly and unambiguously undermines
the prevailing myth of genteel Euro-American womanhood, the most important detail in this passage is its portrayal of white children in the company of
their mothers. The fact that alongside "men, and boys" we see "women *with*
their babes" (emphasis added) suggests the appalling notion of white mothers
accompanying and even shepherding their children to the "the bloody spectacle / Of murder . . . ." This passage is important not only because it exposes
white women's participation in the corruption of their own children (in radical
opposition to woman's traditional responsibility for instilling her offspring with
Christian piety) but also because of what such corruption—of white womanhood, by its own prurient interest in the horror of lynching, and white childhood, by its exposure to this "murder in the style of '33"—reveals about the
southern white household. The notion that the very women and children whose
presence within the Euro-American home is believed to imbue it with its characteristic virtue and civility are themselves actively involved in the perpetu-
ation of racist violence threatens the very foundation upon which the white-
over-Black hierarchy is constructed. Popel replaces the long held myth of the
white household as the seat of American piety and gentility with a new vision
of the white household as originary site for the brutality that manifests itself in
terroristic racial violence.

In the closing lines of "Flag Salute" Popel describes the aftermath of the
Princess Ann lynching. Having divided the remains of the murdered youth
among themselves, the members of the mob disperse to their homes, where
they regale their mothers, wives, and children with grisly souvenirs of the
event, commemorating their battle against the threat of Negro savagery with
keepsakes that underscore their own:[23]

> They cut the rope in bits
> And passed them out,
> For souvenirs, among the men and boys!
> The teeth no doubt, on golden chains
> Will hang

> About the favored necks of sweethearts, wives,
>
> And daughters, mothers, sisters, babies, too! (30–36)

Though its references to Euro-American womanhood are far less direct, Popel's "Blasphemy—American Style," the second of two antilynching poems that she published during the second half of 1934 ("Flag Salute" was the first), shares with its counterpart an interest in highlighting the complicity of white womanhood and the white family in creating and sustaining the culture of the lynch mob. Retreating from the candid portrayal of white women and children's active participation that she offers in "Flag Salute," "Blasphemy—American Style" links the very public act of lynching with the private matter of personal faith. In this poem Popel describes lynching from the perspective of the white male perpetrator. Consistent throughout in content and tone, the poem portrays the irony of the white male perpetrators' grotesque—even profane—misappropriation of Christian doctrine as justification for their crimes. In the opening lines of the poem the speaker calls on God to witness his cruel act:

> Look, God,
> We've got a nigger here
> To burn;
>
> A goddam nigger,
> And we're goin' to plunge
> His cringin' soul
> To Hell! (1–7)

The white male speaker is confident of his privileged position within the Christian order, more exalted than the "goddam nigger" and favored in the eyes of God, whom he perceives as an approving onlooker:

> Now watch him
> Squirm and wriggle
> While we swing him
> From this tree!
>
> And listen, God,
> You'll laugh at this
> I know—
>
> He wants to pray
> Before we stage
> This show!
>
> Imagine, God,
> A nigger tryin'
> To pray!

Lean over, God,
And listen while we tell
This fool

The words
He couldn't even
Spell! (8–26)

Unnamed but complicit in this lynching is white womanhood, whose culpability is rooted in its symbolic and practical function within the Euro-American social order as emblem and source of Christian values. Based on white women's perceived responsibility for instilling their families with piety, humility, and compassion, the white male speaker's misinterpretation of Christian doctrine points to the failure of the white woman in her role as teacher and sustainer of godly compassion or, even worse, her willful and deliberate misrepresentation of biblical teachings to her children.

In her lynching poems Esther Popel takes the freedom (to write beyond the boundaries of acceptable female comportment) that she gains through her focus on the Black male experience of racism beyond the broadly articulated rage that we encounter in Houston, Johnson, and Grimké's demands for resistance and redress, as she uses the powerful image of the lynching scene to indict every constituency within the culture that incubates and sustains the practice. While the strategy of privileging Black male experiences of racism provides access to topics and voices that would otherwise be off limits to Harlem Renaissance women writers, however, this approach also imposes its own limitations.

Tenderness, affection, and concern were difficult to convey through poems depicting or addressing the experience of African American men. Despite the period's unprecedented acknowledgement of sexual diversity, gender roles remained fairly strictly drawn throughout the 1920s, '30s, and even in the progressive urban atmosphere of the New Negro Movement, readers would likely assume that any poem by a woman expressing concern for the well-being of an adult Black man was speaking from the perspective of a woman who, given the prevailing laws and taboos restricting miscegenation, would certainly be perceived as Black. And thus the limitations upon the representation of African American womanhood would again come to bear; any poem that conveyed a Black woman's concern for the safety of her African American male partner in the racially volatile climate of the 1920s and '30s would not only introduce an aspect of Black woman's private life but would also depict an African American female experience of racism.[24] In the poems "My Son" and "Shall I Say, 'My Son, You're Branded'?" Georgia Douglas Johnson writes around this prohibition by clearly identifying as a child the Black male at the center of each of these two commentaries on the future of U.S. racism. The speaker's articulated concern for the male child who is the focus of each work would, in a different context, run the risk of being interpreted as motherly concern which, given the prevailing restrictions on the representation of Black woman subjects, would be rejected as unacceptable. But Johnson renders each of these poems carefully, not only avoiding any specific gender reference to either a mother or a father but focusing the concerns of the parent-speaker on the movements of the son as he negotiates the challenges of the *public* sphere.

"My Son," for example, warns of the likely challenges that await the title character as he comes of age in a racially divided society:

> Stronger than man-made bars, the chain,
> That rounds your life's arena,
> Deeper than hell the anchor sweeps
> That stills your young desires;
> Darker than night the inward look
> That meditation offers,
> Redder than blood the future years
> Roll down the hills of torture! (1–8)

Similarly, "Shall I Say," with its hopeful vision of the speaker's son as a fully matured warrior in the battle against racial prejudice, is as indirect in its gendering of the parent-speaker as it is direct gendering his or her child:

> Shall I say, "My son, you're branded in this country's pageantry,
> By strange subtleties you're tethered, and no forum sets you free?"
> Shall I mark the young light fading through your soul-enchannelled eye,
> As the dusky pall of shadows screens the highway of your sky?
>
> Or shall I, with love prophetic, bid you dauntlessly arise,
> Spurn the handicap that clogs you, taking what the world denies,
> Bid you storm the sullen fortress wrought by prejudice and wrong
> With a faith that shall not falter, in your heart and on your tongue!
> (1–8)

While Johnson stops short of identifying the parent-speaker of the poem as a father, the speaker's emphasis upon the son's skill at battling the forces of racism in his adult life (the speaker urges the young man to "storm the sullen fortress wrought by prejudice and wrong") confirms that the poet behind the speaker supports the understanding that the fight for racial justice is a battle waged between men.[25]

The centrality of the Black male experience of racism to the Harlem Renaissance aesthetic of racial uplift left little room for considering some of the specific effects of prejudice on the lives of African American women, but it did leave open the possibility of treating other nonracialized aspects of women's lives. Thus the female subjects who appear in Black women's poetry of the Harlem Renaissance period are deracinated figures, whose interests, language, and physical characteristics (when described) are carefully selected to avoid any imagery, syntax, subject matter, or setting that might suggest the Blackness or "Coloredness" of the speaking subject. By avoiding specific references to their Blackness, African American women poets of this era were able to address aspects of their womanhood without coming into conflict with the New Negro publishing establishment's preference for submissions depicting Black male experiences and perspectives. This strategy, coupled with the Harlem Renaissance preoccupation with depictions of Black femininity (as a rebuttal to stereotyped images that depicted Black women as boorish and masculine), resulted in female subjects of ambiguous racial identity whose articulated interests coincided with the most conservative interpretations of Euro-American beliefs about woman's true nature and interests.[26] In fact, the only basis for reading the woman subject in such poems as racially or ethnically Black would be the reader's prior knowledge of the poet's ethnicity.

Even poems like Alice Dunbar Nelson's "I Sit and Sew," with its open disdain for certain activities associated with traditional womanhood and bourgeois femininity, achieve little in terms of opening a space for the portrayal of Black women subjects. Nelson writes:

> I sit and sew—a useless task it seems,
> My hands grown tired, my head weighed down with dreams—
> The panoply of war, the martial tread of men,
> Grim-faced, stern-eyed, gazing beyond ken
> Of lesser souls, whose eyes have not seen Death
> Nor learned to hold their lives but as a breath—
> But—I must sit and sew.
>
> . . . .
>
> The little useless seam, the idle patch;
> Why dream I here beneath my homely thatch,
> When there they lie in sodden mud and rain,
> Pitifully calling me, the quick ones and the slain?
> You need, me, Christ! It is no roseate seam
> That beckons me—this pretty futile seam,
> It stifles me—God, must I sit and sew? (1–7, 15–21)

Nelson's disgruntled speaker is unusual, even within the poet's own body of work. In most New Negro women's poetry, the female speaking subjects reaffirm rather than challenge the boundaries of traditional womanhood. Indeed, "I

Sit and Sew" is precisely the type of poetry that Claudia Tate and other recent commentators on the subject of Black Harlem Renaissance women would likely submit as evidence of New Negro women's efforts to create an opening for the emergence of the Black female subject. This reading of Nelson's, Johnson's, or any other Harlem Renaissance woman poet's engagement with the settings and activities associated with traditional womanhood (either for the purposes of critique—as in Nelson—or embrace) is complicated, however, by the fact that the resistance or acceptance of female roles and activities is rarely or never coded to indicate the Blackness of the speaking subject, while descriptions of the activities of African American men almost always call attention their race.[27] In the case of "I Sit and Sew," the speaker takes no steps to locate her statement on gender and domesticity within the context of her African American experience. In so doing, she is, in effect, writing as a woman, to all exclusion of her Blackness. In this way "I Sit and Sew," despite its apparent rejection of woman's role within the home, represents an acceptance of the limited role left open for women within the New Negro literary community.

Nelson's "Violets" replaces disdain for the duties of traditional womanhood, expressed in "I Sit and Sew," with an absolute delight in its settings:

> I had not thought of violets of late,
> The wild, shy kind that spring beneath your feet
> In wistful April days, when lovers mate
> And wander through the fields in raptures sweet.
> The thoughts of violets meant florists' shops,
> And bows and pins, and perfumed papers fine;
> And garish lights, and mincing little fops,
> And cabarets and songs, and deadening wine.
> So far from sweet real things my thoughts had strayed,
> I had forgot wide fields and clear brown streams;
> The perfect loveliness that God had made—
> Wild violets shy and Heaven-mounting dreams
> And now unwittingly, you've made me dream
> Of violets, and my soul's forgotten gleam. (1–14)

Nelson's abrupt transition from the delicate pleasures of the florist's shop (its "bows and pins, and perfumed papers fine") to her focus on its harsh annoyances ("the garish lights, and mincing little fops") is jarring and, on first reading, seems to level a challenge to traditional notions of woman's pleasure. In the end, however, her disgust at these fixtures of urban commerce simply amounts to an impassioned rejection of the worldly in favor of the simple beauty of God-given nature. Juxtaposed against her joy in "the perfect loveliness that God has made," and whose beauty rekindles "her soul's forgotten gleam," the speaker's disdain for the trappings and denizens of worldly commerce suggests a preference for the private over the public, the intensity of which marks her as a true lady. Traditionally, the true lady thrives in only the gentlest, least menacing natural settings. In true ladyhood there are no rivers, but only streams and brooks; there are few rainstorms, but many showers; there are no jungles, but plenty of forests and woods. And the pleasing serenity of field and flower indicates the gentle manners and serene comportment of the woman who finds solace among them, and of the poet who seeks to depict such sweet simplicity.

Georgia Douglas Johnson's "Peace" adopts a similar strategy, using the woman speaker's placement among the idyllic natural features associated with traditional womanhood to create a race-neutral vision of retreat from the worldly affairs of men. Like Nelson's "Violets," Johnson's "Peace" rejects the settings and conditions of the public sphere in favor of the bucolic serenity of nature:

> I rest me deep within the wood,
> Drawn by its silent call;
> Far from the throbbing crowd of men
> On nature's breast I fall.
>
> My couch is sweet with blossoms fair,
> A bed of fragrant dreams,
> And soft upon my ear there falls
> The lullaby of streams.
>
> The tumult of my heart is stilled,
> Within this sheltered spot,
> Deep in the bosom of the wood,
> Forgetting, and—forgot! (1–12)

Clarissa Scott Delany's "Solace" relies on several of the same strategies that Johnson's "Peace" and Nelson's "Violets" employ in creating a space for the representation of female subjects. In the absence of any race-specific coding, the woman speaker's identification of nature as a source of comfort aligns her with the popular association of femininity with a retreat from worldly affairs. Unlike the two previously discussed poems, however, Delany's speaker resides in an urban setting, removed from the rural and suburban settings in which ideal womanhood traditionally becomes visible. In the opening lines of the poem, she describes the limited view from her only window:

> My window opens out into the trees
> And in that small space
> Of branches and sky
> I see the seasons pass (1–4)

The speaker's urban location, however, enhances rather than compromises her display of traditional femininity. She expresses a marked discomfort in this setting:

My life is fevered
And a restlessness at times
An agony—again a vague
And baffling discontent
Possess me. (33–37)

For Delany's disquieted speaker, only the restricted view from her window can alleviate her discontent, and she marks the changing of the seasons in the shifting moods of "that small space of branches and sky." She sees "The glory of the autumn" in "The fragile, golden leaves" and "Cold December" in the "bare, gray branches" (7, 9, 17). The "cold, but gentle rain of spring / Touches them lightly," while "The summer torrents strive / To lash them into a fury / And seek to break them" (27–28, 29–31). Her womanly temperament is evident in the speaker's "baffling discontent" amid the worldly concerns and rapid pace of the urban sphere. That she finds solace only in her limited encounters with nature suggests a yearning and need for those bucolic settings in which True Womanhood flourishes. Her closing thoughts pay homage to the restorative powers of the natural world:

I am thankful for my bit of sky
And trees, and for the shifting Pageant of the seasons.
Such beauty lays upon the heart
A quiet.
Such eternal change and permanence
Take meaning from all turmoil
And leave serenity
Which knows no pain. (38–45)

Like the restless woman at the center of Delany's "Solace," the speaking subject in Angelina Weld Grimké's "Greenness" finds peace in the simple beauty of even the most mundane elements of her natural surroundings. The opening stanza of the poem links the splendor of nature with its capacity to bring calm and relieve anxiety:

Tell me is there anything lovelier,
Anything more quieting
Than the green of little blades of grass
And the green of little leaves? (1–4)

The speaker's association of her "little blades of grass" ("a mothering green finger, / Hushing the heart that beats and beats and beats" [6–7]) with the soothing refuge of maternal love locates the tranquility of the natural environment as a proxy for the comfort and security of the domestic sphere. The unadorned language and naive tone of the poem, from its friendly invitation to the reader ("Tell me is their anything lovelier / . . . . / Than the green . . . / . . . of little leaves?") to the childlike repetition of simple words and phrases ("the green of little blades of grass / And the green of little leaves"; "the heart that beats and beats and beats"), portray the speaker as an innocent, unworldly in her interests and exulting in the pleasures of those remote settings where True Womanhood thrives. Despite her enthusiastic engagement with the womanly theme of nature as respite from worldly concerns, however, the speaker sidesteps any association with Blackness. Juxtaposed against the heavily gendered language and thematics of "Greenness," any reflection of the speaker's race-consciousness is conspicuous by its absence.

Mary Effie Lee Newsome's "Pansy" examines the comparative beauty of three common garden flowers. In "Pansy"—as in "Greenness," "Violets," "Peace," and similar poems—the open engagement by female speaking subjects with the themes and concerns associated with traditional womanhood precludes the racialization of that speaker as African American. Like Grimké's "Greenness," Newsome's poem relies on simple language ("the little pansy's face / That hides away so still and cool" [3–4]) and repetition (the speaker describes the "blue, blue bloom" of the flower [1]) to underscore the speaker's innocence and her pleasure in simple delights. Newsome's poem conveys the speaker's preference, not simply for the carefully tended beauty of garden flowers but for the modestly colored, diminutive pansy over the showy "red lights" and "orange fires" of the rose and the tiger lily (6–7). Choosing the less obtrusive blossoms of "the softest flower that grows," Newsome's speaker voices an aesthetic bias that places her womanhood beyond question or reproach, selecting the most unassuming flower in the garden, a setting already established as a refuge from the public realm of worldly tastes and desires. Safe within the seclusion of her garden, this speaker retreats even further, turning away from the audacious reds and oranges of the larger, showier flowers, toward the subtler, more muted colors of the pansy.

When New Negro women turn their focus to woman's role, they are similarly restrained in their racialization of the speaking subject. In Anne Spencer's "Creed," a short poem that questions the seeming inconsistencies of God's design, the speaker notes proudly her status as loving wife: "my husband loves me til death puts apart, / Less as flesh unto flesh, more as heart unto heart" (15–16); and her description of the events and phenomena that compel her to question God's plan locates her within the isolated setting associated with that role. The speaker's reference to "my garden oak" (1) and "all the wild birds" (3) that surround it places her home in a rural or suburban locale. Her location in a setting far removed from worldly and public concerns is underscored by her description of "a pilgrim stranger" who, "Following an urge . . . / . . . rapped at [her] door" (13–14), an image whose depiction of the lonely wanderer approaching her doorstep suggests a remote, single-family dwelling. Spencer indicates nothing, however, of her speaker's ethnicity. Her open address of woman's concerns and preferred settings displaces any engagement with her likely Blackness.

Just as Spencer's engagement with questions of race and ethnicity is compromised by her reliance on a female speaking subject who occupies a traditional gender role, so too, in "Love's Tendril," is Georgia Douglas Johnson limited from making overt references to Blackness by her decision to portray her speaking subject as a mother. In her other depictions of motherly love and concern ("My Son"; "Shall I Say, 'My Son, You're Branded?'"; and similar poems) Johnson successfully writes around the constraints placed upon the representation of African American women by grounding any race-based assertions in her speaker's concern for the well-being of her Black male children, but she has no such latitude in "Love's Tendril," in which her speaker admires the beauty of her infant daughter:

> Sweeter far than lyric tune
> Is my baby's cooing tune;
> Brighter than the butterflies
> Are the gleams within her eyes;
> Firmer than an iron band
> Serves the zephyr of her hand;
> Deeper than the ocean's roll
> Sounds her heart-beat in my soul. (1–8)

While Johnson's "Ivy" identifies no particular role for the female speaking subject, its focus on defining the limits of womanhood, and its speaker's identification with that category leave no room for the consideration of Blackness in relation to female subjectivity. For Johnson's speaker in this poem, womanhood is defined by the female subject's longing for completion:

> I am woman
> Which means
> I am insufficient
> I need—
> Something to hold me
> Or perhaps uphold.
> I am a woman. (1–7)

THE BLACK WOMAN AS OBJECT AND SYMBOL

Johnson's speaker characterizes womanhood and, by extrapolation, femininity as the state of simultaneously longing to be cared for and needing to care for someone else ("I need / Something to hold me / Or perhaps uphold" [4–6]). Denied the satisfaction of either a caring relationship or a caregiver's role, she is left undone ("I am insufficient / I need—" [3–4]).

Beyond the New Negro establishment's limitations on the portrayal of Black women's lives, Johnson is also constrained in her depiction of female subjects by the fact that, in the broader population, Blackness and womanhood are widely understood as oppositional categories. Johnson, Spencer, Newsome, and others render their delicately articulated explorations of women's concerns with an awareness that any association made by a white reader between their speakers' comprehensive understanding of woman's role and the Black female poet's own achievement of feminine propriety will carry with it the understanding that the Negro woman poet has achieved womanhood and maintains her femininity, not within the context of her Blackness, but despite it.

The female poets of the Harlem Renaissance seem to embrace the same narrowly circumscribed bourgeois femininity that their literary foremothers, the Black women of the post-Reconstruction era, experienced as marginalizing and oppressive. In the racial climate of the first half of the twentieth century, however, their adherence to the limitations of traditional (true) womanhood was also a challenge, if not to the basic notion of a feminine ideal, then certainly to existing beliefs vis-à-vis those groups best and least suited to attaining that goal. To depict Black women subjects who were knowledgeable in and who, by extrapolation, could be interpreted as having embraced European gender norms was to suggest that African American womanhood should be held in the same esteem as white womanhood. The speaking subjects we encounter in "Violets," "Peace," and other, similar poems are deracinated exemplars of traditional womanhood, but the Black woman revealed through such poems—a Black woman whose purity, piety, submissiveness, and humility are so plainly unassailable that the traditional justifications for degrading, misinterpreting, and misappropriating the Black female body and its image no longer seem applicable—is the poet herself, the Negro poetess who modestly sets (or seems to set) aside her own worldly interests in race and political struggle, deferring instead to the more becoming, more feminine concerns of her speaking subject. The womanly interests of the speaking subject—in flowers, childhood, love, and her Christian God—establish and attest to the pious womanhood of the Black woman who created her.

The French aphorism that titles Jessie Fauset's plaintive "La Vie C'est La Vie" links the speaker (and the author) more closely to the elite training of white upper-class women than to the pragmatic vocational instruction that, before

World War II, formed the basis for much of Black higher education.[28] In the body of the poem itself Fauset creates a speaking subject whose idle hours of contemplation in a bucolic park setting suggest both the tranquility of a suburban environment and the leisurely pace of a wealthy lifestyle. These conditions only accentuate the gulf separating the life of the race-neutral woman speaker from the lives of her Black women counterparts:[29]

> On summer afternoons I sit
> Quiescent by you in the park.
> And idly watch the sunbeams gild
> And tint the ash trees' bark.
>
> Or else I watch the squirrels frisk
> And chaffer in the grassy lane[.] (1–6)

In the middle section of the poem, Fauset reveals the conflict at the center of this piece:

> I know a woman who would give
> Her chance of heaven to take my place;
> To see the love light in your eyes,
> The love glow on your face!
>
> And there's a man whose lightest word
> Can set my chilly blood afire;
> Fulfillment of his least behest
> Defines my life's desire.
>
> But he will none of me. (9–17)

The content and subject matter of the poem, a woman's unrequited longing for a man who is inaccessible to her, is a precarious subject for a New Negro woman poet to take on, especially given that her rejection of an available and interested suitor reveals desire, rather than conformity to her expected social role, as her chief motivation. The controversy inherent in the work is counterbalanced, however, by the humble passivity of the woman speaker who, in the final stanza, appears ready to pay the penalty of death for her inappropriate affections:

> . . . he will none of me. Nor I
> Of you. Nor you of her. 'Tis said
> The world is full of jests like these.—
> I wish that I were dead. (17–20)

From Samuel Richardson's *Clarissa* and Thomas Hardy's *Tess of the D'Urbervilles* to Harriet Jacobs's *Incidents in the Life of a Slave Girl* and William Wells Brown's

Clotel and beyond, the authors of popular literature have, in effect, bought permission to explore the more salacious aspects of their female protagonists' lives with the promise of their certain death (including Jacobs's symbolic death in *Incidents*).[30] In "La Vie C'est La Vie" the protagonist's fatal wish communicates an intolerance for extramarital affairs that firmly aligns this poem with a literary tradition that upholds European and Euro-American standards of female sexual propriety, just as it identifies the Black woman poet behind the speaker as a supporter of these established sexual norms.

Despite their restrictions, poems like "La Vie C'est La Vie," "Violets," and "Peace," in which the Black female poet deemphasizes her African American-ness in exchange for the ability to write as a woman, grant their women speakers—and thus the female poets who create them—some degree of freedom to invent themselves as gendered subjects. The speaking subject in each such poem presents her interests and concerns, her sentiments and frustrations, as she perceives them, articulated in her own voice. Poems that depict women and girls who are clearly demarcated as Black trade the humanizing subject status of their deracinated women speakers for a much more limited object status, but of a figure who is specifically coded as a woman of African descent. As object, the Black woman is contemplated, rather than contemplating, analyzed rather than the analyzer, and—most importantly—she is the object of the gaze, but never the objectifier, seen, but never seeing.

Under such constraints, the African American woman poet, confronted with the possibility of depicting a figure who is both woman and Black, in all but a handful of children's poems, elects to prioritize her identity as an African American over her status as a woman. Opting to write as a Black person rather than as a woman, the African American woman poet is obliged in such poems to privilege her Blackness (i.e., those interests, values, and traits that would link her to other African American people, especially those African American writers—largely male—among whom she would have to locate herself in order to secure publication as a New Negro poet) over her gender. And just as the Black woman poet seems to deemphasize her racial difference when writing "as a woman" to depict the deracinated female subject, the same poet deemphasizes her womanhood—that which would separate her from the majority of her peers within the African American literary community of the Harlem Renaissance—when portraying the figure who is woman *and* Black. This is not to suggest that her readers, editors, or publishers were unaware of her gender but rather that the poet took great care to use language and imagery to establish a tone that made clear that the gender difference of the writer was in no way indicative of interests, values, or concerns contradictory to the interests and goals of Black males. Just as the woman poet was obliged to filter her most passionate statements about racism through the experience of Black men, so too was she compelled to depict the Black woman figure in ways that reinforced the elevation of Black manhood as means and goal of the racial uplift movement.

To accomplish this delicate negotiation between the gender identity of the poet and the gendered interests of the New Negro literary establishment, Black female poets often appropriated the male gaze, in effect seeing the Afro-American woman as a Black man would, taking on a male-gendered voice and using the words of her male speaking subject to write "like a man." Once again, this is not to suggest that the gender of the Black female writer of such poems was inconsequential, nor did it go unacknowledged. Both African American and non–African American editors of literary anthologies, for example, freely categorized Black writers by gender, and even marveled at the achievements of those Black writers who overcame both the oppression of their Negro race and the perceived limitations of their female gender in order to create literary poetry.[31] Such acknowledgments of the unique obstacles confronting the woman writer of African descent, however, brought with them neither an embrace of nor a tolerance for any deviation on the part of the woman writer from the agenda put in place by and in accord with the beliefs and interests of African American men. In portraying the African American woman figure as a man would, New Negro women poets followed the example set by their male counterparts, adopting the structure, themes, and images that appear and reappear in Black men's poems about Black women and presenting these figures as the observations of a speaker who is either male or gender-neutral (to whatever degree gender neutrality exists at a cultural moment that assumes maleness as the default or neutral identity, and given a figure of unnamed sex but engaged in actions coded as male—actions like gazing upon the body of a woman, for example).[32]

For the male writers of the New Negro literary scene, the African American woman was a figure rich in symbolism. Looking upon her body with the freshness and optimism born of two generations' removal from bondage and hundreds of miles of distance from the territories held by slavery's last stalwarts, young male poets of the Harlem Renaissance saw in the Black female body a beauty whose departure from the Euro-American ideal reflected the depth and intensity of Black people's journey from freedom and power in Africa to slavery and struggle in the Americas and, finally, back toward freedom. This experience of the African American female body resulted in poems utilizing the Black woman as object and symbol in the exploration of the relationship of New Negro Blacks to the locations and institutions that shaped the lives of their ancestors. In poems like Lucien B. Watkins's "Ebon Maid and Girl of Mine" the male poet's speaker conducts us through an inventory of the Black woman's physical attributes. As Watkins's speaker gazes on the body of his "Ebon Maid," he leads our eye from "the sable beauty of her skin" to the "Glad winds of evening" that "are her face" ("Gentle with love and rich in grace") and the "blazing splendors of her eyes"; like stars, they "Are jewels from the midnight skies" (8–12). Using rich imagery and vivid metaphors to invite readers to re-see her Blackness as her finest attribute, Watkins offers nature-based images associated with darkness—the evening winds, the beauty of sable, the stars in the night sky—as a counterpoint to the centuries-old nature-based metaphors—of snow and milk and ivory—used to idealize white women's paler complexions. Despite his lyrical praise of her body, however, the relationship of the omniscient speaker in this and similar poems can only be described as objectifying the Black female figure, as he leads our eye over the body of a woman who appears passive and unaware of our gaze. Her body is the only aspect of her womanhood that the speaker-poet allows her to bring to the poem; it is this aspect of her womanhood—not her experiences or ideas—that aids the poem in uplifting Blackness without calling attention to the race-based challenges confronting those Black people who are not male.

Gwendolyn B. Bennett's "To a Dark Girl" follows a related trajectory, adopting similar strategies to achieve the same elevation of Blackness without calling attention to particular conflicts and conditions that might point to a distinct Black *female* experience of racism and struggle. In this poem the speaker's slow-moving gaze over the woman-object's body reduces her to a collection of racialized body parts, a dehumanization process into which we as readers are drawn as participants. Our eye follows the direction of the speaker, and before we are able to step away from his objectifying gaze we must first pass through it. In "To a Dark Girl," Bennett's speaker conducts his readers on a survey, from the cherished "brownness" of the dark girl's body ("I love you for your brownness"[1]) to the "rounded darkness of [her] breast" (2).[33] Far removed from the giddy innocence and coy aloofness that generations of European poets and artists have captured in their own maids, Bennett's dark girl wears the burdens of her people heavily on her shoulders, and Bennett's speaker savors the imprint of struggle and survival that he reads in her gloomy temperament, declaring, "I love you for the breaking sadness in your voice / And shadows where your wayward eyelids rest" (3–4). Here, as in Watkins's "Ebon Maid," the speaker praises aspects of African American womanhood that have in past generations been alternately demeaned and ignored, and yet both speakers overlook those layers of woman's experience that might undermine the popular embrace of male perspectives and experiences as universal. Instead, the emphasis in both Watkins and Bennett upon depicting those traits (Blackness in Watkins, Blackness and sadness in Bennett) that the woman-object and male objectifier have in common suggests that each speaker's celebration of the Black female body is not an end in itself but rather is offered as a means of calling attention to new epistemologies of beauty and value that are grounded in African American history and circumstances and that have been overlooked in the past. The Black woman's body becomes a device, introduced to aid the New Negro poet in writing toward a vision of Blackness that, even as it rejects the stereotypes and images that have been used to degrade Black womanhood (the mammy, the jezebel, the tragic mulatto), maintains at its center the interests and struggles of African Americans.

Like Watkins, Bennett uses her speaker's appreciation for the Black female object of his gaze to reconfigure the relationship of U.S. Blacks to both the institution of slavery and the ancestral homeland of West Africa. Her speaker makes a link between the beguiling and seductive melancholy of his African American beauty and Black peoples' historical legacy of struggle and survival. This link, in turn, endows present-day Black (male) subjects with dignity, courage, and strength.

The forgotten dignity of Black struggle against U.S. slavery and the Negro's ancient legacy of dignity and self-determination in Africa are two consistent themes in these depictions of Black women. Between Watkins's "Ebon Maid" and Bennett's "Dark Girl," Bennett's treatment is more subtle, with her speaker's reference to the "sadness" and "shadows" in his dark girl's face serving as an implied reference to the legacy of struggle that creates in Black young people a youthful beauty shaped more by toil and anguish than by the blush of innocence and joy that is often depicted in young white females. Watkins's homage to the beautiful body of his Black woman-object is more explicit, pointing to strong links between the Black female beauty that she embodies and the African heritage of both the female object and her male observer. Watkins's speaker observes that

> Her hair—the darkness caught and curled
> The ancient wonder of the world—
> Seems, in its strange uncertain length,
> A constant crown of queenly strength. (13–16)

His references to "ancient wonder" and "queenly strength" reflect the Jazz Age fascination with the indisputable fact of Black self-rule in precolonial Africa. In particular, Marcus Garvey's invocation, in his pre–Harlem Renaissance campaign for "Negro Improvement," of the necessary reality of Black queens, Black kings, and Black kingdoms captured the imagination of Black and white people alike.[34] Throughout the duration of Garvey's campaign, and for some time after, Black intellectuals and other quarters of the bourgeoisie remained critical of many aspects of his program for racial uplift, especially his drive for African repatriation. The frequency of New Negro poets' references to ancient African greatness and royal bearing suggest, however, that even those African Americans who rejected Garvey's calls for a migration "Back to Africa" found his invocation of the memory of Black kingdoms quite compelling.[35] Still, Watkins's use of the qualifier "seems" ("The ancient wonder of the world— / Seems . . . / A constant crown of queenly strength" [14–16]) strikes a musing tone that leaves room for some doubt, if not about the reality, then certainly about the relevance of ancient African royalty to the African American present.

For male poets like Waring Cuney the speaker's admiring gaze upon the Black female body offers an alternative to dominant epistemologies that refuse to allow for the possibility of beauty and human value within Blackness. In the opening lines of "No Images," Cuney establishes the need for a system of meaning that can recognize and describe Black beauty. Speaking of the African American object of his speaker's gaze, he writes:

> She does not know
> Her beauty,
> She thinks her brown body
> Has no glory. (1–4)

For Cuney and his speaker the inability of even African Americans to recognize Black female beauty stems from African Americans' disconnect from their own history and, in particular, from ways of seeing embedded in an African worldview that would place Black men, women, and children at the sociopolitical and aesthetic center. He writes:

> If she could dance
> Naked,
> Under palm trees
> And see her image in the river
> She would know.

> But there are no palm trees
> On the street
> And dish water gives back no images. (5–12)

If she had the benefit of an alternative point of reference, not embedded in the white supremacist aesthetics of Jazz Age America, Cuney's humble Negro woman might recover the ability to recognize her own and other Blacks' capacity for beauty. Through his gaze upon the body of the Negro woman-object, Cuney's male speaker does recover aspects of that system of meaning, and both speaker and reader achieve an understanding of the woman-object's body that, ironically, she does not have access to. This privileged knowledge—of the woman-object's beauty and the relationship of both her beauty and the capacity to recognize her beauty to the ancestral home of Africa—links reader to speaker as cobeneficiaries of the shift in awareness effected by their gaze upon the Black female body. Objectified by the omniscient gaze that leads reader and speaker over the contours of her body and into her thoughts (speaker and reader are both aware that "She thinks her brown body / Has no glory"), the woman-object at the center of the poem remains as alienated from her meaning and value (including her value to those who are watching her) as any inanimate cultural artifact—an African mask, a painting, a ritual object—would be. For both reader and speaker the body of the Black woman-object functions as a bridge past those conceptions of Blackness and beauty and worth that are rooted in institutionalized white supremacy, backward through the unmaking of African identities that took place during the Middle Passage, and into an encounter with the possibility of an African homeland in which Black-centered ways of seeing and knowing prevail. The body of the Black woman-object becomes a crossing point from those damaging notions of Blackness incubated in the cradle of U.S. slavery and perpetuated through lynching and Jim Crow (and other manifestations of Euro-American dominance) to a physical, historical, and epistemological space in which new and emancipatory meanings and associations—of Blackness with beauty, of Blackness with humanity, of Blackness with joy, and others—become possible.[36]

In "To a Dark Girl" we see the speaker cross into an oppositional perspective in the second stanza, when he recognizes traces of past African splendor in the proud carriage of the title character. The speaker observes that "Something of old forgotten queens / Lurks in the lithe abandon of your walk" (5–6). Bennett makes a similar link in "Song," a poem set among the "heads thrown back in irreverent mirth" and the "moist, dark lips / Where hymns keep company," at "de ole camp-meetin' place" (3, 6–7, 12). Here the speaker notices how "A dancing girl with swaying hips / Sets mad the queen in a harlot's eye" (24–25).

The pattern that we see in Bennett—in which the speaker's recognition of vestigial queenliness in even the most marginalized of Black women (harlots and other "irreverent" types) becomes the catalyst for his transition into an oppositional understanding of Blackness and Africa—is repeated in male poet Andrea Razafkeriefo's "The Negro Woman," but with two minor variations. As in Bennett's and Watkins's pieces, Razafkeriefo's "Negro Woman" offers a narrative of transition into an understanding of Blackness, beauty, and history that opposes the meanings offered up by the white mainstream. In this poem, however, the African American female body serves as a bridge into a new and counterhegemonic understanding of the historical patterns of endurance and strife that have shaped Black life in North America. Also, unlike the other two poems, in which the speaker's evolution into oppositional consciousness begins with his gaze on the Black female body, Razafkeriefo creates a speaker whose emancipatory vision of the Negro begins with his contemplation of Black women's struggles.

In the final stanza of Razafkeriefo's poem the speaker conducts the type of body inventory that characterizes this subcategory of Harlem Renaissance poems:

> What of her sweet, simple nature?
> What of her natural grace?
> Her richness and fullness of color,
>
> That adds to the charm of her face? (17–20)

This homage to African American female beauty affirms the oppositional reading of Black woman's body offered in the opening stanzas. These stanzas detail the speaker's recognition of the Black woman-object's residual queenliness (an artifact of her African past), not in the contours of her body, however, but in the conditions of her life:

> Were it mine to select a woman
> As queen of the hall of fame;
> One who has fought the gamest fight
> And climbed from the depths of shame;
> I would have to give the scepter
> To the lowliest of them all;
> She who has struggled through the years,
> With her back against the wall.
>
> Wronged by the men of an alien race,
> Deserted by those of her own;
> With a prayer in her heart, a song on her lips
> She has carried the fight alone.
> In spite of the snares all around her;
> Her marvelous pluck has prevailed
> And kept her home together—
> When even her men have failed. (1–16)

Among Harlem Renaissance depictions of the Black female object, "The Negro Woman" is unique in its open description of African American women's suffering, not only at the hands of white men, but in relation to Black men as well (the Negro woman is "Wronged by men of an alien race" and "Deserted by men of her own"). With its focus on Black women's relationships with men, this poem incorporates one of the central themes of the blues, the one poetic form of the period in which Black women speak freely and audaciously about the details of their lives.[37]

Razafkeriefo's address of the circumstances that shape some Black women's lives relies, in part, on his privilege as a male writer, especially given the restrictions against the depiction of Black women's daily lives observed by Black female poets. While Razafkeriefo opens a small window for some aspects Black woman's experiences to come briefly into view, however, the paternalistic tone and strident omniscience of the piece reinforces her status as object, both in the eyes of the speaker and in the experience of the reader. By confining the woman at the center of his poem to object status, Razafkeriefo models a strategy for exploring limited aspects of African American women's lives that is adaptable to the constraints imposed on Black women poets' depictions of Black female subjects. Indeed, while Gwendolyn Bennett's "To a Dark Girl" follows the example of those male poets who engage the African American female body as a conduit into an oppositional understanding of the legacy of their African ancestors, most New Negro women poets' depictions of the African American woman use that figure in the same way that Razafkeriefo does, as a tool for reimagining of the legacy of their U.S.-based slave ancestors. Similar to Watkins and Cuney in their exploitation of the African American woman-object as a vehicle for renegotiating the relationship of Jazz Age conceptions of Blackness to those key locations, experiences, and institutions that have shaped U.S. Black history, Harlem Renaissance women poets tend to deviate from their male counterparts' emphasis on the idealization of Africa, choosing instead to focus on the history of African American struggle in the United States. Like Razafkeriefo's, such poems take advantage of the limited space that their emphasis on the legacy of slavery and segregation opens up for the address of Black women's experiences.

In Joyce Sims Carrington's "An Old Slave Woman" the speaker's reevaluation of African Americanness (by way of his reevaluation of Black womanhood) takes into account both the body and the experiences of the female figure at the center of the poem. The object of his gaze is not, however, the idealized young beauty that Bennett and her male counterparts depict. Instead, Carrington conducts her readers through a renegotiation of the temporal and discursive barriers that have alienated U.S. Blacks from their history, using the deteriorating body of a female former slave as the bridge between the speaker's Jazz Age present and an emancipatory encounter with the Negro's historical past. Here, though, the emphasis is upon transforming the relationship of twentieth-century Black people, not to the distant specter of African self-rule, but to the more recent memory of U.S. slavery. The poem begins with a description of the aging title character:

> She
> Is like
> A wrinkled apple,

> Old and brown,
> Clinging
> By its fragile stem
> To life. (1–7)

For Carrington's speaker, this wrinkled old woman embodies the legacy of U.S. slavery; and as the speaker gazes upon her old, Black body his narrative assessment of her legacy becomes a way of interpreting and assessing the Negro heritage that she symbolizes.

Like Razafkeriefo's "The Negro Woman," the gendered nature of whose experience is revealed in the details of her relationships with men (in this case, her alternate subjugation to and alienation from white and Black men), "An Old Slave Woman" provides unusual visibility for experiences that the poem takes specific steps to specify as female. Emphasizing the slave woman's role as a mother to her sons, Carrington draws on traditional associations of motherhood with affection and expectation in order to recast the death of the last surviving generation of former slaves, not as the close of a painful chapter in African American history, but as the wellspring for a promising future. Thus the speaker concludes,

> You
> Cannot say
> That hers
> Were
> Empty hands;
> For,
> About her sons
> Is wound
> The golden thread
> Of Hope and Love,
> And
> In their faces
> Shines
> The rising sun. (8–21)

"The golden thread / Of Hope and Love" that binds her to her sons, and the "rising sun" reflected "In their faces" each suggest the promise and possibility that the old woman and other former slaves leave behind for their heirs. In order to find in the final moments of this aging generation hope for the future and reverence for the dignified struggles of the past, the speaker must reexamine the institution that distinguished their lives from his own and from the lives of future generations. Yet this poem does not in any way represent an attempt to recast slavery as benign or just. Rather, in developing a view of Black history that opposes the interests of white supremacy, this poem seeks to lift the lives of the enslaved out of the silent obscurity into which the rage and shame of subsequent generations has cast them and to raise them up as examples of survival and persistence. An integral part of this recuperative effort is the recognition, not simply of Black motherhood but of the persistence of Black woman's nurture and love, even under the bonds of slavery. Such praise for this aspect of Black women's everyday lives does not carry with it, however, a tolerance for the depiction of Black women subjects. As in Razafkeriefo's "The Negro Woman," whose glimpse of one aspect Black woman's struggle is crafted to maintain the object status of that figure, Carrington's "Old Slave Woman" uses the omniscient perspective, reinforced by the speaker's tone of mild repulsion, to maintain the hierarchy of speaking subject over gazed-upon object. Carrington's focus on the slave woman's sons is, of course, a response to the prevailing social framework of 1920s, in which the relative progress or, in this case, promise of a race, was measured primarily through the achievements of its men.

Like "The Negro Woman," "To a Dark Girl," and other New Negro Renaissance poems that make use of the speaker's gaze upon the Black female body, Jesse Fauset's "Oriflamme" limits the African American woman at the center of the poem to object status. "Oriflamme," however, shares the interest of "An Old Slave Woman" in exploring the meanings that can be gleaned from the elderly Black female body. Here, as in Carrington's piece, the speaker's evaluation of the Black woman's life of struggle—inscribed in the contours and details of her aging body—becomes the speaker's passage or bridge from his Jazz Age Negro reality (that is, an understanding of his Black subjectivity that is wholly limited by the context of his immediate temporal environs) to an emancipatory rereading of the slave past. This, in turn, ushers the speaker into a progressive reinterpretation of his own Black present.

"Oriflamme" begins with a quoted passage from Sojourner Truth:

> I can remember when I was a little, young girl, how my old mammy would sit out of doors in the evenings and look up at the stars and groan, and I would say, "Mammy, what makes you groan so?" And she would say, "I am groaning to think of my poor children; they do not know where I be and I don't know where they be. I look up at the stars and they look up at the stars!" (epigraph)

Like Carrington's "An Old Slave Woman," in which the "golden thread" of "Hope" refers to the speaker's commitment to rising above the bonds of racial prejudice, "Oriflamme" emphasizes the theme of transcendence. Sojourner Truth's cherished memory of her "old mammy" looking up at the stars is not the heavenward gaze of the Protestant faithful, a cherished image among slavery's apologists for its suggestion of the childlike and submissive faith of Black "uncles" and "aunties." Rather, this image, of the African American woman with eyes focused on points far above the earth—focused, quite literally, above and beyond the mundanities of daily existence—refers to the power of willful transcendence, the act of deliberately looking beyond the everyday realities of race, class, and caste, to deliver the Black figure beyond the routine humiliations and losses of slave life.

Looking with the aid of his own mind's eye at the scene that Truth describes, Fauset's speaker encounters the dramatic and painful legacy of chattel slavery as he gazes at the realities of dehumanization literally written on the body of the grieving Black mother. We follow his gaze as his visual inventory of the elderly Black woman's body moves him toward a new understanding of slave history and his own Negro past:

> I think I see her sitting bowed and black,
> Stricken and seared with slavery's mortal scars,
> Reft of her children, lonely, anguished, yet
> Still looking at the stars. (1–4)

Beyond its more obvious role as a symbol of her exploitation, the old woman's scars bear witness to her courage and resolve. She is "Stricken and seared," "lonely," and "anguished," and yet her resistance quite literally marks her as a tenacious survivor, battered and forsaken but "Still looking at the stars."

Inspired by the defiance and fortitude of his "Symbolic mother," the speaker pledges to bring her steadfastness to his own battle for freedom and equality:

> Symbolic mother, we thy myriad sons,
> Pounding our *stubborn hearts* on Freedom's bars,
> Clutching our birthright, fight with faces set,
> Still visioning the stars! (5–8, emphasis added)[38]

Like his counterpart in "Oriflamme," the speaker in Mae Smith Johnson's "To My Grandmother" uses his consideration of the body of a Black woman elder to gain an understanding of both the legacy of slavery and its relationship to his own life, two generations out of bondage. The marks and wounds of the peculiar institution have literally molded and colored the old woman's body, from the forced miscegenation of her foremothers ("Dark Africa with Caucasian blood / To tinge your veins combined" [1–2]) to her years of manual labor (Your proud head bowed to slavery's thrall, / Your hands to toil consigned" [5–6]), and the speaker's understanding of Black slave life grows more complex as he considers its toll on her elderly frame.[39] From the chaos of the Civil War ("Your ears have heard the din of war, / The martial tramp of feet" [9–10]) to the melodies of the old Negro spirituals ("Your voice has risen to your God / In supplications sweet" [11–12]), Johnson's speaker imagines each detail of the woman's slave body as a physical response to her environment. She sings and calls out to her God, listens to the sounds of battle, lowers her head under the burdens of her labor, and works her fingers to exhaustion. And when Johnson's speaker turns to the question of transcendence, he forms his reply in the language of the body. In the tradition of spirituals like "Shout All Over God's Heaven," with its jubilant inventory of the material rewards awaiting the righteous in Paradise, "To My Grandmother" seeks both physical and spiritual comforts for the aging title character.[40] The implication is clear: the humble dignity of her earthly struggles has proven her worthy of heavenly blessings and bodily rest in this world and divine comfort and peaceful reward in the next:

> May angels kiss each furrowed scar
> Upon your brow where care has trod.
>
> God bless the hands all withered now
> By age and weary care.
> God rest the feet that sought the way
> To freedom bright and fair.
> God bless thy life and e'er endow
> Thee with strength each new-born day. (17–24)

In this closing passage, "To My Grandmother" becomes a praise song, uplifting the soul of the aging slave, and even as our status as readers makes us complicit in the speaker's objectification of this figure, so too, in this final moment, are we complicit in his loving adoration.

Indeed, a central concern in the exploration of New Negro depictions of Afro-American women is the relationship of the reader to the interaction between the male-gendered or gender-neutral speaker and the woman-object. Even those who find themselves reading the objectifying, exoticizing poem primarily in order to critique it must first enter into the speaker's perspective and share in his experience as objectifying, omniscient observer. In Gladys Casely Hayford's popular and widely published "The Palm Wine Seller" the reader is made complicit in two distinct and almost contradictory acts of objectification.[41]

In the first six stanzas of "The Palm Wine Seller" the omniscient speaker conducts the reader through a surprisingly candid inventory of wine seller Akosua's "charms." Thus speaker directs reader through an experience of objectification once removed, beginning with Akosua's "jet black hair" and continuing with the following roster of attributes:

> [The] Roundness of her bosom,
> Brilliance of her eyes

THE BLACK WOMAN AS OBJECT AND SYMBOL

Lips that form a cupid's bow,
Whereon love's dew lies.

Velvet gleam of shoulder
Arch of bare black feet;
Soft caressing hands . . . . (13–19)

This lurid vision is not the perspective of the speaker, however, but of the intoxicated boatmen who are watching her progress down the harbor street:

Akosua selling palm wine,
In the broiling heat;
Akosua selling palm wine
Down our street.

Frothing calabashes
Filled unto the brim,
Boatmen quaffing palm wine
In toil's interim.

Tossing off their palm wine,
Boatmen deem her fair:
Through the haze of palm wine,
Note her jet black hair. (1–12)

Beginning in the seventh stanza, the speaker, drawing upon his omniscience to elevate himself above both the ogled wine seller and the ogling boatmen alike, probes beneath the idealized beauty that the boatmen perceive to another, truer vision of Akosua, unenhanced by the consumption of her wares. This time the speaker's gaze reveals

Lips creased in by wrinkles,
Eyes dimmed with the years,
Feet whose arch was altered
Treading vales of tears.

Hair whose roots life's madness
Knotted and turned wild
On her heart a load of care;
On her back a child. (25–32)

Thus Hayford oversees the passage of her Black woman-object from one form of objectification and symbolism to another, neither of which delivers her—even momentarily—into the realm of subjecthood. The first six stanzas of "The Palm Wine Seller" portray Akosua as the idealized Black Venus, a figure whose beauty, like the gloomy splendor of Bennett's unnamed dark girl, suggests the dignity and grandeur of a forgotten African past. In the second portion of the poem, however, Hayford's speaker uses his omniscience—his capacity to see and know not only the body and mind of the wine seller but the vision and motivations of the boatmen—to reevaluate the meanings assigned to Akosua's Black body. Dismissing the boatmen's appraisal of the wine seller's body as the bleary-eyed imaginings of drunken laborers, the speaker casts his own gaze on both the woman-object and her objectifiers and derives a far different understanding of the wine seller's body and of her role in symbolizing the links between past and present. Where the boatmen perceive in her lush beauty a reminder of the grandeur and dignity of precolonial Africa, he sees the reality of her broken, burdened body, with very different implications for Black people's present as well as their ancestors' past.

Where Cuney's and Watkins's and Bennett's speakers each see in the Black female body an ancient, ancestral splendor that suggests the return of the present-day Negro to the power and glory of the past, and where Johnson's and Carrington's speakers see courage, persistence, and a basis for hope in the worn, aging bodies of Black female slaves, Hayford's speaker communicates a bleaker vision, based on the defeat that he reads in the scars and creases of the wine seller's body. In the woman-object poems, beauty is a symbol of greatness and worth and an emblem of hope. That the hardships which shaped the life of this apparently young Black woman (she carries her infant child on her back) have stripped her of her beauty suggests the defeat of African Americans by the cruelties that have distanced them from any possible legacy of precolonial freedom and power. That the only people who recognize her as beautiful do so in a state of drunken illusion suggests the foolishness of seeing strength and glory—or the basis of hope for these things—in the lives of everyday Black people. Thus while Hayford limits her African American woman to the object status common in New Negro Renaissance depictions of that figure, her deviation from the characteristics and conclusions most often associated with Black womanhood takes its symbolism to a very different place.

"The Palm Wine Seller" is among the darkest of the poems that use the Black woman-object to speak about the condition of African American people. While "Oriflamme," "To My Grandmother," and "An Old Slave Woman," make similar use of the imagery of the scarred, broken body of a Black woman, such poems differ from "The Palm Wine Seller" in that they depict elderly Black women (the suggestion is that they were former slaves) and associate their marked bodies with the struggles of the past. Such women are depicted as living history, and the poems that depict them do so to honor their status as living memorials to the struggles of the ancestors of present-day African Americans. Indeed, most of the poems that depict the woman-object use that figure to symbolize and establish a positive link with the past. And although this role does, at times, seem to be a retreat from the audacious speaking subjects of the previous era, its appearance, barely fifty years after the end of slavery, as a tool for reconciling the relations of Renaissance-era Blacks to both their slave and African pasts, also constitutes a great step forward.

CHAPTER 3

REVOLUTIONARY DREAMS
AFRICAN AMERICAN WOMEN POETS
IN THE BLACK ARTS MOVEMENT

just like that I woke up one morning
and looked at my self
and what I saw was
carolyn
not imani ma jua or soul sister poetess of
the moment
i saw more than a "sister" . . .
i saw a Woman. human.
and black
i felt a spiritual transformation
a root revival of love
and I knew that many things
were   over
and some me of—beauty—
was about to begin. . . .

CAROLYN RODGERS
"Some Me of Beauty"

When U.S. scholars have turned their attention to the Black Arts Movement, it has most often been to scrutinize how its emphasis on the Black male experience of racism marginalized African American womanhood and ignored some of the specific ways that the racial terrorism and enforced segregation of the mid- to late 1960s shaped Black women's lives.[1] Indeed, many African American women poets writing during the 1960s articulated their frustration with the androcentric focus of "the movement" and the patriarchal bias of some its most prominent texts.[2] Too often, however, the label of "sexist" has been applied to male poets of the Black Arts Movement as a justification for dismissing the entire possibility of an emancipatory Black nationalist politics. And in the rush to address the overt gender prejudice expressed by many of the period's male, separatist poet-revolutionaries, many scholars have overlooked some of the important ways that the link between masculinity and resistance made in poems by Imamu Amiri Baraka, Don Lee, Everett Hoagland, and other Black Arts men opened the door for all African American poets to revisit the transgression inherent in representing their own lives and communities. This chapter describes the moment when African American women poets first entered the discourse of resistant Black manhood and how they utilized its most revered images, initially to establish a role for Black womanhood within the patriarchal landscape of nationalism, but eventually in order to critique and transcend it.

The Black Arts Movement inherited its infamous male-centeredness from the poets and theorists of the Harlem Renaissance who, in turn, inherited their masculinist bias from some of the more prominent male artists and intellectuals of the post-Reconstruction era. Possibly the earliest African Americans to identify as part of a Black artistic and intellectual community, these late-nineteenth- and early-twentieth-century pioneers saw it as their duty to shape and define the nature and focus of Black artistic and scholarly pursuits. In carrying out this charge, James Weldon Johnson and other African American intellectual trailblazers shunned Black women writers and their propensity for treating subjects related to Black woman's domestic life, based on what they perceived as the limited relevance of women's daily activities to broader political concerns; for Johnson and his contemporaries, representations of domestic labor, child rearing, and intramarital relations were far too narrow in scope and appeal to advance the goals of a movement that sought to implement a broad program of racial uplift.

The revolutionary nationalism of the 1960s added to this established predisposition against the representation of Black women's lives an emphasis on Black power and self-defense. This emphasis evolved out of a need and even a hunger on the part of young urban Blacks in the northern and West Coast states for African American images that would counteract the fear and vulnerability that was introduced into and maintained at the center of Black life through the gruesome spectacle of lynching. For the young Black writers and activists who would shape the 1960s movement in the arts, the link between Black manhood, power, and resistance was clear. Since the end of the nineteenth century, the lynched, mutilated Black male body had functioned in the collective imagination of both Afro- and Euro-Americans as the most widely recognized symbol of white dominance, in much the same way that the sexually ravaged body of the African American woman slave had served as the primary symbol of white control over Black people during the antebellum period. In a society that had, since the end of Reconstruction, justified the practice of lynching (a practice evolved to suppress freedom and dissent in Black communities) with false and exaggerated claims of the social threat posed by the alleged predatory sexuality of Black men, poems depicting Black men as virile, masculine, and powerful held special appeal for a rising generation of Black activists who wished not merely to reject and disrupt white dominance but to reject and disrupt it audaciously.

To the young urban Blacks of the northern and West Coast cities of the United States, the passive resistance of the civil rights movement in the South and the images of African Americans answering violent white aggression with passivity, songs, and prayer came across not as empowered resistance but as timid reinforcement of the old dispensation. The young activists who would form the Black Power movement and its artistic offshoot, the Black Arts Movement, demanded actions and images that would answer white terroristic violence with fearlessness, power, and rage.

Poems like Baraka's "Black Dada Nihilismus" are emblematic of this new aesthetic of masculine anger and might. Baraka's poem locates the power within the Black male body to disrupt the institutions of Euro-dominance. His speaker's open articulation of the threat inherent in the body of his nihilistic Black antihero—"the simple striking arm under / the streetlamp" (38–39)—is a bold affront to a sociopolitical order that leaves no space for African American rage and resistance. Baraka's narrator summons the Black Dada Nihilismus into action ("Come up, black dada / nihilismus" [40–41]), his words literally drawing the antihero up from beneath the economic forces that have nursed his undiscriminating wrath. Baraka's knife-wielding antiheroes are "the cutters' from under / their rented earth" (35–36), their characteristic impulse to destroy forged out of the explosive interaction between racism, poverty, and urbanization (implied in the characterization of the renter as simultaneously living within and buried— or dying—beneath the weighty control of their white landlords). The violent nihilism of Baraka's antihero is most dramatically symbolized in his open rejection of the white-over-Black hierarchy and its sacred boundaries. At the poem's climax, the speaker incites the nihilismus to "Rape the white girls. Rape / their fathers. Cut the mothers' throats" (41–42). These three penetrative acts—two acts of rape and one knifing—deliver the anguish and rageful alienation of the 1960s Black urban male literally and forcibly into white America's field of vision, with a drama and tragedy that forces the interests and demands of this liminal figure literally into the center of white consciousness.

Like Baraka, poet Everett Hoagland offers challenging and excessive images of the Black male as an antidote to the silencing image of the mutilated, stationary body. Where Baraka uses rage to write past the limitations imposed on Black masculinity, however, Hoagland draws on the power of the erotic. In "love

Child—a black aesthetic" Hoagland's speaker exults in the generative power of his own sexual climax:

> . . . we love screaming and curdled creaming cradled in crisis
> of our now we love now we love now my love now my love now my love
> love me now my love my love My Love Now!!
> glob globs of tapioca textured essence of nascence ice-cream
> fire yellow white hot maggots seeming more than semen
> sperm jellied germ of god the rich pudding of love tiring tadpole
> couriers of destiny coursing toward the heaven halo aborrea
> of egg sun like yolk wonder deep in the night time of belly love . . . (19–25)

Though divergent in their approaches, Hoagland and Baraka share an interest in exploring the transgression inherent in their life-affirming images of African American manhood. The Black Arts Movement has come to be known for the intrepid literary experimentation of its men, each of whom developed, revised, and then honed his own strategies and approaches to writing against U.S. white racism and its killing intolerance for the living Black male body. The unifying theme in all such representations, however, is the overt link that each writer makes between his celebrations of the vigorous, unfettered male body and the disruption of a mainstream culture that tolerates only weakness and submission in its African American men and that affirms (in such bodies) only stasis and death.

For African American women in the Black Arts Movement, the location of antiracist Black resistance in the body of the African American man was both a benefit and a hindrance. On the one hand, the link made in revolutionary nationalist thought between the idea of white power and the image of the dead, mutilated Black male precipitated the recuperation of the everyday as site of resistance; if the idea of the dead Afro-American male reinforced white power, then any depiction of a thriving, defiant Black man, engaged in any of his life's activities (walking, loving, speaking, "styling") was perceived by both the men and the women of the nationalist movement as a rejection of white domination. And thus for the first time since the post-Reconstruction era, Black daily life emerged as a suitable topic—beneficial or germane to the larger interests of the race—for address by African American poets. Less auspicious for the interests of Black women writers was the fact that the emphasis in the Black Arts Movement upon lynching and imprisonment as the primary manifestations of white dominance perpetuated the tendency to define racism as the denial of Black manhood, a trend detrimental to the reintroduction of African American women's experiences as viable subjects for representation within the context of a larger aesthetic of antiracist social change.[3] Thus while many of the aspects of African American men's lives that find their way into the new Black poetry of the 1960s are quite indistinguishable from similar aspects of Black women's lives (for example, in "Breakthrough" John Sinclair describes "Men, at work at simple human business," like "getting food, making ourselves se- / cure in our homes, making such things as / poems, babies, music, houses, tools" [41, 42–44]), the popular link between manhood, racism, and Black resistance placed new roadblocks to women's representation.[4]

During the earliest years of the Black Arts Movement the primary form of participation left open for African American women poets was the creation of works that portrayed Black maleness as defiant and empowered. Representations of the African American female were limited, for the most part, to those that buttressed the image of the Black male as intrepid and commanding, and such poems continued to dominate depictions of African American womanhood even into the latest years of the Black Arts period.[5] In such poems Black women appear in one of two traditional roles, as either homemaker/helpmate or lover, each of which is portrayed to maximize the impact of the Black male subject's performance of masculinity. When Black Arts women poets create images of the African American female as wife or helpmate, the woman figure is not the focus of the poem but rather the vehicle either for the representation of the Black male or the expression of his power.[6]

In "To My Mate (Wherever He May Be)," poet-speaker Zubena (Cynthia M. Conley) understands her own role as woman revolutionary solely in terms of the needs of her future "mate," the nationalist Black male.[7] Although Zubena's position as speaker might seem at first to subvert the conventional roles of male gazer and woman as focus of that gaze, the relationship that she describes—her fantasy of the ideal romance between the Black revolutionary and his female partner and helpmate—reinforces the gendered hierarchy of male subject over woman-object. As subject, her mate will order his actions (including his interactions with the speaker-poet) according to his interests and his mood.[8] Zubena envisions some of the ways that his activities would determine the atmosphere and the shape of communication within their household:

> He'll be
> moody at times
> cause he'll
> be thinking
> some beautiful
> mental music.
>
> His ideas
> will have some

way out rhythms
his expressions,
some of his own timings.

And he won't
have to say
i love you
to me
for his presence
will say it
for him. (1–18)

So, too, would his needs and desires shape her own performance of revolutionary womanhood. Zubena's list of her responsibilities as revolutionary mate privileges not the imagined the needs of the woman poet and speaker but the likely wants and concerns of her Black man:

And he'll want me
To Be
Myself
Hisself

        or

a lady
a queen
a good mother
a good housekeeper
a good cook
a good thinker
            and
HIS GOOD WOMAN. (19–31)

Even in her own thoughts and fantasies the speaker-poet confines herself to a female role governed by the demands of masculine subjecthood. Toward the end of her poem, Zubena confirms her commitment to this position, defined by and in support of the interests of male, revolutionary privilege. She writes:

i will be
whatever he wants
me to be.

i will go
wherever he wants
me to go
i will do
whatever he tells
me to do (32–40)

In locating the African American woman as helpmate to the male revolutionary, Black Arts women create portraits of the Afro-American wife and mother that affirm the vision of Black womanhood offered in the writings of their male counterparts. Though such pieces do, literally, represent a Black female voice, that voice is employed in the articulation of what is essentially an African American masculinist vision. Zubena's grateful objecthood, for example, is consistent with Baraka's call for "Black/queens" (4–5) to "lift me up" (18) and "Help us [African American men] get back what was always ours." (16)[9]

In her capacity as lover to the Black male subject, the African American woman functions as object in the elevation of Black manhood and, especially, Black male virility. In many such poems the African American woman is presented as a passive figure whose connection to, interest in, and even awareness of the need and substance of the (nationalist, anticapitalist) revolution is either minimal or nonexistent until her body is acted upon by her Black male lover. Such an action might be as inconspicuous as the male gaze upon the Black female body. In Sandy Robinson's "I Had to Be Told" for example, the speaker-poet is able to challenge and reject Euro-dominant conceptions of female beauty and aesthetic value only once she comes to see herself through the gaze of her male lover. Robinson's pronouncement, in the final line of the poem, that her true life has begun only since adopting an African American male revolutionary stance on the subject of Black women's beauty, invests the Black male gaze with the capacity to overcome the false consciousness imposed by her exposure to Euro-American beauty standards:

> I HAD TO BE TOLD THAT BLACK WAS BEAUTIFUL
> I HAD TO BE TOLD THAT MY BLACK SKIN WAS SEXY AND EXCITING
> I HAD TO BE TOLD THAT MY BIG LIPS AND WIDE
>   FLAT NOSE WERE NOT UGLY MISTAKES OF NATURE,
>   BUT BEAUTIFUL TRAITS OF A BEAUTIFUL PEOPLE.
> I HAD TO BE TOLD NOT TO WORRY ABOUT THE NAPS
>   AND KINKS OF MY HAIR AND
>   WEAR IT NATURALLY.
> I HAD TO BE TOLD MY SMILE COULD INSPIRE OR A
>   LOOK FROM ME COULD SILENCE.
>   I WAS TOLD AND I ALMOST DID NOT BELIEVE.
>   BUT A BEAUTIFUL BLACK MAN TOLD ME AGAIN AND
>   AGAIN, AND ONLY NOW HAVE I BEGUN TO LIVE. (1–13)

In "An Ex Carbon Copy of White Women Speaks," Wanda Coleman's speaker describes a similar transformation. For Coleman's speaker, however, the rejection of Euro-American beauty standards is only one component in a larger rejection of established norms (including belief in the state, Christian doctrine, and social hierarchies):

> I sent my sons to war
> went on state relief
> pressed my hair,
> affected airs;
> went to church. (17–21)

Coleman's speaker experiences the Black male gaze upon her hair—especially his appreciation for its natural texture—as an invitation to reexamine every aspect of her conformity to social and aesthetic norms:

> I met a black man.
> He said he cared,
> liked my hair;
> said I needn't imitate
> I was born to innovate. (23–27)

The loving attentions of her African American man enable her to set aside the traditional meanings and restrictions imposed on those Blacks who are women, creating an unencumbered position from which she is able to reassess her relationship to the prevailing social order: "He raised me high enough / to see I wasn't / what I ought to be" (28–30).

It is noteworthy that neither Coleman's "An Ex Carbon Copy of White Women Speaks" nor Robinson's "I Had to Be Told" depicts the newly aware Black woman engaged in revolutionary action. Instead, each poem leaves its readers just after the speaker's awakening. We stand beside her, sharing her joy in the new awareness of her own self-worth, but neither she nor we—as observers—are permitted to pass fully into the promise of this ideological new day. To depict the Black woman acting autonomously, in accordance with her newly aroused consciousness would pose an unwelcome challenge to the widespread support for maintaining a gendered separation between African American women's limited role as lover-object and the role of the Black male as redeemer-liberator. The goal of Coleman's and Robinson's "gaze poems" is not to explore the activist potential of the awakened Black female consciousness but to underscore the authority and power of the African American man. In each of these two poems, the seeming contradiction between the subtlety and simplicity of his action—a mere gaze, a recognition—and its stunning capacity to transform highlights the force of resistance inherent in the Black male subject position.

Frequently, however, such poems rely on more explicit manifestations of male desire, like the passionate, life-giving touch that Sonia Sanchez describes in "black magic":

magic
> my man
is you
> turning
my body into
a thousand

smiles.
> black
magic is your
touch
> making
me breathe. (1–12)

Once again the Black male action upon the passive and even lifeless Black female (she recalls his touch "making / me breathe") delivers her into a new and enhanced experience of her own African American identity. Sanchez, as poet-speaker, emerges with a new joy in her Blackness as her partner's touch turns her Black body "into / a thousand / smiles."

Sanchez's brief homage to the male touch resonates with a pleasing simplicity that is subtly provocative. Many lover-object poems are considerably more explicit, however, using references to the male subject's sexual penetration of the Black female body, and to the ejaculation and implantation of his "seed," all as a means of highlighting the critical role of Black manhood in awakening the poet-speaker to the radical anti-racist movement in her midst. In "Black Cultural Confrontation (During)," Jeanette Adams begs her unnamed male partner to "fill my being with the seed of knowledge of life" (23) and in "My Man," Nia Na Imani proclaims, "when my man comes in&out of me my whole world expands" (9). Like his gaze and his touch, the Black male subject's ejaculation introduces into the mind of the receptive woman beneath him a new framework for understanding herself, her African American people, and the world in which they struggle.

Writes Imani, "when my man plants his seed in the warmth of my body / I know he is the Creator God; as all Black men are" (10–11). Her newfound faith in the Black man as her one true god sets aside centuries of African American faith in the supreme omnipotence of the holy King of Kings in favor of a new understanding that locates the divine within the speaker's own community.[10] Imani's speaker is capable of making this stunning break with African American religious tradition only after she has progressed through a sequence of acts of ideological and sexual foreplay that, in challenging traditional U.S. social and political thought, gradually push her towards the counter-hegemonic understanding of Black female beauty (stanza two) and the coming revolution (stanza one) that she articulates in this poem:[11]

> when i lay next to my man he makes me realize
> that we don't have time to suc&jive playing the man's games/
> 'cause there's too much of the business of the nation to deal with
> on our hands.
>
> when my black man wraps his arms 'round me
> it makes me know that i don't have to readmadamoselle [sic] or
> even catch up with revlon's latestbeautyhints. (2–8)

Like Imani, Johari Amini (Jewel Latimore) experiences the capacity of African American love and sexuality to undermine the centuries-old conventions of U.S. Black Christian thought. In "About Man" she describes her lover as a "demigod," identifiable by the power of creation inherent in his "ejaculated extensions of black . . . love creating black / life" (8–9). Despite her own developing revolutionary consciousness, however, Amini imagines for herself a role within the nationalist movement that is largely passive; in the final assessment she becomes

> . . . the black pulsating
> fundus throbbing
> dark receptive warmth
> existing for
> implantation. (19–23)

Johari Amini's willful, prideful embrace of her own object status within the Black Power movement underscores the contrast between the success of Black Arts representations of women in the traditional roles of lover/wife/mother in resisting perceived attacks on Black manhood, and the same poems' failure to address limitations on and obstacles to Black women's visibility.

At the same time that poems like Amini's "About Man" reinforce existing gender hierarchies, they also create a pathway for the emergence of the Black female as subject. The focus in the lover-object poems on African American women's adoration of their Black male lovers establishes a place within the prevailing revolutionary discourse for the consideration of at least one aspect of Black women's daily lives, their love for and attraction to Black men. This small opening for the voice of the Black woman-as-lover-object gives rise to some of the period's earliest efforts to resist white supremacy with scenes from the lives of Black women subjects. Rather than positioning the African American woman as object in the construction of a discursive setting in which the Black male subject (or the white male or female subject, for that matter) is dominant, these poems draw upon lover-object poems like Imani's "My Man" and Amini's "About Man" and then move beyond them to locate the Black woman as desiring subject at the center of her own discursive setting, the politically charged urban erotic landscape. Active instead of acted upon, and gazing instead of being gazed upon, the African American woman, as desiring subject, populates her surroundings with those figures—the Black male in particular—who exacerbate the capacity of her image to challenge and transform.

Black Arts poets reembrace the everyday experiences of African American people as a suitable topic for poetic exploration, based on their assessment of the usefulness of Black daily life as a site of antiracist resistance.[12] To identify the African American everyday as a site of revolutionary struggle is to locate the power to create social change not only in the daily lives of Black people but also in the very act of seeing Black people. When an African American writer composes texts in praise of an aspect of Blackness that has traditionally been despised, he or she throws into relief the divide between Black and white systems of meaning, thus (re)inventing each identity group (Black and not-Black) based upon its relationship to the act of seeing Blackness. The speaking subject in such poems undertakes active resistance of white supremacy, a move that aligns him or her with the social and political interests of 1960s revolutionary nationalism. Indeed Black Arts literature and Black revolutionary thought both come to depend on a definition that understands Blackness primarily as a way of seeing Black people and communities.

In the poetry of the Black Arts Movement, African American women first achieve subjecthood as seers. Revolutionary nationalist women's representations of the desiring Black female gaze upon the revolutionary male play a critical role in establishing the usefulness of African American women subjects to the movement for nationalist resistance. It is easy to mistake the expressions of admiration and appreciation for Black manhood in the lover-object poems for articulations of desire by Black women whose perceptions of African American masculinity locate them as desiring subjects. In fact, though, the lover-object poems construct no such figure. In those poems, the agent who initiates the female speaker's evolution into revolutionary consciousness is not the African American woman herself but the Black male, through the introduction of his "seed" into her passive, (racially) unconscious body.

Those desire poems that invent the African American woman as revolutionary subject show the female poet-speaker committing *speech acts of desire* upon the men who populate her surroundings. This desire for the Black male shapes and distinguishes her everyday experiences as that Black subject who is female from the daily experiences of those Black subjects who are men.[13] At the same time, African American women's desire identifies the Black woman's everyday as a site of resistance and redefines the African American female revolutionary, not as object desired (and acted upon) by her male counterpart, but rather as subject whose vision of Black manhood and masculinity opposes those meanings offered up within the discourse of white supremacy.

Such poems appear, at first glance, to be solely concerned with reinforcing Afro-masculine conceptions of revolutionary Black subjectivity. In her highly anthologized tribute poem "Beautiful Black Men," for example, there seems to be little room for an exploration of Black women's daily lives in poet Nikki Giovanni's enthusiastic praise for the men she sees "sitting on stoops, in bars, going to offices / running numbers, watching for their whores" (8–9). Even Carolyn Rodgers (who, with her poem "The Last M.F.," became one of the most outspoken African American critics of sexism and gender exclusion in the Black Arts Movement) appears, in the opening lines of the short poem "Yuh Lookin GOOD," to place men and women in the familiar roles of active male subject and passive female object:

> Meetings meeting meetings
> rooms crowded spaces
> sweaty smoki rapping
> and the brothas, the brothas
> the oh so fine brothas
> with the hair, the fuzz,
> the nat'chal kinky hair
> and the beards and goatees
> and the rapping to us sisters
> to each otha, can u dig it? (1–10)

In both poems, however, the elevation of the masculine is the vehicle, not the focus. And both Giovanni and Rodgers quickly establish that their admiration for African American manhood is, above all else, a foundation for indulging and exulting in their own Black female desire. Giovanni loves her "Beautiful Black Men" and the power of their erotic appeal, but no more than she relishes the challenge posed to Euro-dominance by her bold demonstration of African American woman's playful sexual longing. This joyful indulgence in her own unabashed wantonness is apparent in Giovanni's shameless and deliberate inventory of the bodies that she craves:

> i wanta say just gotta say something
> bout those beautiful beautiful beautiful outasight
> black men
> with they afros
> walking down the street
> is the same old danger

but a brand new pleasure

. . . .

in their fire red, lime green, burnt orange
royal blue tight tight pants that hug
what i like to hug

. . . .

dashiki suits with shirts that match
the lining that compliments the ties
that smile at the sandals
where dirty toes peek at me
and i scream and stamp and shout
for more beautiful beautiful
black men with outasight afros (1–7, 12–14, 21–27)

So, too, does Rodgers relish the sheer audacity and transgression in her expressions of desire, and not only in terms of its challenge to Euro-dominant ways of seeing. For Rodgers, desire and gender and revolution combine audaciously, her female gaze taking on an overt political function within the discourse of nationalism. Rodgers explains that

. . . if the cause, the movement
don't make us sisters militant, (about somethin!)
the brothas, the beautiful brothas
sho will! (16–19)

She undercuts her readers' assumptions about nature of Black sexuality, offering a scenario that begins in street corner cliché (with "the oh so fine brothas / . . . / . . . rapping to us sisters"), but ends in an expression of the undeniable links—in a social order that constructs Blackness as undesirable—between desire and social change. Eschewing the banalities of seduction, Rodgers's fine Black "brothas" are "rapping"

about us making it,
as a people
as a nation
a Third World (11–14)

Like Giovanni, she identifies and eroticizes those aspects of Black masculinity farthest outside of the norms established by whiteness. Euro-dominance rests in part upon the relegation of Blackness to the abnormal—Blackness-as-aberration— and the internalization of this racialized understanding of normality (and its cohorts, worth and desirability), by African Americans as well as whites.

But Giovanni's pleasure in the "danger" of the African American male (all the way down to his "dirty toes"), and Rodgers's "sweaty, smoki" revelry in the "nat'chal kinky hair" of her brothers each challenge the limitations placed on the ways that Blackness becomes visible on two distinct levels: first by contesting the designation of Blackness as a male identity category, and second by challenging the aberration, undesirability, and other meanings assigned to the male subject who is Black.[14]

Despite their relative audacity and overall effectiveness, however, these poems still create a rather narrow vision of Black woman's political role. In both "Beautiful Black Men" and "Yuh Lookin GOOD," Black woman's desire is transgressive, challenging the erasure of African American womanhood itself, as well as the meanings assigned to the more visible identity category of African American manhood, but the Black male remains the sole embodiment of the insurgent, the disruptive, and the revolutionary. In each poem, the African American woman's expression of a desire that contravenes Euro-American conceptions of beauty, value, and desirability is dependent upon his (the Black male's) performance of masculinity. Thus, while the woman speaker's own open expression of desire for the African American male does, at last, introduce a Black female subjectivity whose resistance to white supremacy (and, thus, support for the Black Power agenda) is unequivocal, her daily acts of transgression are undertaken on Black men's terms. Her expressed attraction to the revolutionary male becomes the defining feature in a model of Black female subjectivity whose portrayal, in maintaining the center status of the male, affirms the masculinist vision and goals of revolutionary nationalist movement.

Indeed, the desire poems fail to identify any points of conflict between the male-centered mainstream of nationalist discourse and the conceptions of transgression and challenge that rise out of the experience of the Black female subject, a figure whose womanhood might create a relationship to the institutions and identity categories that support Euro-dominance quite distinct from that of her male counterpart.

The desire poems pose a challenge to the long-held notion that, for the purposes of discourse, activism, and visibility, Blackness is gendered male—that strategies of resistance are undertaken in response to the understanding of Blackness generated from out of the male gaze upon, and experience of, African American subjects and spaces—by highlighting the perspective of the subject who is Black and not man. At the same time, they advocate the seemingly contradictory notion that any revolutionary re-visioning of African American subjectivity that would challenge the white-over-Black hierarchy depends upon the representation of strong Black men.

The absence from the desire poems of any critique either of Black masculinist revolutionary ideology or the limits that it places upon women's representation seems to affirm recent scholarly consensus on the Black Arts Movement that it inhibits African American women's expression and confines the depiction of Black women to those spaces in which her visibility does not detract from its preferred emphasis upon African American men. Indeed, combined with the enthusiastic tone of both pieces, this failure to even acknowledge the male bias inherent in the Black Arts community comes across as powerful evidence of the internalization of a male-centered worldview by both men *and* women of the period. Might Black Arts women have so thoroughly absorbed the phallocentric, masculinist views of their era that they produced their art thoroughly unaware of their own marginalization within a movement that privileged the experiences and perspectives of its males?

Such an interpretation would hinge on the notion that Black women poets, in a bizarre twist on the pre-Oedipal, were unable to see themselves as distinct from the male subjects whose representation dominated the Black Arts literary scene.[15] And while poems like Rodgers's "Yuh Lookin GOOD" and Giovanni's "Beautiful Black Men" affirm the power of Black male sexuality and its function as both expression of Black male power and vehicle of Black woman's revolutionary empowerment, when African American women poets respond to other aspects of their relationships to and interactions with the nationalist male, their poems depart from and offer perspectives far more complex than the affirmation and wonder of the desire pieces. Specifically, such poems focus on those moments when masculinist revolutionary ideology and action fail Black women. The identification of these lapses in the efficacy of revolutionary nationalist thought forms the basis for poems that complicate and challenge those notions about gender, subjectivity, and representation that have been central to the development of an African American literary aesthetic that privileges Black men's struggles. These poems, in their bold and unprecedented exploration of the difficult terrain of sexuality and politics within the African American community, came about because the compelling links made between Black female subjectivity and antiracist resistance in poems like "Yuh Lookin GOOD" and "Beautiful Black Men" opened the door for further exploration of Black woman's everyday experience within the context of a revolutionary nationalist literary movement.

The desire poems, in turn, owe a debt to the image of the empowered Black male and to male poets like Imamu Amiri Baraka and Everett Hoagland, who deploy those images with such effectiveness. The unflinching rage portrayed in poems like "Black Dada Nihilismus" and the phalloerotic abandon in pieces like "Lovechild" opened the door for all African American men and women—poets and nonpoets alike—to reevaluate the capacity of their daily choices and actions (and the representations of those choices and actions) to resist white supremacy. In short, what I am suggesting is that rather than limiting Black women's representation to that of marginalized object, poems offering the image of the empowered Black man opened up, for Black women writers, an avenue to revisit, for the first time since the post-Reconstruction era, the capacity for resistance inherent in their depictions of African American women.

While a handful of Black female poets writing between the end of World War II and the beginning of the Black Arts period did undertake to write African American women's lives into the discourse around racism and social change (most notably, Gwendolyn Brooks and Margaret Walker), their work did not precipitate a transformation in the larger community's understanding of the relationship between womanhood, poetry, and antiracist struggle.[16] Brooks's and Walker's powerful portraits of Black women's joys and adversities were very well received, even by key voices in the literary establishment, but this enthusiastic reception, especially for Brooks's work, was also a reflection on the singularity of her work, a condition which the awarding of her Pulitzer Prize and other literary accolades only served to highlight. While Brooks's and Walker's portraits of African American womanhood reflect each woman's unique line of artistic inquiry, Black Arts women's depictions of African American female life emerged out of a what was, in effect, a community-wide inquiry, both artistic and political in scope.

When Black Arts women's poetry looks beyond the desiring gaze of the African American woman speaker to focus on actual interactions between the Black female subject and the male revolutionary, it often does so in order to expose those moments when the rhetoric and practice of masculinist revolutionary resistance neglects the interests of African American women. Poems like Carolyn Rodgers's "The Last M.F." and Sonia Sanchez's "Memorial: 3. rev pimps" move beyond the simple practice of reporting Black women's desire for the male revolutionary, to interrogate the impact of masculinist rhetoric upon Black women within the movement. "Memorial: 3 rev pimps," "The Last M.F.," and similar poems highlight those moments when the interests and methods of revolutionary nationalism collide with the interests of African American women, to suggest that, despite both Black women's attraction to Black men and their appreciation for the power of the image of the Black male subject as tool for resistance, the mechanisms put in place to support, depict, and advance Black masculinity and manhood may not always meet the needs of those Black people who are women.

In particular, these poems emphasize the often very different ways that African American women and African American men encounter those figures who populate the radical nationalist landscape. By emphasizing the link between the movement's adherence to a male-centered ideology of sexual difference and the very wide gulf between the ways that Black men and Black women experience and understand concepts like revolution and identity categories like white womanhood, these poems introduce the notion of distinct, gendered subjectivities within Blackness, the very notion of which contradicts the idea—central to nationalist politics and literature—of a single perspective that is uniformly and universally Black. In so doing, these poems not only challenge the gendering of Blackness as male and the related acceptance of Black male experience as universal; by exploring those instances when the interests and the pleasures of the Black male subject restrict, constrain, or alienate the Black woman speaker, poems depicting the interaction between African American women and the masculinist ideology of Black nationalism assign a particularity to the daily experiences of Black men that was previously attributed only to the lives of African American women.[17] Having debunked the notion of "universal" Black manhood, such poems introduce the notion of multiple identities with Blackness, highlighting the different and often opposing interests of African American subjects who are women and African American subjects who are men.

In "Memorial: 3. rev pimps," Sanchez urges African American women to remain aware of the possibility of sexual exploitation by Black men who use nationalist rhetoric as a tool for sexual conquest:

> hey.
>   Sisters
> git yr/blk/asses
> out of that re/
>   volution/
>   ary's
> bed.
>   that ain't no revolutionary
> thing com/munal
>   fuck/ing
> ain't nothing political
> bout fucking.
>   that's a white/
> thing u doing Sisters. (1–14)

Sanchez uses uneven lines and the fragmentation of words like "re / volution / ary" and "com/munal" to convey the divisive effect that the sexual exploitation of African American women has on any efforts to build and mobilize the Black community.[18]

The significance of Sanchez's critique is not so much in its exposure of Black women's sexual exploitation within the revolutionary nationalist movement as it is in its clear location of a Black woman's subject position relative to the categories of race and sex that is distinct from the relationship of her Black male counterparts to those very same groupings; certain aspects of nationalist masculinity that are affirming and even liberatory for African American men are marginalizing and oppressive to her. "Memorial" pokes fun at the so-called revolutionary, highlighting how his (mis)use of nationalist rhetoric betrays his disregard for the very ideas (in this instance the antiracist philosophies of Frantz Fanon) that he appropriates:

> and that so/
> called/brother there
> screwing u in tune to
>> fanon
>> and fanon
> and fanon
>> ain't no re
>> vo/lution/
>> ary (16–24)

The humor and irony of Sanchez's "Memorial" is that in using Fanon's analysis of race and the distribution of power to seduce his Black women comrades, the "so / called/brother" transforms the scholar's powerful challenge to one hierarchy (white over black) into a tool for reinforcing another (man over woman).[19] For the faux-revolutionary, Blackness remains an inherently male identity category, with the African American woman functioning only as object and symbol of his power. It is important to note that Sanchez's critique is not leveled at revolutionary nationalism itself but at the meanings assigned to the term *revolutionary* by some of the men who take on that label. Even so, the address of her poem to "sisters," in general, suggests both the pervasiveness of this phenomenon, and—in light of the frequency of this occurrence—the need for "sisters" to address some of the specific ways that they are marginalized as African American women.

Carolyn Rodgers exposes similar flaws in the use nationalist rhetoric in her humorous poem "The Last M.F." A direct response to those (mostly male) critics who condemned her for her use of vulgarities, this piece highlights the absurd contradictions of a rhetoric of Black freedom that seeks to limit the expression of half of its followers:[20]

> they say,
> that i should not use the word
> muthafucka anymo
> in my poetry or in any speech i give.
> they say,
> that i must and can only say it to myself

as the new Black Womanhood suggests
a softer self
a more reserved speaking self. they say,
that respect is hard won by a woman
who throws a word like muthafucka around
and so they say because we love you
throw that word away, Black Woman . . .
i say,
that i only call muthafuckas, muthafuckas
so no one should be insulted. (1–16)

Poems that depict the interaction between the African American woman speaker, the Black male revolutionary, and his white woman lover further complicate the notion of multiple identities within Blackness. Such poems not only underscore the existence of Black females as African Americans who are not male, but as women who are not white, a theme that Carolyn Rodgers seizes upon in "I Have Been Hungry," one of the earliest critiques of racism in white liberal feminism:

and you white girl
shall I call you sister now?
Can we share any secrets of sameness,
any singularity of goals
you, white girl
with the head that perpetually tosses over-rated curls
while i religiously toss my over-rated behind
    you white girl
i am yet suspicious of
for deep inside of me
there is the still belief that
i am
a road
you would travel
to my man. (1–15)

In "I Have Been Hungry," Rodgers's skepticism about the viability of a true feminist alliance between white and African American women hinges on her understanding of Black men's and white women's shared investment in the relegation of African American women to object status. Rodgers's poem implies the existence of common ground between white women and Black men, based on each constituency's utilitarian relationship to African American womanhood, with Black men using the African American female body to elevate their masculinity, and white women using Black women to gain access to Black men.

Sonia Sanchez's poems about the relationship between white women and Black men further illustrate the need for a distinct Black women's poetics of resistance. Her poems link the Euro-dominant conception of womanhood as a white identity category with some Black men's embrace of a revolutionary nationalist politics that marginalizes Black women. In "to all brothers" and "to all sisters" Sanchez suggests that an African American man's acceptance of a white female lover represents the failure of revolutionary nationalism. Each of these two poems highlights the contradiction between revolutionary nationalism and the politics of white privilege, as it captures the Euro-American female exercising her race privilege to the detriment of the Black power movement's cultural nationalist and anticapitalist principles.

In the cautionary poem "to all brothers," Sanchez scorns white women's sexual advances toward Black men, warning African American males of white women's desire to "in / tegrate your / blackness" (13–15). The similarly titled "to all sisters" deconstructs white female allure in a way that shifts the discussion of Black men's perceived preference for white women from its more common focus on white female beauty and onto the topic of white women's economic and social power. The poem begins with an enumeration of the qualities that distinguish white women's allure from its Black female counterpart. Along with the expected attributes of "white pussy" and "straight hair," the poem also lists the white male as a feature whose presence contributes to white women's attractiveness to nonwhite men. Sanchez asks,

> what a white woman got
> cept her white pussy
> always sucking after blackness
> what a white woman got
> cept her straight hair
> covering her fucked up mind
> what a white woman got
> cept her faggoty white man
> who goes to sleep in her
> without
> coming (1–11)

That the white man is listed as an attribute, despite his "faggoty" impotence, points to the irony of the power struggle between Black and white men. Even as African American males of the Black Arts period seek to assert their virility as strong, heterosexual men, white males retain a level of institutionalized social and economic control, beside which individual claims of superior potency or muscle are largely irrelevant. Sanchez's inclusion among those elements that contribute to white female allure white women's access to white men forges a link between the perceived physical attractiveness of white female bodies and the association of that body with socioeconomic privilege and political control. In the final stanza, Sanchez emphasizes the link between white women's bodies and white women's economic power, as she summarizes her analysis of white women's appeal:

> what a white woman got
> > cept money trying to buy up
> > a blk/man?
> > > > Yeah.
> what a white woman got? (12–16)

For Sanchez, white woman's value and attractiveness to African American men rests on the popular acceptance of both her body and her social position (her proximity to white males) as a marker of wealth and power.

Although Sanchez's Black Arts writings do, on one level, constitute an invective against relationships between Black men and white women, of far greater significance is her characterization of such relationships as a power exchange between two figures who enjoy center status within each of the identity categories that they share with African American women (Blackness and womanhood, respectively). In this exchange of power, the maleness of the Black figure and the whiteness of the female figure each elevate the status of the other. The African American woman's absence from this equation, despite her unique position of sharing at least one identity category with each figure in the pairing, dramatizes the vulnerability to erasure of the subject whose very existence exposes the fallacy inherent in both the racialization of womanhood and the gendering of Blackness. Neither white nor male, the Black woman speaker in these poems is rendered powerless by her white and male counterparts, her recourse limited either to passivity and hope in "to all brothers" ("this sister knows / and waits" [18–19]), or to an impassioned but ultimately ineffectual belittling in "to all sisters" ("what a white woman got / cept money").

Given that they constitute a response to established conventions within the movement, it is no surprise that "Memorial: 3. rev pimps," "to all brothers," and other poems suggesting the possibility of multiple perspectives within Blackness appear, for the most part, during the later years of the Black Arts period.[21] Nor does their emergence signal a wholesale departure from all self-objectifying poetry by all Black women in the movement. Even so, Sanchez's and Rodgers's focus on the rift between Black male and Black female experiences of both nationalist rhetoric and white-skin privilege demonstrates the absolute necessity of an antiracist poetics that addresses the interests of African American women.

Poems describing some of the gender-specific ways that racism touches the lives of African American women further expose the divide between Black men's nationalist ideology and Black women's subjugation at the hands of its advocates. They accomplish this by drawing attention to forms of bigotry and sites of antiracist struggle not accounted for in a movement that frames racial progress in terms Black men's quest for patriarchal power. In "On My First Trip to Mississippi" Linda Brown Bragg's portrayal of her mother's and grandmother's daily struggles against white southern racism moves the discussion of prejudice beyond those spaces associated with male power and privilege (the workplace, the ballot box, the courtroom) and into the more private settings where Black women have traditionally battled its effects. Bragg describes her mother's and grandmother's dignity under attack:

> Here I am in Mississippi,
>> Where my mama fought with her
>> eight year old fists
>> and learned with tears that feminine
>> fragility was a luxury enjoyed by
>> white blossom belles of the south
>> (after they had stoned her down
>> Lynch St. and down Rose St. and
>> all the way to her porch, softly, of course,
>> and with lady-like refinement).
>
> Here I am in Mississippi,
>> Where my grandma stood in her doorway,
>> bones grinding in her cheeks,
>> while she offered to blow the heads
>> off those little white knots of hatred
>> who called themselves children, who
>> screamed "nigger," in chorus, and who
>> didn't believe she'd pull the trigger even if
>> they *had* touched my mama. (1–19)

In revisiting the trials of her forebears, Bragg creates a legacy of Black female power and resistance in which African American women's everyday struggles and victories shape and inform the poet's own antiracist actions and thought. Other poems of the period link the specific ways that racism and poverty shape Black women's lives to the larger discourse on revolution, as in "U Name This One," Carolyn Rodgers's brief inventory of African American female struggle, first published in 1969, just as the 1960s were drawing to a close:

> let uh revolution come. uh
> state of peace is not known to me
> anyway

> since i grew up uhround in chi town
> . . . .
>> where pee wee cut lonnell fuh fuckin wid
>> his sistuh and blood baptized the street
>> a least twice ev'ry week and judy got
>> kicked outa grammar school fuh being pregnant
>> and died trying to ungrow the seed (1–4, 8–12)

She summarizes her female experience using the masculinist language of war and revolution ("just livin was guerilla warfare" [14]) in order to reinforce the link between the daily experiences of African American women and the interests of the radical Black social movement. Having established this link, however, she seems both impatient for and frustrated with what must have seemed at the time to be increasingly hollow demands for revolt (by 1975, nearly ten years had passed since the founding of the Black Panther Party for Self-Defense). Rodgers writes, "let uh revolution come. / couldn't be no action like what / i dun already seen" (15–17).

The reification of masculinity and male power by some Black Arts writers has resulted in the devaluation and, in some instances, the wholesale dismissal of the entire movement, all based on the perception that its male focus slowed the development of a Black woman–centered literature. In truth, however, Black Arts poets' awareness of the transgression inherent in creating portraits of African American manhood that exceed the narrow spaces in which the Black male subject becomes tolerable within a white supremacist social framework precipitated the reidentification of everyday life as a site of resistance for an entire generation of Black women poets. This chapter has explored how, using poems that in turns celebrate, scrutinize, and eventually challenge their relationship to the image of revolutionary male, Black Arts women expanded conceptions of identity sufficiently to include the possibility of multiple experiences of Blackness.

Nikki Giovanni's and Carolyn Rodgers's desire poems represent a developmental stage in Black Arts women writers' exploration of the transgressive capacity inherent in depictions of their everyday lives.[22] To express love, admiration, and desire for Black men is to challenge the sociopolitical order in which such figures are demeaned as undesirable and worthless. Such poems take an important first step in establishing African American women's visibility, depicting a Black female subject distinct from Black manhood and yet opposed to the interests and ideologies of white mainstream culture. Sanchez's "Memorial: 3" and other, similar poems represent an important next step, in which Black women's poetry begins to expose the limits of Black men's revolutionary thought and action in addressing the needs and concerns of the Black female subject.

Carolyn Rodgers's and Sonia Sanchez's poetic critiques of romantic relationships between Black men and white women further dramatize the limited capacity of revolutionary thought to address the needs of African American women, as they use representations of the links between Black men's gender privilege and white women's race privilege to expose some of the gaps between nationalist rhetoric and nationalist practice. These poems underscore the often stark differences in the ways that Black people who are women and Black people who are men experience power, even as they demonstrate the usefulness of the Black female everyday—the experiences and perspectives of the subject who enjoys neither white nor male privilege—as a tool for interrogating white supremacy. Such poems pave the way for (and even justify) pieces like "U Name This One" and "On My First Trip to Mississippi," in which African American women writers re-view the concept of resistance through the lens of Black women's experiences of racism.

Free, at last, to reimagine the texture and substance of revolution (after having exposed the weaknesses in male-centered nationalist discourse), Black Arts women indulge in the type of exploration and realization that Giovanni describes in her poem "Revolutionary Dreams":

> i used to dream militant
> dreams of taking
> over america to show
> these white folks how it should be
> done
> i used to dream radical dreams
> of blowing everyone away with my perceptive powers
> of correct analysis
> i even used to think i'd be the one
> to stop the riot and negotiate the peace
> then i awoke and dug
> that if i dreamed natural
> dreams of being a natural
> woman doing what a woman
> does when she's natural
> i would have a revolution (1–16)

Having recovered the power to define and readjust the boundaries of the "revolutionary" (embodied in the image of "a natural / woman doing what a woman / does when she's natural"), Giovanni moves on to explore the boundaries of the "natural," the "real," and other fundamental notions in the literature of transgression. "Ego Tripping (there may be a reason why)" (1970), with its bold reconfiguration of concepts like "natural," historical," and "true," rejects those constructions of the historical and the real that have traditionally supported white and male dominance, and in so doing culminates a process begun in the early desire poems:

> My oldest daughter is nefertiti
>> the tears from my birth pains
>> created the nile
> I am a beautiful woman
>
> I gazed on the forest and burned
>> out the sahara desert
>> with a packet of goat's meat
>> and a change of clothes
> I crossed it in two hours
> I am a gazelle so swift
>> so swift you can't catch me
>
>> For a birthday present when he was three
> I gave my son hannibal an elephant
>> He gave me rome for mother's day
> My strength flows ever on
>
> My son noah built new/ark and
> I stood proudly at the helm
>> as we sailed on a soft summer day
> I turned myself into myself and was
>> jesus
>> men intone my loving name
>> All praises All praises
> I am the one who would save
>
> I sowed diamonds in my back yard
> My bowels deliver uranium
>> the filings from my fingernails are
>> semi-precious jewels
> On a trip north
> I caught a cold and blew
> My nose giving oil to the arab world
> I am so hip even my errors are correct
> I sailed west to reach east and had to round off
>> the earth as I went
> The hair from my head thinned and gold was laid
>> across three continents (12–46)

Irreverently collapsing space-time boundaries and geographic distances to re-write a history of civilization embedded in events culled from the daily lives of Black women (birth, child rearing, bowel movements, common colds, and the thinning hair of old age), "Ego Tripping" represents a turning point in African American women's poetry. In this moment the Black female poet throws off the shackles of white- and/or male-centered notions of civilization, power, and historical progress, in favor of a Black woman–centered discourse of sociopolitical change. In appropriating the power to (re)make history, "Ego Tripping" foresees African American women poets' recuperation of the power of mythmaking in post–Black Arts collections like Ntozake Shange's *A Daughter's Geography*, Audre Lorde's *The Black Unicorn*, and Lucille Clifton's *Two-Headed Woman*. Having recovered the power to create, Giovanni-as-time-traveler locates herself beyond the small questions of any given historical moment. The issue of nationalism no longer pertains once her narrative exposes the ultimate inadequacy of any one nation to account for or contain the all-encompassing breadth of her Black experience. Similarly the question of African American women's marginalization—as passive object or desiring subject—is, finally, of little consequence. There is neither margin nor center for the "ego-tripping" Giovanni. As a Black woman, she is the wellspring—the origin—of all things; to de-center her influence or deny her power is to privilege the relative truth of a given moment (in this case, the twelve-year period of the Black Arts Movement) over the ageless truth of Giovanni's woman creator. "Ego Tripping" stands on the threshold of a new era, in which absolute truth is located in the power of language and African American women poets draw on the creative power of their words to renegotiate the terms of their own visibility, within Blackness, and beyond.

CHAPTER 4

LOCATING THE BLACK FEMALE SUBJECT
LATE-TWENTIETH-CENTURY AFRICAN AMERICAN WOMEN POETS AND THE LANDSCAPE OF THE BODY

> Indeed, a fundamental task of black critical thinkers has been
> the struggle to break with the hegemonic modes of seeing,
> thinking, and being that block our capacity to see ourselves
> oppositionally, to imagine, describe, and invent ourselves in
> ways that are liberatory.
>
> BELL HOOKS
> "Loving Blackness as Political Resistance"

> When women write to praise the body rather than to attack
> or joke about it, their most significant technique is revisionist
> metaphor. Water, moon earth, and living things, the natural
> as opposed to the artificial, provide the common sources
> of imagery for women poets engaged in commending the
> physical self, just as they always have for men describing
> women; but the images are turned to new directions.
>
> ALICIA OSTRIKER
> *Stealing the Language*

By the mid-1970s the era of the Black Arts Movement had passed, ushered into
obsolescence by the dramatic cultural and political shifts that marked the transition of the United States away from the volatile social upheaval of the 1960s
and into the increasingly tolerant social climate of the late twentieth century.[1]
Among those developments that contributed most significantly to the diminishing influence of Black nationalism on both literature and politics were the passage
of federal civil rights legislation, the government infiltration of revolutionary

nationalist organizations, and—at a time when U.S. Black women were growing in number and influence in African American political and cultural organizations—the challenge posed to that movement's androcentrism by poets like
Nikki Giovanni, Sonia Sanchez, and Carolyn Rodgers, whose Black Arts writings exposed the deleterious effects of its male-centered vision on the status and
advancement of African American women.[2] The next twenty-five years saw the
emergence of unprecedented numbers of African American women poets writing the Black female subject into poems whose topics and themes (such as racism,
political activism, and socioeconomic equality) would have, in earlier decades,
precluded the mention of any black subjects who were not male. Amidst the late
twentieth century's extraordinary range of representations of African American
womanhood, a smaller subtrend developed whose depictions of the Black female
subject engage the specific question of her position at the intersection of two identities traditionally viewed as oppositional. Such poems address African American
female subjectivity in ways that speak to the very roots of those conventional
notions of the relationship between gender, race, and space that have consistently
marginalized those figures who have sought visibility as both woman and Black.
In so doing, these works establish a poetics of wicked excess that embraces and
reinterprets the Black female subject's contravention of those roles and restrictions that have defined mainstream conceptions of U.S. womanhood.

A crucial step in African American women writers' pursuit of an aesthetic
that embraces the Black female subject's simultaneous location within womanhood and Blackness has been the identification of a symbolic or figurative
setting for African American womanhood that is liberatory and transformative. This chapter explores how those late-twentieth-century poems in which
African American women writers take up the question of Black woman's dual
identity create Black female subjects whose willful defiance of the physical and
discursive boundaries that have limited African American women's visibility
disrupts and destabilizes those established relationships between subject and
setting and those institutions, roles, and discourses (history, science, Eurocen-
trically based conceptions of the "real") that have maintained womanhood as a
white, middle-class identity category. Such poems locate Black womanhood as
a counterhegemonic subject position, and in so doing, reclaim transgression as
a celebrated feature of Black female subjectivity.

While most exaggerated in the literature and rhetoric of the Black Arts
Movement, the androcentic bias in African American literature can be traced
as far back as the Harlem Renaissance era, and before. In *Black Women, Writing and Identity: Migrations of the Subject,* Carole Boyce Davies describes the
capacity of African American women's literature to disrupt and transform prevailing social structures: "Black women's writing re-negotiates the questions of

identity; once Black women's experience is accounted for, assumptions about identity, community and theory have to be reconsidered" (Davies 3). The poems that appeared during the last quarter of the twentieth century introduced the Black female subject into areas of artistic inquiry that had previously been closed to her, depicting her engaged in activities and negotiating circumstances and settings whose representation was previously considered incompatible with the political and aesthetic goals of the Black literary establishment. Writing both as African Americans and as women, Black women poets of the late twentieth century renegotiated those "assumptions about identity" that understood anti-racist action and thought in terms of the interests of African American males, reading some of the defining themes, issues, and events shaping the historical and present-day circumstances of U.S. Black people through the experiences of African American women.

Sanchez, Giovanni, and Rodgers, whose Black Arts poems were instrumental in writing the African American woman out of more than fifty years of relegation to object status, emerged into the literary landscape of the late twentieth century retaining many of the same thematic and aesthetic interests that they had explored in their nationalist poetry. Their post–Black Arts poems, however, expand their address of these topics, applying them to a broader range of frameworks than had been acceptable within the constraints of that movement. In *A Blues Book for Blue Black Magical Women,* for example, Sonia Sanchez's first volume to write beyond the constraints of Black Arts prohibitions on African American female subjectivity, the poet adapts the Black Arts theme of the embrace of Islam to the specific interests of African American women, deploying it as an epistemology through which to reexamine motherhood while simultaneously deploying motherhood as an epistemology through which to examine Islam, all toward the end of emancipating Black womanhood from Euro-American notions of femininity and women's role.[3] In late-twentieth-century volumes like *The Heart as Ever Green* (1978), *Morning Glory* (1989), and *A Train Called Judah* (1996), Carolyn Rodgers makes similar use of spiritually based systems of meaning, as she undertakes a comparable redefinition of social transformation and political change, but rooted in her embrace of Christianity. Like Sanchez's reciprocal explorations of Islam and motherhood, each through the lens of the other, Carolyn Rodgers's adoption of Christianity as a mode through which to achieve and explore notions of personal transformation and individual freedom resists not only the androcentrism of the Black Arts Movement of her youth but also its narrowly defined notions of "revolution" and "social change."[4]

In the title poem of *The Heart as Ever Green,* for example, Rodgers uses nature-based metaphors to illustrate the human potential for spiritual rebirth and individual growth. She describes her heart as

ever green. green
like a season of emeralds
green as in tender & like buds or shoots
determined to grow
determined to be (2–6)[5]

Rodgers uses the familiar biblical metaphor of Jesus as the "light of the world" to compare the deliverance associated with the embrace of Christian faith to the liberation inherent in nature's capacity for change and renewal.[6] Her heart, she explains, is "green / like a light in the world, for freedom" (9–10).[7]

In Nikki Giovanni's post–Black Arts poems and in Sonia Sanchez's poetry since *Blues Book*, the reintroduction of the Black female subject is manifest most dramatically in each poet's treatment of political and cultural figures, topics, and phenomena through speaking subjects whose perspectives are shaped by their simultaneous identification, either implicitly or explicitly, as women and as Black. Giovanni's "Linkage (for Phillis Wheatley)," for example, published in *Those Who Ride the Night Winds* (1983), submits the abduction, enslavement, and exploitation of Black woman poet Phillis Wheatley as the paradigm against which to measure and comprehend the exploitation of women and children of all races and nationalities, past and present. Giovanni imagines the pioneering writer—who was kidnapped from Africa at around the age of six, transported to the United States, and sold to a wealthy Boston socialite—as "a little Black girl . . . / standing on a stage . . . waiting to be purchased" (27–28).[8] She emphasizes the powerlessness of Wheatley's position and offers her vulnerability and absolute loss of agency as a framework through which to understand the circumstances, not only of child slaves in the antebellum period, but of exploited children in the present day. Giovanni explains that "Little white boys . . . stalking Park Avenue . . . little white / girls . . . on the Minnesota Strip . . . are also slaves . . . to the / uncaring . . . of a nation" (42–44).

Sonia Sanchez makes similar use of notable Black women's experiences of racism and exploitation in works like her 1992 poem "Introduction of Toni Morrison, and Others, on the Occasion of the Publication of Her Book *Race-ing Justice, En-Gendering Power: Essays on Anita Hill, Clarence Thomas, and the Construction of Social Reality*."[9] Here Black woman attorney Anita Hill's experience of both racism and sexism during the period surrounding the Hill-Thomas hearings forms the framework of Sanchez's retrospective analysis of the objectification and dehumanization of African American women *and* men that characterized both public expressions of support for Thomas and the public campaign to discredit Hill. Sanchez interprets the *New York Times*'s "delight" in Thomas's "accomplishment of weight lifting" as but another incarnation of the United States' historic obsession with African American male bodies (12).[10] She explains,

> We all know that Black men's bodies are important
> to them, to women, other men, Phil Donahue, academics,
> voyeurs, scientists, journalists, oprahwinfrey, undertakers,
> prisons, long winding trees (13–16)

For Sanchez, newspapers' and senators' objectification of Thomas was as insidious and damaging as the public attempts to portray Hill as "crazy or jealous or deranged or / a scorned lover or jealous or a lesbian or insane / or disturbed or a hater of lighter-complexioned women" (30–32), in that both phenomena resulted in the sacrifice of Hill's *and* Thomas's humanity to

> . . . the homicidal nature
> of a country that continues to pit Black men and women
> in arenas of combat so the executioners can cream
> in private . . . (57–60)

The post–Black Arts writings of Sanchez, Rodgers, and Giovanni are part of the larger trend in late-twentieth-century African American women's poetry toward deploying Black womanhood as a device for expanding the discourse around race, identity, and social change. Their poems join those of other late-twentieth-century African American women writers—June Jordan in *Passion* (1980), Rita Dove in *Thomas and Beulah* (1986), Elizabeth Alexander in *The Venus Hottentot* (1990), Alice Walker in *Revolutionary Petunias* (1973), and many more—in using the events and conditions of African American women's daily lives as a lens through which to reexamine and reimagine the social hierarchies, historical developments, cultural institutions, political phenomena, and personal relationships that have shaped the meaning and experience of Blackness in the United States.[11] Such poems are most compelling in their transgression of conventionally drawn identities and established sociopolitical hierarchies when they portray Black women's navigation of those relationships, settings, circumstances, and events whose representation during previous periods in African American literary history reinforced the location of Black women's lives and experiences at the margin of African American literary concerns.

Despite their success both in introducing Black women's experiences into the center of African American scholarly and literary discourse, and in reestablishing the African American woman as subject within Blackness, U.S. Black women poets remained, throughout the late twentieth century, challenged in their visibility as women by the continuing association of womanhood with the space of the middle-class nuclear-family home. Ushered in by the 1960s confessional movement, with its indicting portrayals of domestic—often middle-class—dysfunction, and by the rise of bourgeois feminism in both artistic and academic circles, a white female poetry of resistance and transgression rose to increasing prominence during the same period in which African American women poets were exercising their newly acquired subjecthood. Euro-American poets like Louise Glück, Sharon Olds, and Marge Piercy carved out a space for the emergence of an oppositional female subject position within whiteness, based on their rejection of the traditional roles and spaces associated with Euro-American womanhood and femininity.[12] Even as their poems challenged the notion of bourgeois domesticity as the endowed role for white female adults, however, the focus in many of their most highly regarded works on exposing the myth of serene domesticity, its preferred setting of the single-family home, and its constituent relationships as universally fulfilling and safe for all women served as a reminder of the ongoing hegemony of that model—the ideal of middle-class, home-centered (true) womanhood—as a fundamental influence on women's lives.

Thus African American women poets and the figures and circumstances that their poems depicted remained marginalized, and for the same fundamental reason that their visibility as women had been compromised in previous periods. The subjects, issues, and locations that late-twentieth-century Black women poets treated in their depictions of African American women's lives fell far outside of the limits that defined womanhood not only in the popular imagination but also among artistic and academic considerations of womanhood where, based on their historically troubled relationship to ideal womanhood and the pastoral homescape, Black women's poems of testimony and resistance were often tokenized and exoticized as glimpses into "the other womanhood."[13]

In writing beyond the traditional boundaries that maintained womanhood as a white identity category, late-twentieth-century African American women poets employed many of the same tactics that they were using to write beyond the traditional boundaries that maintained Blackness as male, introducing African American womanhood into the center of poems that engaged issues like sexual harassment and rape, institutions like marriage, and roles like mother, sister, and daughter, which had traditionally been framed by the positionality of white women. Many of the same collections—and poems—that sought to expand the consideration of race beyond the experience of Black men also include depictions family life, female sexuality, and personal transformation that write womanhood beyond its association with whiteness. Volumes like Sapphire's *American Dreams* (1994), with its focus on Black women's physical and sexual abuse; Thylias Moss's *Small Congregations* (1993), an exploration of faith, motherhood, and stereotypes; Toi Derricotte's *Captivity* (1989), whose opening section, "Black Bottom," chronicles the spiritual, racial, and cultural dimensions of suburban isolation; and Rita Dove's *Thomas and Beulah* (1986), which examines how gender and race shape the female subject's experience of "universal" life events (marriage, birth, aging, death) each played an instrumental role in writing African American womanhood into the broader dialogue on feminism and social change. Only a smaller number of African American women poets, however, and even then in only some of their poems, took up the question of Black female subjectivity itself, not as a context against which to explore a broader sociopolitical or historical question, nor as a lens through which to revisit a relationship or event, but as the focal point of their poetic inquiry.

The emergence of a body of poems that engages the specific question of Black female subjectivity represents one of the most significant development in late-twentieth-century African American women's poetry. It is in these poems alone that we see Black women poets not only challenging the more recent association of women's emancipation and empowerment with the positionality of the middle-class white female but also confronting the very root of this construction (of womanhood as a white identity category), the designation of the single-family home as that site in which womanhood becomes visible. In identifying a metaphorical "setting" for the African American woman subject that transcends the limits of any single physical space and allows the Black female subject to become visible as African American and as woman in any context in which she is portrayed, such poems draw on many of the same strategies used by those very poets whose nineteenth-century depictions of middle-class domesticity helped to establish the racially exclusive vision of female subjectivity that late-twentieth-century Black women poets are writing against. In the poems of this late-twentieth-century subtrend, however, those strategies take on a subversive quality, as African American women writers apply them in poems that celebrate the very "failure" to conform to mainstream notions of femininity and women's role that had for so long consigned Black women to silence and invisibility.

Ntozake Shange, Lucille Clifton, and Audre Lorde are three of the most prominent figures among those late-twentieth-century African American women poets for whom the reappraisal of the Black female body is both goal and means in a line of artistic inquiry that emphasizes the counterhegemonic position of the Black female subject. For these poets, the Black female body displaces the private suburban home to become that site whose features, traits, and interactions with its physical setting most accurately reflect the relationship of the African American female subject to the institutions and identity groups that constitute her discursive surroundings. Unlike the mid-nineteenth-century poems of the pastoral homescape, whose depictions of that setting support a notion of female identity based on woman's thorough compliance with established social norms, the portraits of the Black female body created by Shange, Clifton, and Lorde point to a vision of womanhood that depends on the female subject's willful transgression of traditional settings and roles.

Indeed, in a social order that has previously recognized only white woman-hood and male Blackness, to achieve visibility as both woman and Black is to exist in excess of each of those identities and in defiance of the institutions and discourses which have supported the exclusion of African American women from each of those categories. For Betsy Erkkila, "wicked excess" refers to female poets' use of fantasy, myth, sarcasm, exaggeration, and other techniques to call attention to their willful existence outside of the narrow spaces left open for traditional womanhood. Since the mid-1970s, Shange, Clifton, and Lorde have each used mythical language and imagery to create portraits of the Black female body that, in resisting the narrow definitions of womanhood that have hidden the Afro-American woman from view, undermine the system of socio-political hierarchies that perpetuates Black women's invisibility.[14] These poets attribute to their bodies and the bodies of those Black women who populate their surroundings (family, friends, ancestors) an array of features and char-acteristics ranging from the mundane to the magical. These traits reflect each poet's vision of the relationship of the Black female subject to the institutions and identity groups that have determined her position and meaning.

Karla Holloway describes the use of myth in literature by Black women writ-ers as "a metaphorical revisioning of experiential knowledge" (Holloway 87). For African American women poets the deliberate incorporation of language and images associated with myth becomes a way to articulate commonalities in Black women's experience without collapsing into essentialism.[15] Jacqueline De Weever describes the impact of this process on the world outside of the mythic text: "If fiction establishes lines to a world other than the real . . . [then] the mythic narrative establishes lines to a world that is not only beyond the real world, but that, at the same time, transforms it" (De Weever 4). Building upon the frame-work of common experience, Black women writers use myth to control and redirect the way that the African American woman subject becomes visible. For late-twentieth-century African American women poets, to depict actual people and events in poems that incorporate magic and other elements of fantasy, and then to demand the reader's interaction with elements as real that are tradition-ally engaged as fantastic or unreal is to transform the reader. Jane Campbell car-ries this notion one step further, as she goes on to identify the specific effect of mythmaking upon race relations in the United States: "[M]ythmaking . . . con-stitutes a radical act, inviting the audience to subvert the racist mythology that thwarts and defeats Afro-Americans, and to replace it with a new mythology rooted in the black perspective" (Campbell x). When the reader interacts with and accepts the mythic landscape arranged by the Black woman poet, he or she abandons the mythic landscape organized and presented by white Americans and other privileged constituencies. The African American woman poet offers myths explaining Black woman's subjectivity as an alternative to the marginalizing sociopolitical constructs which aid those identity groups who enjoy "center" status in maintaining their privileged discursive position.

When African American women poets assign to their Black female subjects fantastic traits and mythical capabilities that exceed the boundaries of traditional womanhood, their flagrant disregard for the roles and restrictions that would limit their function and meaning challenges the positionality of those institutions and identity groups whose visibility depends upon the preservation of Blackness and womanhood as opposing categories. Their Black bodies replace the marginalizing system of binary relations (man/woman, Black/white, margin/center, public/private) that perpetuates the confinement of womanhood to exclusionary spaces (like the middle-class suburban home) with a paradigm of meaning based upon simultaneity. Within this new paradigm of meaning the African American female subject comes into view, not by virtue of her relationship to the institutions (womanhood, domesticity, marriage) and identity categories (whiteness, maleness, etc.) located outside of Black womanhood, but through those institutions, identities, and ideas that coexist within the boundaries of that position.[16] Within the paradigm of simultaneity, the coexistence within the African American female subject of Blackness and womanhood is indicated through each poet's use of images suggesting duality. The notion, central to the Afro-mythic cosmology that these poets construct, that history, culture, and memory position U.S. Black women and their African ancestors as different manifestations of the same subject position is represented through images evoking the idea of timelessness. These images depict the space and time that separates late-twentieth-century African Americans from their ancestry as virtually inconsequential, so that Black women's subjectivity becomes simultaneously a fact of the past and a condition of the present. Other seemingly contradictory qualities that converge within African American womanhood—the seen and the unseen, the possible and the impossible—are opposing pairs whose coexistence within Black womanhood is indicated through each poet's invocation of the magical.[17] Ntozake Shange, Lucille Clifton, and Audre Lorde write lyrical body portraits that, in emphasizing the ways in which the Black female subject exceeds the traditional boundaries that have defined each of her most visible identities, disrupt conventional notions of Blackness and womanhood, not merely resisting but rejecting those systems of meaning that would preclude her embodiment of both categories.

Ntozake Shange was the first of these poets to gain national renown. A playwright and novelist as well as a poet, she is most widely known for the unflinching realism with which she portrayed the lives of ordinary African American women in *For Colored Girls Who Have Considered Suicide When the Rainbow Is*

Enuf (1976). The author herself labeled this unique stage production a "choreo-poem," a name evolved to emphasize its hybrid construction. *For Colored Girls* consists of twenty short pieces, written in free verse and arranged into a single book-length dramatic poem in seven voices, to be performed by seven Black women. Its lengthy run at Broadway's Booth Theater made Ntozake Shange a household name in the New York metropolitan area and among theater goers nationwide. Compared to the wide impact of and broad-based interest in *For Colored Girls*, however, Shange's subsequent forays into magical realism have gone virtually unnoticed.

Ironically, *For Colored Girls* in many respects represents a developmental phase in Shange's work. In it she exhausts the possibilities of realism as her seven speakers each expose the details of their lives at the intersection of Black-ness and womanhood in a series of monologues that are as heart wrenching as they are life-affirming. At the close of her choreopoem, each of Shange's women appears strengthened by the act of telling (her story), but these are individual transformations, born of the catharsis of confession and testimony. While each woman's monologue bears poignant witness to the complications that arise when a subject who is Black and woman finds herself trapped in a sociopoliti-cal order that resists such ambiguities, these eloquent accounts of struggle and survival do little to address the capacity of the Black woman's emergence as speaking subject to transform and disrupt those binaries, sociopolitical frame-works, and systems of meaning whose existence both maintains and depends on her silence and invisibility.

In the poems of Shange's *Nappy Edges* (1978) we see her vision expand from that of *For Colored Girls*, which frames its Black female characters' transcendence of conventional notions of gender and race as individual transformations collec-tively voiced, and into an interest in depicting African American women sub-jects whose representation rewrites the meaning and function of Black woman-hood as an identity category. In the poems of Shange's magical realist collection, *A Daughter's Geography* (1983), we see her interests expand once again, as she explores the manner in which the Black female subject's reemergence into visi-bility and voice disrupts and reconfigures those identity categories, institutions, and ideologies that exist outside of African American womanhood. Like Nikki Giovanni's "Ego Tripping," the explorations of the intersection between Black-ness and womanhood in Shange's *Nappy Edges* and *A Daughter's Geography* establish not only that the voice in all of her poems is Black and female—from the "word paintings" of *Ridin' the Moon in Texas* (1987) to her meditations on the complexity and challenge of loving Black men in *The Love Space Demands* (1991)—but also that, in each of Shange's poems, the racial, sexual, geographi-cal, and aesthetic landscape revealed and inhabited by her Black woman speaker observes neither the boundaries that have limited each of her constituent identities nor the established social frameworks that have obscured her from view.

The *Nappy Edges* collection opens with a short poem defining the idiom that serves as its title.[18] The expression "nappy edges" refers to that portion of African American, heat-straightened hair that grows closest to the scalp, "turning back" to its tightly curled natural state upon exposure to water, humidity, and especially the sweat of vigorous activity. Thus the term names an experience—hair straightening and the management of its transitory state—that sits firmly at the intersection of Blackness and womanhood. Shange defines "nappy edges" as

> the roots of your hair/ what
> turns back when we sweat, run,
> make love, dance, get afraid, get
> happy: the tell-tale sign of living/ (1–4)

In choosing as her title an idiom so intimately associated with African American women's bodies, activities, and standards of beauty, Shange locates the voices of and the intended audience for her book as Black and female. Similarly, the definition she provides serves not as an invitation to those who exist outside of that dual identity but as a notice that those who inhabit bodies in whom Blackness and womanhood do not intersect are entering the space of the text not as addressees but only as observers of a conversation framed by and concerned with the interests and experiences of African American women.

This notion is most dramatically represented in the poem "resurrection of the daughter." This poem traces a young African American woman's journey to self-invention and discovery, having freed herself from what the poet characterizes as the priggish constraints of the Black bourgeoisie. The early stanzas of the poem highlight the stifling effects on female autonomy of an African American middle-class whose understanding of the sexuality of unmarried women is grounded in a binary that poses modest virginity as the sole acceptable alternative to prurience and lust. The daughter's family is "quarantined / socially restricted // to bridge & sunday brunch by the pool," (2–3) and proud of its daughters who

> . . . cd set a formal table
> curtsey as if not descendants of slaves
> & speak English with no accent at all
> they were virgins for a long time (11–14)

The hostility toward young African American women's sexuality that is implicit in this passage is confirmed in an anecdote in which the speaker recalls how "one [daughter] wuz on punishment for a month / cuz she closed her eyes while dancing on the wrong / side of town" (15–17). Her parents' distrust of the sexuality of their unmarried Black daughter is linked to their own class anxiety; her "mama . . . came from there" (the "wrong" side of town), and "knew too well / a cheap pleasure cd spell remorse / for an upwardly mobile girl" (18–20).

These parents value their daughters' middle-class decorum (the etiquette of table setting and curtseying and the mastery of non-accented English), based on the perception that it disassociates their family from the slave status of their ancestors (the daughters could "curtsey as if not descendants of slaves / & speak English with no accent at all"), a legacy that links them even to those African Americans who are poor and working class. This belief distinguishes their class anxiety from the larger transethnic phenomenon of class anxiety among the newly middle-class, complicating it with a racial anxiety that manifests itself in a suspicion and intolerance of any form of Black female sexuality not confined within the boundaries of those social institutions—marriage and the nuclear-family home—that signify women's propriety within the Black bourgeoisie.

The second portion of the poem follows the one daughter who has chosen to reject the limitations imposed on her Blackness and her womanhood by the intertwined class and race anxieties of her family, as she reconfigures the meaning of each of those identities in opposition to the conventions of propriety and visibility maintained within the confines of the African American middle class. Shange describes the beginnings of her transformation:

> a daughter convinced her beauty an aberration
> . . . .
> left the asylum of her home on a hunch
> . . . .
> & she was last seen in the arms of herself
> blushing
> having come to herself
> in the heat of herself (42, 44, 53–56)

This passage appropriates the sensationalist tone of the newspaper headline or missing person's report ("*she was last seen in* the arms of herself" [emphasis added]) to capture the urgency of the daughter's retreat from her childhood home. At the same time, the language of sexual release (the "blushing" and "heat" as she "come[s] to herself") frames her journey as an act of resistance at odds with the prudish convictions of her bourgeois upbringing. The intrepid "daughter" of this poem is a fugitive from the chaste sensibilities of an African American middle class that, in leaving no space for the sexual expression of single Black women, rejects the very body in which the Black female subject becomes visible. Such figures are thus condemned to a discursive no-man's land between the chastity-based positionality of the girl and the subject status, conferred upon marriage, of the woman.

The daughter's pursuit of a subject position that accommodates all of her identities (middle-class, inhabiting a body in which Blackness and womanhood intersect, and yet also unmarried)—against the backdrop of a bourgeois social order which tolerates only chaste objecthood (the manners, elocution, and virginity of the daughters function primarily to enhance the visibility of their parents as middle-class African Americans) or married subjecthood in its women and girls—parallels Black Arts male poets' pursuit of subjecthood in a white-dominated social order that tolerates African American men only in the positions of subjugated object or dead symbol (the lynched body of the Black male as symbol of white power and supremacy). Her male Black Arts predecessors created poems whose demands for Black women's deference and fierce threats of vengeance against the white mainstream suggest a route to subjecthood that depends upon recognition of their African American manhood by constituencies external to that subject position. For the daughter in Shange's poem, however, subjectivity depends not on her recognition and acknowledgment by others but instead on her own understanding that, despite the failure of conventional notions of Blackness and womanhood to account for her possibility, the figure in whom those identities intersect does, in fact, exist as a subject, Black and woman, in willful transgression of the spaces left open for each of those categories. Indeed, this daughter turns away from those whose vision of Black womanhood have limited her ("she a daughter refused to answer her mother's calls" [49]) and disregards the disapproval and rejection of others ("she refused to believe in the enmity of her sisters" [50]). Inasmuch as her male Black Arts predecessors chose the subjecthood of men, she chooses its female counterpart, taking her place among those "daughters choosin to be women" (59). For this daughter, however, the full capacity to emerge as a Black subject—not simply the declaration and undertaking of that pursuit, but the success of seeing it to completion—lies simply in her own appropriation of the power to confer that status upon herself.

In the closing lines of the poem, having rejected her family's bourgeois anxiety and its manifestation in their denial of Black female sexuality, the daughter seeks not the embrace of the male lovers from whom she, as a vessel of the family's propriety, was once protected. Instead, she finds affirmation and release in her own embrace and healing in the tender ministrations of her own tongue against her flesh, discovering in her efforts to repair the psychic wounds of her middle-class confinement the capacity to reinvent herself. The final passage of this poem repeats the possessive pronoun in order to underscore Black women's agency to effect their own emergence as female subjects, as well as to heal the wounds of invisibility and silence borne of their occupation of a subject position for which there is no acknowledged sociocultural context or setting: "daughters choosin to be women / lick *their* own wounds with *their* own spit / til they heal" (59–61, emphasis added).

"Resurrection of the daughter" offers its description of the constraints imposed upon unmarried women of the Black middle class by their families' faith in and reliance on conventional notions of propriety and success as a context for understanding the relationship of the renegade daughter's rejection of such beliefs to her emergence as a liberated subject. The contrast between her experience prior to and after having abandoned the systems of meaning that circumscribed her middle-class upbringing underscores the necessity to African American women's visibility (as subjects in excess of both Blackness and womanhood) of transformative means that circumvent, confound, and defy established notions of social progress and prosperity.

The body portraits of Shange's *A Daughter's Geography* build on this premise, using magical realism and its inherent challenge to conventional modes of understanding to highlight Black women's willful departure from traditional paths to empowerment. The poems of *A Daughter's Geography* combine myth with words and images culled from diverse language and folklore traditions of the Black Atlantic cultures (in this text Shange is particularly interested in incorporating elements of Afro-Cuban and Afro-Brazilian culture and tradition) to propose a new vision of African Americanness as a transnational designation whose subjects are historically and ethnically unified, despite the physical distances and geographic boundaries that divide them. Two poems in this volume are of particular interest to this study, in that they apply magical realism and myth to the specific task of rewriting African American women's subjectivity and reconfiguring the role of language—the written and spoken word—in making and remaking identities. In "We Need a God Who Bleeds Now," we see Shange using the language and images of religion and myth in new ways, to write into view an emancipatory vision of the fertile woman-as-god. In this poem she offers several unique, and sometimes shocking, images of her goddess in opposition to what she perceives as the detrimental limitations upon woman's subjectivity presented in the Word (Logos) of Scripture. In "Oh, I'm 10 Months Pregnant" we see a woman writer whose commitment to language (words are the creative medium of her vocation) is acted out literally by her unborn daughter, who refuses to observe the distinction that her mother so willingly accepts, between living in the body and living in the discourse.

In "We Need a God Who Bleeds Now," Ntozake Shange offers her vision of an omnipotent Black woman god as a challenge to traditional conceptions of female subjectivity that recognize only a limited number of possibilities within that identity category. Shange's bold and graphic image of the woman god, bleeding copiously and unabashedly, opposes the long-standing equation of woman's fertility cycle with diminishment, frailty, and shame:

> we need a god who bleeds now
> a god whose wounds are not
> some small male vengeance
> some pitiful concession to humility
> a desert swept with drying marrow in honor of the lord
>
> we need a god who bleeds
> spreads her lunar vulva & showers us in shades of scarlet
> thick & warm like the breath of her (1–8)

Shange juxtaposes the vivid image of her bleeding woman god against images invoking death and sacrifice to reinscribe the symbolic meaning of blood. Instead of conjuring up notions of weakness, death, and defeat, Shange's representations of bleeding and, in particular, menstruation call up notions of vigor, renewal, and life.

In another, similar reconfiguration, the poet call for a god "whose wounds are not the end of anything." This passage recalls the link between wounds and renewal in Shange's earlier "resurrection of the daughter," as it pokes fun at the canonical Christian association of bodily wounds—and especially bleeding—with somber sacrifice through real, mortal death. Instead the poet associates her bleeding god with the breath of life itself: "[she] showers us in shades of scarlet / thick & warm like the breath of her." The image of moon and sea struggling to restrain the god reads like playful slapstick: "the moon tugs the seas / to hold her" (13–14).

Shange's "Oh, I'm 10 Months Pregnant" is a whimsical allegory in which the poet uses the unlikely image of the Black woman writer in her tenth month of pregnancy to explore the relationship between visibility, representation, articulation, and Black female subjectivity. In this postmodern fable, African American womanhood is embodied in the figure of the unborn girl child developing within the Black female body of the mother. The relationship between the African American woman speaker and her unborn daughter becomes a metaphor for the centrality of language in Black woman's pursuit of visibility. The speaker begins her unusual tale:

> i tried to tell the doctor
> i really tried to tell her
>
> . . . .
> i tried
> to tell her the baby was confused

>   the baby doesnt know
>   she's not another poem. (1–2, 5–8)

The problem, she explains, is that her unborn child believes that she is to be articulated—spoken or written—into being:

>   "doctor/the baby doesnt think she shd
>   come out that way!"
>   . . . .
>   this baby wants to jump out of my mouth
>   at a reading someplace/
>   the baby's refusing to come out/down
>   she wants to come out a spoken word (18–19, 27–30)

For the unborn girl child the relationship between mother and daughter is discursive, rather than biological:

>   i mean/she thinks she shd come up/not down
>   into the ground/she thinks her mother makes up things
>   nice things ugly things but made up things nonetheless
>   unprovable irrational subjective fantastic things
>   not subject to objective or clinical investigation/
>   she believes the uterine cave is a metaphor (20–25)

Eventually, wearily Shange's writer-mother capitulates to the wishes of her unborn daughter to emerge not merely as a physical being but as a discursive figure:

>   i finally figured out what to say
>   to this literary die-hard of a child of mine
>   "you are an imperative my dear"/& i felt her startle
>   toward my left ovary then I said/"as an imperative
>   it is incumbent upon you to present yrself" (37–41)

Thus, like all fables, this fantastic tale, too, has a moral: eventually, humorously the speaker comes to understand that to speak of Black womanhood is to deliver it into being.

Like Shange, poet Lucille Clifton creates playful revisionist images of reproduction and other themes and events associated with Black women's lives. Also integral to Clifton's myth-play is her appropriation and subversion of the oldest forms of sacred and ritual expression. Her poems read like incantations, short parables, and invocations, except that rather than explaining how the oceans were made or where the sun goes when it sets, her mythic texts explain the nature of Black women's subjectivity. In addition, while allegories, invocations, praise songs, and other sacred forms generally reinforce established hierarchies, Clifton's poems subvert the dominant paradigm.[19] Her explanations of Black womanhood cast that identity category as oppositional; her incantations and invocations are written to incite resistance, not to maintain order.

Clifton has maintained the specific question of the intersection between Blackness and womanhood in the African American female body as a recurring theme throughout her post–Black Arts poetry. "Sisters: For Elaine Philip on Her Birthday," in *An Ordinary Woman* (1975), marks one of the poet's earliest explorations, not simply of African American women's perspectives, struggles, or politics, but of the African American female body as a tool for resisting and then reconfiguring those ideologies, hegemonies, and epistemologies that have silenced and marginalized Black women.[20] The aging Black women friends in Clifton's "Sisters" recognize each other by their bodies. The appearance of their bodies indicates not shared genes or common bloodlines, however, but shared rituals or cultural practices. Clifton describes the rites with which both women marked their youth. The phrases that she uses to describe these shared activities are culled from Black vernacular and suggest the shared language that figured so prominently in the previous discussion. She writes: "me and you / be greasing our legs / touching up our edges" (5–7).

Clifton recalls the rituals with which both women marked their transition to maturity and motherhood:

> me and you
> got babies
> got thirty-five
> got black
> let our hair go back (15–19)

Their common rituals denote the sisters' shared signification as African American women, an identity group that becomes visible through the vehicle of the body, not by virtue of the essential or physical qualities that it exhibits, but through the cultural practices that the Black woman subject performs on that body and the values and interests that these practices suggest. Clifton's emphasis on ritual is a deliberate departure from notions of African American identity that rely on false and bigoted notions of biological "race." She writes: "me and you be sisters. / we be the same. / me and you / coming from the same place" (1–4).

As she advocates a vision of African American women's subjectivity that is based in the Black female body and the rituals that mark and maintain it, Clifton is careful not to reduce identity or sameness to monoliths. Thus, despite the similar processes by which she and Elaine Philip invent themselves as Black—that is, through the exercise of body rituals which link them to the larger community of U.S. Black women—Clifton closes the poem with a passage highlighting important *differences* between the two. Her brief focus on each woman's chosen medium of expression calls attention to the persistence of distinctions even among subjects within a single common identity group:

> me and you
> . . . .
> be loving ourselves
> be loving ourselves
> be sisters
> only where you sing
> i poet. (14, 20–24)

Without undermining Clifton's larger theme of connections between Black women, the notion that some women "sing" and some women "poet" challenges the assumption that subjects within a marginalized group are indistinguishable from one another, an idea that gives rise to stereotyping and other forms of bias.

In Clifton's "to merle," the profound connection between Black female speaker and addressee is evident in the speaker's capacity to recognize, in the body of her companion, the duality that frames their shared subjectivity as African American women. In "to merle" Clifton-as-speaker greets her beloved friend, named in the title, with words whose playful excess locate the Black woman subject simultaneously in the contradictory moments of present and past:

> say skinny manysided tall on the ball
> brown downtown woman
> last time i saw you was on the corner of
> pyramid and sphinx (1–4)

Clifton's greeting juxtaposes the seemingly opposing traits that coexist within the body of her Black woman friend. Beyond the obvious reference to physical size, skinny implies thinness or simplicity—thin as inconsequential, or the antithesis of complex. For Merle, however, thinness and complexity coexist without contradiction; she is simultaneously "skinny" *and* "manysided." Similarly she is both brown (i.e., Black) and a woman, a pairing unacknowledged within a system of meaning that understands womanhood as inherently white. Even the circumstances under which Clifton offers her greeting suggest the pairing of opposites. Clifton and Merle are friends in the present but linked by an ancient bond, forged when the pyramids were new; they are American, but their shared subjectivity looks to the physical and symbolic space of Africa as its setting of origin.

Clifton-as-speaker recognizes her long absent friend not only by her "skinny," "brown" body, but by her language:

ten thousand years have interrupted our conversation
but I have kept most of my words
til you came back. (5–7)

In this passage, Clifton's relationship with Merle takes on a broader, more historical function, as a symbol of the bonds that exist between Black women separated by time and space. The notion that the contradictions, characteristics,
and language ("words") by which Clifton and Merle recognize each other have
survived for "ten thousand years" locates the African American woman subject
outside of the dominant systems of meaning that do not allow for such temporal excesses. The idea of a friendship whose roots lie at the "corner of / pyra-
mid and sphinx" suggests that the connections between late-twentieth-century
U.S. Black women have a basis far beyond the temporal and spatial boundaries which define the circumstances of their lives. Indeed, the relationship that
Clifton shares with Merle and, by extrapolation, with all women of African
descent, is rooted in the persistence of her own cultural memory—her stubborn
refusal to abandon those long-established systems of meaning ("my words") by
which she is able to identify herself and others as women who are Black. In fact,
when Clifton writes that "I have kept most of my words / til you came back," she
is essentially bearing witness to the enduring power of remembrance.

In the end, the long-anticipated reunion between poet and friend ("I have
kept most of my words / til you came back") symbolizes the reconnection of
African history-as-memory with those Black women of the present who are its
inheritors. Ironically, the symbolic reunion depicted in "to merle" only becomes
possible when writers like Clifton use representations similar to and including
that which we see in "to merle" to create a historical framework which privileges
developments in the status of Afro-American women. Clifton, like many of her
contemporaries, uses myth to fill in those circumstances and events in the history of the African American female subject that traditional western forms of
documentation have failed to record. Hence the memory which forms the basis
of her reestablished link with Merle (as representative of all Black women) is
imperfect; Clifton reports that she has kept "most," but not all of her words.

That the women in this poem are joined in sisterhood, not by marriage or
blood but by shared language and locus (instead of the single-family suburban
home, which leaves no space for the woman who is not white, the figures in this
poem become visible in the space of the Black female body) suggests the social
and political constructedness of Black womanhood and other identity categories that are usually perceived as essential or causal. The poem concludes:

what i'm trying to say is
i recognize your language and

let me call you sister, sister,
i been waiting for you. (8–11)

Clifton's emphasis, in her closing, upon language ("i recognize your language") and naming ("let me call you sister") locates Black women's power and struggle ("what i'm *trying* to say" [emphasis added]) to relocate the boundaries that circumscribe each of her interlocking identities in the very acts of recognition (identification and greeting) that this poem portrays. These acts of seeing highlight, by contrast, the resistance within prevailing social structures to seeing or even acknowledging the possibility of women subjects who are not white.

In "i was born with twelve fingers," Clifton places images of the Black female body at the center of an allegory that explains aspects of the encounter between African American women and those sociopolitical forces (from the nineteenth-century Cult of Domesticity to Eurocentrism in the mainstream of today's feminist movement) that have sought to limit or exclude them.[21] Like "Sisters: For Elaine Philip on her Birthday," this poem emphasizes the body as a reflection of the discursive link that exists between Afro-American women. But while "Sisters" relies on the imagery of the colloquial body, rendered familiar within the community of Black women by the cultural practices it manifests (the figures in the poem are "touching up [their] edges," "let [their] hair go back," etc.), "i was born with twelve fingers" depicts a Black woman figure whose physical traits initially seem strange and unfamiliar. More specifically, "i was born with twelve fingers" replaces the image of Black sisterhood made manifest through African American women's exercise of common cultural practices, offering instead the surprising image of a family of Black women, each of whom exhibits the physical anomaly of a sixth finger on each hand: "i was born with twelve fingers / like my mother and my daughter" (1–2).

These six-fingered hands exceed our expectations for the "normal" body in the same way that African American women's dual, interlocking identities exceed mainstream expectations for normal (i.e., white) womanhood. Like the six-fingered hands of the women of Clifton's family, the Black woman subject confounds the American cultural imagination; her simultaneous embodiment of both Blackness and womanhood transforms the spaces left open for the signification of each.

Clifton uses an image of the strange black fingers poking into a pool of fresh milk to dramatize how the dual, interlocking identities exemplified by the African American female subject and her "strange" Black body intervene in and disrupt efforts to maintain the idea of woman as a racialized category with which Blackness may neither coexist nor intersect:

each of us
born wearing strange black gloves

LOCATING THE BLACK FEMALE SUBJECT

extra baby fingers hanging over the sides of our cribs and
dipping into the milk (3–6)

The haunting image of Clifton's small, twelve-fingered hands (her "strange black gloves") reaching over the side of the crib disrupts popular and cherished notions of infant beauty and childhood innocence—the pure simplicity of babyhood and life in the nursery—and lays the foundation for renegotiating the boundaries that define motherhood and other identities within womanhood.

Clifton remembers the cosmetic, "normalizing" surgery to remove the sixth fingers as a great loss for all of the women in her family. "[O]ur wonders were cut off" (8) because, she explains, "somebody was afraid we would learn to cast spells" (7). Clifton offers this recollection as a metaphor for how identities and institutions at the center rely on the erasure of difference, or assimilation, as a means to lessen the challenge to hegemony issued by those whose difference positions them as marginal (in "Sisters" a comparable move would be to describe Black women being discouraged from practicing the body rituals that enable them to recognize one another). Such attempts eventually fail, however, because those who wish to separate the women of Clifton's family from their difference grossly underestimate the persistence of historical and cultural memory. The poet explains, "they didn't understand / the powerful memory of ghosts" (9–10). "They," of course, refers to those figures whose social and economic privilege depends upon the suppression of difference, while Clifton's allusion to the "memory of ghosts" conjures up notions of the common West African belief that the spirits of the ancestors dwell among the living. Unseen but ever present, the ancestors live among their descendants, eating, sleeping, and otherwise participating in the daily lives of their communities, where their presence as living manifestations of tribal history is cherished and cultivated.[22] Their advice is often sought on issues of culture, tradition, and genealogy. A somewhat modified version of this belief remains a powerful element in the belief system of many of America's oldest Black enclaves.

In "daughters," another semiautobiographical meditation on the question of ancestry, Clifton depicts the potential of the Black woman subject to transform her discursive surroundings as a secret passed from one generation to the next. Where "i was born with twelve fingers" is allegorical, "daughters" is literal. The text of "daughters" consists of the poet's meditation on an old photograph of her great-grandmother. She is the "woman who shines at the head / of my grandmother's bed, / brilliant woman" (1–3). Though unnamed in the poem, this woman ancestor is based on the poet's great-grandmother, a Dahomey woman who was kidnapped from Africa and sold into slavery in the United States.[23] This in itself would appear to be of great interest to the poet, whose ability to trace her ancestry to a particular place and people on the African continent is a rare and coveted privilege within the African American community. For Clifton, however, the significance of her great-grandmother's position as conduit of cultural and historical memory clearly surpasses the importance of any blood ties that she and her female ancestors may share. Clifton is interested in the secrets of culture, history, and memory that, when passed down among women of African descent, perpetuate in the daughters of the present the values, interests, and practices that defined Black womanhood in the past.

To pass these fragments of ritual and ancestry from one generation of women to the next is to transmit a system of meaning, so that each generation of daughters locates the subject position of Black woman at the same intersection of gender, history, and race that their mothers did before them. Clifton imagines her great-grandmother sharing this secret knowledge with her own daughter, the poet's grandmother: "i like to think / you whispered into her ear / instructions" (3–5). Passed down from great-grandmother to grandmother to mother to daughter (Clifton-as-speaker), these secrets distinguish the women in this family group as unique and magical figures who wear their difference—their power to transform—on their bodies: "i like to think / you are the oddness in us" (5–6). Clifton understands the transmission of this "oddness" in terms that suggest a link with the ancient West African practice of ceremonial scarification: "you are the arrow / that pierced our plain skin / and made us fancy women" (7–9). During scarification, tribal and familial patterns are etched into the skin (identity and history are literally written on the body) in a painful ritual that elides the process of beautification with the application into the flesh of traditional, ancestral markings. Like the recipients of scarification, Clifton and her daughters are marked women who inherit their unique ancestral legacy as both painful burden and transforming pleasure. As in the scarification rituals of sub-Saharan Africa, the metaphorical piercing of flesh that turns Clifton and her kin from plain women into fancy Black daughters processes transformations in the abstract realm of status and meaning through the embodied realm of blood and flesh. Touched by the legacy of their ancestor's difference, Clifton, her grandmother, mother, and daughters become "my wild witch gran, my magic mama, / and even these gaudy girls" (10–11).

As the poem draws to a close, the poet leaves us with the image of her great-grandmother as a living ancestral presence who wishes no more elaborate honor than simply to be remembered:

> it is enough,
> you must have murmured,
> to remember that i was
> and that you are (16–19)

Thus Clifton offers this benediction as her promise to perpetuate the memory of the women who preceded her:

> woman, i am
> lucille, which stands for light,
> daughter of thelma, daughter
> of georgia, daughter of
> dazzling you (19–23)

Like the metaphorical piercing of the skin that unites poet with her kin, and all to the enduring legacy of their ancestors, Clifton writes her literal, real-life experiences of surgical scarification—first through hysterectomy (addressed in *Quilting* [1991]) and later through lumpectomy (described in *The Terrible Stories* [1996])—as sacred rituals, establishing her link to the wisdom and power of her foremothers. The markings that remain at each point of excision signify not diminishment but rather the painful yet ultimately life-affirming recontextualization of the female body within the larger cycle of strength, survival, restoration, and change. Only in the breast cancer poems of *The Terrible Stories*, however, do these experiences function as a vehicle for engaging the specific question of Black female subjectivity.

The widely praised hysterectomy poems of *Quilting* ("poem in praise of menstruation," "poem to my uterus," and "to my last period") depict the poet's journey through hysterectomy, the end of menstruation, and the passage of her fertility as a gendered experience, linking her memories of thirty-eight years of menstrual periods with those of all women transitioning out of their reproductive years.[24] Scrupulously avoiding language that would mark her meditation on this life passage as a consideration of the specific impact of hysterectomy on African American women, Clifton instead draws on race-neutral icons and archetypal roles. Thus in "poem in praise of menstruation" menstruation is described as "this / daughter of eve / mother of cain and abel" (14–16), and in "to my last period" the speaker-poet feels like

> the grandmothers who
> after the hussy has gone
> sit holding her photograph
> and sighing *wasn't she*
> *beautiful? wasn't she beautiful?* (10–14)

Clifton's reliance on these deracinated and archetypal figures (Eve) and roles (grandmothers and "the hussy") frames her assertions and observations as applicable to all women, most dramatically illustrated in "poem in praise of menstruation." Building on its ecumenical and transethnic association of women's monthly reproductive cycle with the figure of Eve, Clifton concludes this poem with praise for menstruation as a unifying force, marking each woman who has experienced its persistent retreats and returns, and uniting them, "beautiful and faithful and ancient / and female and brave" (23–24).

In *Quilting* Lucille Clifton uses her own experience of hysterectomy as a starting point from which to explore the significance of reproductivity and its passage in all women's lives. Her poems on this topic deemphasize the specificity of Clifton's own diagnosis and treatment and, instead, serve as a basis for her inquiry into the broader meaning of menstruation, fertility, aging, and transition.[25] Clifton's exploration of the similarly gendered experience of diagnosis and treatment for breast cancer, in *The Terrible Stories,* replaces the unifying poetics of cyclical renewal and the inevitability of passage with a race-specific poetics of battle and survival. The poems "amazons" and "1994" engage Clifton's journey through excision and recovery not as a trans-ethnic odyssey, linking the poet's experience with that of all female breast cancer survivors, but rather as a vehicle for exploring the specific question of Black female subjectivity. Instead of using her experiences to emphasize those dimensions of women's cancer treatment that link female survivors across racial groups, the poet-speaker offers her diagnosis and treatment as a pathway to an understanding of Black women's survival that challenges not only the traditional meanings assigned to the Black female body but also conventional notions of illness, wholeness, and health.

In "1994" the poet-speaker presents her breast cancer diagnosis as a confirmation of the perils of existence at the intersection of Blackness and womanhood. She writes,

> you know how dangerous it is
>
> to be born with breasts
> you know how dangerous it is
> to wear dark skin (9–12)

In "amazons" the poet positions these legendary women warriors as both her predecessors and her kin in the adoption of excision of the breast as a mark of strength and heritage. Their unwavering support at all points of her journey through diagnosis and excision is Clifton's inheritance as an African American woman and, more specifically, as a "daughter of dahomey," a direct descendant of the Fon of West Africa, among whom amazons served as an elite military unit for two centuries.[26] Their sudden presence at her side points to the poet's embrace of those African and Afro-diasporic belief systems whose understanding of the absolute importance of communication between descendants and their ancestors defies conventional notions of space, time, and mortality. Clifton's recollection of her initial encounter with the amazons confounds Western notions of time and possibility:

> . . . they each
> with one nipple lifted
> beckoned to me
> five generations removed (11–14)

Her memory of the amazons' approach, "each / with one nipple lifted," is an allusion to the legendary belief that these warriors practiced voluntary mastectomy, with each woman either cutting or burning off one of her breasts in order to aim her bow with more precision and efficiency.[27]

Clifton portrays the moment of her diagnosis as an intrusion of present-day notions of science and reason (in which generations are not crossed and the loss of one breast does not leave the mark of a warrior) into the time-transcendent realm of her one-breasted ancestors:

> i rose
> and ran to the telephone
> to hear
>
> cancer   early detection   no
> mastectomy   not yet (15–19)

This recollection juxtaposes the grim scientific notions of wholeness and the body advocated in the allopathic discourse of her doctors (note the stark, spare language with which she recounts her diagnosis) against those meanings recognized and understood in the spirit world of her warrior sisters.

The final image of the poem, in which Clifton steps away from the phone and returns to the shelter of her Amazon forebears, collapses the distance of the Middle Passage and the centuries separating the poet from her African foremothers in a moment's gesture. The boundaries between the imagined and the lived, celebration and mourning, and life and death are blurred in a ritual whose ambiguities (is the living truly dancing among the dead?) bespeak a breadth of possibilities as rich and full of promise as the doctor's analysis is guarded and detached:

> there was nothing to say
> my sisters swooped in a circle dance
> audre was with them and I
> had already written this poem (20–23)

In the end, the true nature of Clifton's encounter—a dream or a vision or a physical meeting—is unimportant. The significance is in the gathering of Black women, their capacity to reach out across space and time to give to and draw strength from each other and—in their common experience of the failure of conventional notions of the real, the scientific, the possible, the valuable, and the necessary to account for their existence—their shared capacity to transcend the conventional boundaries of distance and death. In the third stanza of "amazons" Clifton recalls,

> when they came to ask
> who knows what you might have
> to *sacrifice* poet amazon
> there is no choice (7–10, emphasis added)

Given the limits imposed on African American female subjectivity within a social order that marginalizes even "healthy" Black female bodies, it is only in the company of women of African descent that Clifton is able to abandon the conventional reading of scarring and mastectomy as tragic diminishment and create new meanings. Reconceptualized as "sacrifice" rather than subtraction, and embraced as a signifier of belonging and connection, Clifton's new understanding of lumpectomy and mastectomy reinscribes the marked body of the breast cancer survivor as strengthened and whole.

In the closing line of this poem, Clifton-as-poet-speaker recounts her discovery, after the close of the amazons' dance, that she "had already written this poem." In locating Audre Lorde among the amazons who lend their support to the newly diagnosed Clifton ("my sisters swooped in a circle dance / audre was with them . . . "), this poem suggests an alternative meaning for the term. Having received her diagnosis in the clinical terms of late-twentieth-century medicine, the amazons—ancient Dahomean ancestors and more recent comrades like Audre Lorde—use their "circle dance" to lift the poet-speaker beyond the limited understanding of the loss of a breast as a marker of deterioration and weakness and into a new set of meanings that define her as (Black woman) warrior, sister, and daughter. Just as their ritual dance reinvents Clifton-as-speaker, so too does her poem reinvent the amazon sisterhood, if not for the poet herself, then for those for whom her words of witness will serve as a conduit to a new meaning for the scarred body of the Black woman cancer survivor.

In "my dream of being white" Clifton shifts her focus from relationships between Black women and onto the complex interaction between the African American female subject and the idea of white womanhood. In describing the bond between the Black woman speaker and other women of African descent, Clifton highlights the shared features and practices by which the African American speaker is able to recognize her and others' Black female subjecthood. In this poem, however, the speaker encounters in the white female body a collection of traits that define her own Blackness by opposition. "My dream of being white" describes white womanhood from the rarely articulated perspective of the Black female gaze:

> me
> only white,
> hair a flutter of
> fall leaves
> circling my perfect
> line of a nose,
> no lips,
> no behind,
> hey white me (2–10)

The word "white," repeated at the beginning and the end of this description of the Euro-American female body, frames the speaker's account of her experience in that body as one characterized by absence or lack ("a flutter of / fall leaves," instead of hair; "a perfect / line" in place of a nose; "no lips, / no behind"). This characterization contrasts sharply with her waking experience of Blackness, whose physical characteristics are perceived within both African American and non-Black ethnic groups alike as embodying fullness, and it is reinforced by her portrayal of the relationship of whiteness to time. Clifton's speaker feels the burden of Euro-American history ("I'm wearing / white history," she explains [11–12]) but sees no promise in that legacy and concludes that "there's no future / in those clothes" (13–14). The closing image of the poem, in which the speaker shrugs off the mantle of whiteness to "wake up/ dancing," juxtaposes her tentative wonder at what she perceives as the limited potential of whiteness with her unfettered joy in the infinite possibility of Blackness (16–17).

Lucille Clifton's short praise poems "homage to my hair" and "homage to my hips" turn away from an emphasis on relationships between women (African American women to each other in "daughters," "Sisters," "i was born with twelve fingers, "to merle," and "amazons"; and African American women to white women in "my dream of being white") to focus on the interaction between the Black woman subject and the African American man. The poems discussed thus far in this study use the relationship between Black women joined in camaraderie and kinship to explore the substance of Clifton's mythic womanhood. These brief "homage" poems use the cross-gender relationship between African American women and men to revise and explore the meanings assigned to the Black female body. In particular, the poems "homage to my hair" and "homage to my hips" celebrate the capacity of the African American woman subject to transform and disrupt those figures whose visibility depends on the confinement or erasure of Black female subjectivity simply by reinscribing either or both of her constituent identities (Blackness and womanhood) with new meaning.

In "homage to my hair," Clifton focuses on changing the meaning of Blackness by transforming the language and images linked with "nappy," tightly curled hair, a characteristic whose association with Black bodies has been used both to single out and ostracize African American women and men. For Clifton's speaker, nappy hair is neither primitive nor comical, alien nor exotic. She writes into visibility a head of bushy, Black hair whose movement and texture simply overwhelm the narrow spaces in which such derogatory characterizations are conceived. It is unruly and excessive; it "jump[s] and dance[s] / . . . my God" (1–2) with powers that derive from its propensity to overrun neatly drawn boundaries and challenge expectations. The Black male figure in the poem becomes the friendly opposition on whom Clifton's speaker illustrates the reconstructive power of this feature that they share:

> i'm talking about my nappy hair!
> she is a challenge to your hand
> Black man,
> she is as tasty on your tongue as good greens
> Black man,
> she can touch your mind
> with her electric fingers (3–9)

In "homage to my hips," Clifton continues her pursuit of a new and emancipatory vision of the Black female body, shifting her focus downward to its notorious midsection. Like "homage to my hair," the woman speaker of "homage to my hips" uses the suggestion of a male addressee as the background against which to convey her new vision of a frequently stereotyped Black feature. Clifton reinterprets the outrageousness and excess associated with the African American female body as a source of power and a point of pride. Epitomized in the notorious swing of her "big," "free hips," Black woman's failure to conform to conventional notions of womanliness and femininity is recast as deliberate resistance. Far from hiding her difference, Clifton celebrates her excess, openly proclaiming that her broad hips overwhelm the "little / petty places" created to contain her:

> these hips are big hips
> they need space to
> move around in.
> they don't fit into little
> petty places. these hips
> are free hips.
> they don't like to be held back.

these hips have never been enslaved,
they go where they want to go
they do what they want to do. (1–10)

Like her nappy hair, Clifton's audacious hips have been known to unsettle the men who engage with their powers:

these hips are mighty hips.
these hips are magic hips.
i have known them
to put a spell on a man and
spin him like a top! (11–15)

In leaving her readers with this playful image of a man, stunned and reeling at the sheer majesty of her Black body, the poet reintroduces the same attitude of friendly opposition that we first encountered in "homage to my hair." Clifton invites the unnamed men to whom her poem is addressed to reexamine the symbolic position of the Black woman's corpus, not as oppressors, but as allies. Indeed, Clifton's emphasis upon recasting the Black female corpus—once a symbol of the physical and sexual oppression of all Black bodies—as an emblem of freedom suggests that her attempt to rewrite the positionality and meaning of the African American female body may prove equally liberating for Black men and Black women. Certainly, Clifton's boast that "these hips have never been enslaved" ("they go where they want to go / they do what they want to do") positions Black woman's body as a symbolic link for all Black people to the distant precolonial past.

Like the two previously discussed poems, "song at midnight" uses the relationship between African American women and men as a context for generating new meanings for the Black female body. Addressed to her "brothers" in the U.S. Black community, and adopting a persuasive, beseeching tone that is absent from the "homage" poems, "song at midnight" bears a superficial resemblance to the lover-object poems of the Black Arts period, as it calls on African American men to recognize the beauty of Black women. This resemblance is reinforced in the epigraph to this piece, a brief passage from Sonia Sanchez's autobiographical "Poem at Thirty," written and published in 1966, at the height of the Black Arts Movement. The passage reads, "do not send me out among strangers," and represents the culmination of Sanchez's plea for that specific brand of consolation and sanctuary which the poet-speaker can find only in the company of African American men. In "Poem at Thirty," speaker Sanchez is empowered and emboldened through the symbolic act of joining hands with her Black brothers, and she finishes the poem with the image of forward movement, the unnamed Black male figure in the poem "stretching scraping / the mold from [his] body," reawakening to his strength after a long period of inaction, and the poet-speaker herself stepping boldly out into the night, stirred by the courage she draws from his renewed authority and power:

> you you black man
> stretching scraping
> the mold from your body.
> here is my hand.
> i am not afraid
> of the night. (27–32)

Clifton creates "song at midnight" in dialogue with Sanchez's "Poem at Thirty," whose portrayal of the Black woman revolutionary poet drawing courage from the companionship of an African American man is itself a variation on the Black Arts lover-object poems. Like many such poems, "song at midnight" draws a link between the Black woman speaker's growing self-confidence and the loving approval of a Black male companion. For Clifton's speaker, however, the approving male gaze and the loving male embrace neither confer meaning on nor establish the subjecthood of African American women. Instead, the woman speaker herself establishes the terms on which she emerges as a Black female subject, applying her own gaze as she describes the characteristics of her body and interprets the meaning that reveals itself in its textures and curves:

> brothers,
> this big woman
> carries much sweetness
> in the folds of her flesh.
> her hair
> is white with wonderful.
> she is rounder than the moon
> and far more faithful. (1–8)

This enumeration by the speaker of her own attributes frames the subsequent inquiry less as a plea than as an invitation. Her closing query, "who will hold her, / who will find her beautiful / if you do not" (10–12), in posing the question of Black woman's beauty, functions less as an appeal than a proposal to her male addressees that they join her in taking pleasure and power from the abundant "sweetness" and enduring grace of the African American female body.

Clifton's "song at midnight" approaches African American men as allies coexisting within Blackness and offers them privileged entry into a form of gratification—the appreciation of Black female beauty—which "brothers" are uniquely positioned to enjoy. Implicit in this equation is the notion that, rather than validating Black women with their male gaze and their embrace, it is African American men who are exalted and affirmed by the speaker's invitation to share her pleasure in the wonders of her own Black body. To welcome the Black male gaze is to extend to African American men access to a form of beauty from which Euro-American males have, by virtue of their investment in mainstream epistemologies that define womanhood and female beauty as white, largely remained disconnected. In offering not only the pleasure of her embrace but an interpretation of her body that facilitates Black males' appreciation of its exquisite beauty and mythic power, the African American woman speaker is offering her "brothers" a form of privilege—knowledge of and access to the Black female body—from which white males are barred. Having established the terms on which she will become visible and be loved, the African American woman speaker underscores the greatest distinction between her positionality as subject and the object status of that figure with which she is in dialogue (the poet-speaker-as-lover-object in Sanchez's "Poem at Thirty"). While Sanchez's speaker looks to the recognition and companionship of Black men to invest her with the qualities that create her as powerful and transgressive, Clifton's speaker sets the conditions of her own emergence and empowerment.

In *The Book of Light*, "song at midnight" is immediately followed by Clifton's "won't you celebrate with me," whose similar theme and similar tone of invitation position it as an extension of the preceding work. That the second poem is untitled (and referred to in this context by its first line) bolsters this interpretation. Read as a companion piece to the preceding poem, "won't you celebrate with me" emerges as an elaboration on the process by which the Black woman subject, whose salient features are described in "song at midnight," invented herself.

The call to Black men at the close of "song at midnight" to "hold" the African American woman and to "find her beautiful" is followed immediately in the opening lines of "won't you celebrate with me" by the Black woman speaker's broader invitation to all of her readers to "celebrate with me / what I have shaped into / a kind of life" (1–3). Clifton's speaker declares, "i had no model" (3), and points to her existence at the intersection of the perceived oppositional identities of African American and woman as both the root of her singularity and the explanation for the absence of existing frameworks that might account for her existence. She asks, rhetorically, "born . . . / both nonwhite and woman / what did I see to be except myself" (4–6)?

Clifton's speaker describes African American womanhood in terms that reflect its embodiment within a form that marks its perpetual existence in a body that unites two identity categories still perceived as contradictory. She explains, "i made it up / here on this bridge between / starshine and clay" (7–9). This intradependence—of Black womanhood upon Black women for its origination—is reflected in the image of the African American woman speaker's "one hand holding tight / [to her] other hand" (10–11), an image whose depiction of the African American woman drawing herself out of herself is—given Clifton's interest in midrash poetry and the prior suggestion of Black woman's emergence out of "starshine and clay"—certainly a comment on the traditional Judeo-Christian account of God creating woman by drawing her out of the body of a man.[28]

The speaker's restatement, at the end of the poem, of her call for all readers to celebrate the courageous self-invention of the Black female subject echoes the theme of invitation in "song at midnight," but with an added reference to the implications of the African American woman's existence at the intersection of perceived opposites (for her survival in a larger socio-cultural landscape that continues to resist such possibilities):

> . . . come celebrate
> with me that everyday
> something has tried to kill me
> and has failed. (11–14)

In "homage to my hair," "homage to my hips," and "song at midnight" / "won't you celebrate with me" Lucille Clifton applies the imagery and language of myth to highlight the extraordinary transformations that occur when ordinary Black women write to demand visibility. In the Kali poems, a trilogy of short verses published in *An Ordinary Woman*, Clifton accentuates the ordinary (those features that Kali shares with mortal Black women) in the extraordinary figure of Kali, the black-skinned Hindu goddess of creation and destruction. The overall effect of this pairing is to link the discursive mechanisms by which the Black woman subject disrupts and transforms to the supernatural methods that Kali employs in her infamous acts of destruction. In "Kali," the first of Clifton's three poems in honor of the warrior goddess, the poet identifies this ancient figure by the attributes that she shares with the present-day African American women she has been called upon to represent:

> terrible Hindu Woman God
> Kali
> who is Black. (1–3)

As a Black woman, Kali's power to effect change in the lives of others ("she determines the destiny of things" [5]) is derived from her embodiment of two identity categories, each of which experiences the other as marginal within its bounds (Blackness is marginalized within womanhood, womanhood is marginalized within Blackness). Clifton's portrayal of Kali as "the permanent guest / within ourselves" (7–8) and as "the mystery / ever present in us and outside us" (11–12) recalls Mae Gwendolyn Henderson's explication of African American women's experience of interlocking identities: "[t]he complex situatedness of the black woman as not only the 'Other' of the Same, but also as the 'other' of the other(s)" (Henderson 118). Henderson goes on to explain in further detail:

> What I propose is a theory of interpretation based on what I refer to as the "simultaneity of discourse". . . . Such an approach is intended to acknowledge and overcome the limitations imposed by assumptions of internal identity (homogeneity) and the repression of internal difference (heterogeneity) in racial and gendered readings of works by black women writers. (Henderson 117)

"The Coming of Kali," the second poem in the trilogy, begins with an allusion to the two interlocking identities that Kali represents: "it is the *Black God*, Kali, / *a woman God* and terrible" (1–2, emphasis added). Clifton underscores the theme of duality with a striking description of emblems of life and death juxtaposed: "Kali . . . / . . . / with her skulls and breasts" (1–3). Kali's two-ness exposes the dualities in others, just as Black woman's duality—her construction out of the fusion of two opposing identity groups—exposes the constructed nature of all identity categories: "i am one side of your skin, / she sings" (4–5).

Kali's position at the margins of both Blackness and womanhood imbues her with a rare perspective on the sociopolitical relationships and hierarchies that structure her surroundings. In the final lines of this poem, the speaker concedes that Kali "knows places in my bones / i never sing about" (11–12). This admission, from the very figure through whose words Kali becomes visible, sets up a relationship that functions as a metaphor for the interaction that Clifton perceives between Black woman and her sociopolitical environs. Kali's subordinate position relative to the speaker, whose vision determines the parameters within which she may come into view, grants her access to knowledge that is apparently either withheld from or unfamiliar to the speaker (this is knowledge that the speaker "never sing[s] about"). And like Kali, the African American woman subject occupies a marginal position within both Blackness and womanhood that affords her a more detailed insight into the sociopolitical relationships and hierarchies that structure and regulate her visibility than individuals and identity groups at the center are required to develop.

"Calming Kali," the third and final poem in Clifton's Kali series, shifts focus from the two identities which coexist within Black womanhood, outward, to the relationship of Black women to one another, as figures who become visible from within the common space of the Black female body:

> be quiet awful woman,
> lonely as hell,
> and i will comfort you
> when i can

and give you my bones
and my blood to feed on (1–6)

That the "awful woman" Kali is calmed, comforted, and nourished by the body of another suggests that the Black woman subject experiences the Black female body in much the same way that the husband and children experience the pastoral homescape of the mid-nineteenth century. Unlike the pastoral of the American homescape, however, in which the Euro-American woman's location within the remote, single-family dwelling indicates that others who achieve visibility primarily in spaces outside of the home will experience that space as sanctuary, Black woman's position within and signification from the space of the Black female body is linked with her own comfort and affirmation; the body is her sanctuary and her refuge.

As the poem draws to a close, Clifton's speaker offers these conciliatory words, recognizing, at last, her kinship with the ancient black-skinned goddess:

gently gently now
awful woman,
i know i am your sister (7–9)

To acknowledge her kinship with the terrible woman god is, in effect, to recognize the terrible—the vast power to disrupt and transform—within herself.

Best known for her autobiographical writings and essays, Audre Lorde also produced a considerable body of poetry that, likewise, focuses on themes and experiences drawn from the life of the poet. Both her poetry and her prose explore and celebrate the challenge to Euro-dominance leveled by the artist's representation of the multiply identified subject (the figure who locates herself within two or more identity categories simultaneously). Lorde herself demanded recognition for all of her identities, making a practice in her public presentations and interviews of listing several of the subject positions that she occupied.[29] The poems in Lorde's 1978 collection, *The Black Unicorn,* feature African American female subjects whose Blackness, like that of the mythic creature named in the title, simultaneously opposes and coexists alongside their other identities.

In the essay "Poetry Is Not a Luxury," Audre Lorde offers that "The quality of light by which we scrutinize our lives has direct bearing upon the product which we live, and upon the changes which we hope to bring about through those lives" (Lorde, "Poetry" 37). In late-twentieth century representations of the Black female body, African American women poets do, in effect, transform the "quality of light" by which Black womanhood becomes visible. In the context of Lorde's work, "quality of light" refers to ways of seeing and knowing a place or a people and how those ways of seeing and knowing inform and direct one's vision and sense of possibility (governing, for example, what degree of accommodation and transformation one might demand from her environment). If, for example, one embraces an epistemology that only allows for the understanding of time as a linear progression, moving in a single direction, from past through present and into the future, then a reality in which ancestors and descendants coexist and interact is incomprehensible. Nor will someone who accepts this way of knowing confront and challenge those discourses—science, history, reason—that understand a clear and impermeable divide between past and present.

In a 1990 interview with Charles Rowell, Lorde elaborates on her decision, described in the introduction to *Chosen Poems*, not to include any poems from *The Black Unicorn* in her only volume of selected works.[30] She explains, "The poems in *The Black Unicorn* have always felt to me like a conversation between myself and an ancestor Audre. The sequence began in Dahomey when I visited that country with my children in 1974, and continued for the next three years, resulting in *The Black Unicorn*" (Rowell 58). Thus *The Black Unicorn* is a transitional text, whose depictions of the poet's interaction with the deities and ancestors that define her Afro-diasporic past represent the culmination of her journey beyond those epistemologies that resist Black woman's simultaneous occupation of multiple—and, at times, oppositional—subject positions. The excessive, outrageous Black female bodies that appear in this volume, and that defy conventional Western conceptions not only of Blackness and womanhood but of time and space and nation, emerge in the wake of Lorde's experiences in Dahomey, the impact of which deeply transformed the "quality of light" that she was able to bring to her scrutiny of African American womanhood and the Black female body.

The Black Unicorn represents Lorde's embrace of sources of wisdom and power—communion with her ancestors (a central element in Dahomean religious practice), prayers to the gods and goddesses of the Yoruba—that exist beyond the boundaries that define traditional Western conceptions of the knowable and the "real."[31] In this volume, the Black female body serves as a conduit into these sources of vision and understanding; such forms of knowledge, which resist the orthodoxy of contemporary Western scientific and philosophical discourse, are most accessible (and most useful) to women, whose empowerment and enlightenment oppose and resist the accepted social hierarchy of male over female. African American women, whose education and enlightenment resist established hierarchies of both race and gender, are uniquely poised to take advantage of these sources of wisdom. Eventually Lorde would name these ways of knowing—which only become comprehensible through the occupation of the female body and which serve as a source of women's (em)power(ment)— "the erotic."[32] Embodied in sexuality but *not* primarily sexual, the erotic is "a resource within each of us [women] that lies in a deeply female and spiritual plane, firmly rooted in the power of our unexpressed or unrecognized feeling" (Lorde, "Uses" 53). We can read "unexpressed or unrecognizable" as *inexpressible or unrecognizable within the constraints of traditional systems of meaning*. Lorde explains that "our erotic knowledge empowers us, becomes a lens through which we scrutinize all aspects of our existence" (Lorde, "Uses" 57).

Dahomey functioned in the life and work of the poet as a catalyst, inspiring her reconceptualization of the Black female body as both symbol of and vehicle for Black women's challenge to and transcendence of those North American and western European systems of meaning that resist her dual subjectivity. The poems of *The Black Unicorn* mark Lorde's reappraisal of the meaning and function of the Black female body, based on her encounter with Dahomean and Yoruban belief systems and cultural practices, and each is embedded in ways of seeing and knowing that predate the enslavement of her ancestors. Describing Lorde's 1980 essay collection *The Cancer Journals*, Jeanne Perrault asserts that Lorde engages in "a writing of self that makes the female body a site and source of written subjectivity, yet inhabits that body with the ethics of a deeply and precisely historical, political, sexual, and racial consciousness" (Perrault 1). As such, the prose of *The Cancer Journals* builds on the role and placement of the Black female body (as vessel of power, knowledge, and connection) that originated in the poems of *The Black Unicorn*. The mythic bodies that emerge in this text reflect the poet's readjustment of her gaze upon the Black female subject, having viewed that figure "in a new light" based upon her encounter with Dahomean deities and beliefs systems and the Afro-diasporic history embedded in those ways of seeing and knowing, and they mark Lorde's unequivocal embrace of simultaneity as the paradigm for engaging and depicting Black female identity, not only as Black and woman, but as present and past, ancestor and daughter, earthly and divine.

In the poems of *The Black Unicorn*, Black woman's dual subjectivity is manifest in many forms, appearing as any of a number of oppositional pairings. In "From the House of Yemanja" the transgressive duality of Black womanhood is evident in the burdened body of the Black woman speaker who must carry two "mothers," one Black and one white, on her back:[33]

> I bear two women upon my back
> one dark and rich and hidden
> in the ivory hungers of the other
> mother
> pale as a witch (11–15)

Like her own, her mother's two-ness is evident in the features of her body: "My mother had two faces" (5).

Later, Lorde's speaker uses the images of sun and moon to indicate her two-ness as that aspect of their shared identity as Black women for which she most desperately wants her mother's acknowledgment: "I am the sun and moon and forever hungry / for her eyes" (9–10).[34] She privileges this discursive link that she and her mother share as Black women over their biological link as parent and child.

In the final stanza Lorde's speaker uses the relationship between sun and moon to suggest the limitations of the interaction between unlike elements—like the opposing identities that meet within the Black female subject—that are forced to coexist:

> I am
> the sun and moon and forever hungry
> the sharpened edge
> where day and night shall meet
> and not be
> one (31–36)

Like "sun and moon" and "day and night," pairs whose distinct elements "shall meet / and not be / one," Blackness and womanhood remain distinct despite their coexistence within the African American woman subject.

In "A Woman Speaks" Audre Lorde uses the themes of magic and timeless nature (elements within nature that are older than humanity, and that are diminished and renewed in a regular, cyclical pattern) to explain the Black woman's subject's capacity to transform. The opening images of the poem reemphasize the duality of Black womanhood and then go on to suggest that nature and woman are part of one another, that woman's body is inscribed on nature:

> Moon marked and touched by sun
> my magic is unwritten
> but when the sea turns back
> it will leave my shape behind. (1–4)

To examine or study the movement of nature, its cycles, and its periods of renewal is to understand Black women's subjectivity:

> and if you would know me
> look into the entrails of Uranus
> where the restless oceans pound. (13–15)

Black womanhood endures, after all, in the same way that the seas and the planets endure, rebuilding and renewing regularly and/or in response to periods of invisibility or diminishment. Lorde's speaker confirms the long-term survival of Black womanhood as an identity category: "I have been woman / for a long time" (25–26).

Blackness and womanhood combine in the African American female body to create a subjectivity that is marked by its enduring capacity to effect change. The warning by the Black woman speaker to "beware" and her confession that she is "treacherous" are offered ironically, in acknowledgment and contempt of the fear and apprehension which often greet the transformations and disruptions she precipitates:

> beware my smile
> I am treacherous with old magic
> and the moon's new fury
> with all your wide futures
> promised
> I am
> woman
> and not white (27–34)

While African American woman's endurance—expressed here as her ability to transcend the bounds separating past and present from future—links her with women across time, her capacity to transform, equated here with sorcery and magic, links her with Black women separated by distance and culture:[35]

> my sisters
> witches in Dahomey
> wear me inside their coiled cloths (20–22)

"From the House of Yemanja" and "A Woman Speaks" address the capacity of the African American woman subject to disrupt and rearrange the systems of meaning that would seek to limit the terms of her visibility. The poems "Seasoning" and "Scar" focus upon Black women's use of emancipatory speech as a tool with which to reconstruct themselves. Similar to Shange's humorous "Oh, I'm 10 Months Pregnant," Lorde's "Seasoning" uses the theme of the writer's craft to express the relationship between articulation, visibility, and being. The events of the poem take place during "this advancing summer" (1), as "solstice is passing" (9), so that the condition of the earth in the late stages of its annual renewal is linked with the struggle of the speaker to articulate her being. As she speaks herself into subjectivity,

> [her] mouth stumbles
> crammed with cribsheets and flowers
> dimestore photographs
> of loving in stages
> choked by flinty nuggets of old friends
> undigested enemies (10–15)

For the speaker, to articulate—to testify to—the friendships, liaisons, and animosities that circumscribe and define her experience is to deliver herself into visibility as subject at the center of her own social, political, and cultural surroundings.

In "Scar" Lorde explains the relationship between recognition, visibility, and being as she describes African American women's experience of the constructive power of the Black female gaze. Like Clifton's "i was born with twelve fingers" and "Sisters: For Elaine Philip on Her Birthday," "Scar" emphasizes the ways that Black women locate one another. However, "Scar" moves beyond the celebration so prominent in Clifton's poems to suggest a more significant role for these forms of intragroup recognition. The most prominent phase in the Black female subject's emergence into visibility is her pursuit of context and meaning among or in opposition to the institutions and identity groups which constitute the U.S. mainstream. However, the female subject must seek placement within the identity group of African American women before she can pursue visibility as such. What initially designates the subject as Black woman? How does the subject know that she is Black?

In "Scar" Lorde proposes that the subject is marked as Black woman when other Black women recognize her as such. Their acknowledgment is, in turn, based on their recognition that she displays the traits and participates in the rituals that defined their own emergence as African American women. The "mothers sisters daughters girls" to whom Lorde dedicates this "simple poem"—"the women who clean the Staten Island ferry," "the sleek witches," and others—identify or designate the speaker as Black woman simply by recognizing (looking at or seeing) her (1–3). She describes her experience of their identifying gaze; she feels them "whittling me with your . . . eyes / laughing me out of your skin" (12–13). A crucial moment in Black woman's struggle toward subjectivity takes place when other African American women acknowledge that she shares with them a common site of origin. She emerges into visibility and meaning from out of the same "skin" (the Black female body) that they do.

The emphasis in this poem is upon the ways and conditions under which women subjects invent each other. Lorde provides this scene of women dancing together by moonlight as an allegory for the transmission of the traits of Black womanhood, not from elder to daughter, but among women of the same generation. We see

> only a tideless ocean of moonlit women
> in all shades of loving
> learning the dance of open and closing
> learning a dance of electrical tenderness
> no father no mother would teach them. (45–49)

Here, as in many other poems by late-twentieth-century African American women writers, the poet offers a metaphor for how the sisterhood that links Black women based on their shared subjectivity develops entirely outside of the bonds of kinship. For African American women, bonds based on a shared relationship to the identities and institutions of the mainstream play a more significant role in their resistance to invisibility than do familial ties to biological kin.

At the end of the poem Lorde describes her vision of the kind of powerful, enduring, and transforming African American woman who is granted subjectivity by the acknowledgment and recognition of her sisters. In this final passage Lorde imagines a Black goddess in the style of Clifton's Kali and Shange's god "whose wounds are not the end of anything," whose joyful abandon positions her in wicked and willful excess of the narrow space designated for the signification of woman. Both goddess and poem originate in her mind, in the realm of her imagination. When Lorde speaks them simultaneously, speaking the poem to articulate the goddess into being, they enter the realm of discourse, in which poem and Black woman goddess use each other to challenge the systems of meaning that seek to limit their very existence (that resist the possibility of Black goddesses *and* Black poets):

> This is a simple poem
> sharing my head with dreams
> of a big black woman with jewels in her eyes
> she dances
> her head in a gold helmet
> arrogant
> plumed
> her name is Colossa
> her thighs are like stanchions
> or flayed hickory trees
> embraced in armour
> she dances
> slow earth-shaking motions
> that suddenly alter and lighten
> as she whirls laughing
> the tooled metal over her hips
> comes to an end
> and at the shining edge
> an astonishment
> of soft, black curly hair (68–87)

Lorde's enormous dancing goddess embodies the playful spirit of indulgence that links African American women poets' representations of the Black female body. When Lucille Clifton, Audre Lorde, and Ntozake Shange collapse the distinctions between history and myth, sorcery and science, conjuring and creativity, they assert—mischievously, unabashedly, self-indulgently, and with pleasure—the newly reclaimed power to define the limits of their own subjectivity. Black women's joy in their newly recovered authority to dictate the terms of their own visibility is evident in their writings, which bend and taunt the conventions of the mainstream, not wholly eliminating or exploding traditional identity categories, but alleviating them, so that other possibilities may come into view.[36] It is this pleasure in resistance and reconstruction that is intimated in Betsy Erkkila's phrase "wicked excess," a term which implies willful mischief. The interaction between each Black woman poet's self-awareness as creator and her playful unrestraint appears in her poetry as deliberate, pleasurable, and often wicked self-indulgence in the act of remaking. Excessive display is one of the means by which late-twentieth-century Black women poets writing against the hegemony of the mainstream highlight the role of process—of creating—in those institutions and identity categories most commonly understood as absolute.

I have come to describe such literary acts of resistance and re-creation as *myth-play*, a term that connotes the joy and euphoria which accompany African American women poets' recuperation and exercise of the power of making identity. In this context, "myth" establishes identity as fabrication-in-progress; rather than a fixed position, identity is a process. I use "myth" instead of "fiction" or "tale" to acknowledge that, although identity categories are not material, essential, or otherwise empirical, they explain material conditions and power relationships that are quite concrete. Like story myths (Kipling's "How the Camel Got His Hump," the biblical creation myths, and others) the identity categories to which "myth" refers comprise a discourse created and engaged in order to explain some "real" aspect of the world in which the mythmakers live. Similarly, in this context the word "play" refers to the exercise of reclaimed power in the process of identity construction. The term "play" is particularly relevant to the poets' exercise of power reclaimed because it connotes indulgence. Play implies the self-conscious exercise of agency, not merely in responsible service to the emancipation of the group (though that certainly is a significant part of Black women poets' re-presentation of the Black female body as landscape), but in celebration of visibility, empowerment, and the return to voice. Thus "myth-play" expresses the Black woman poet's engagement in the construction of her identity category, not only in accordance with the needs of African American women as they write to disrupt social-political relationships that deny them subjectivity, but in response to their desires and pleasures as well.

In the early twentieth century, African American poet James Weldon Johnson urged young Black writers to take on the "serious work" of "wearing away the stereotyped ideas about the Negro" (qtd. in Birch 34). Today, Black women poets encourage each other in the "serious work" of play—playing with gender, race, and other frameworks traditionally used to impose limits upon signification and subjecthood. African American women poets create a new vision of the African American female subject to replace the old and constraining notions that have limited womanhood on the basis of race and class. In so doing, Black women poets like Ntozake Shange, Lucille Clifton, and Audre Lorde destroy old myths that refuse to acknowledge their existence and create new myths that, in rejecting discursive formulations that resist Black women's subjectivity, write the Black female subject into view.

Play is, above all else, the recuperation of the prerogative and power to create and re-create meaning; it is rooted in the writer's reassertion of ownership, so that play becomes a way of reclaiming. In the last quarter of the twentieth century, African American women poets reclaimed the Black woman's body by re-creating the meaning of its component parts, Blackness and womanhood. The transforming influence of African American women poets' playful revisions of Black female subjectivity are not, however, limited to these categories. In "Eating the Other," bell hooks describes several strategies through which African Americans and other nonwhite peoples might reinscribe the historical meanings assigned to Black and brown bodies. Hooks explains that members of nondominant identity groups can use their histories of struggle against Euro-dominance to reconstruct themselves so that tragic losses and defeats are recast in ways that encourage celebration:

> The contemporary crises of identity in the west, especially as experienced by white youth, are eased when the "primitive" is recouped via a focus on diversity and pluralism which suggests the Other can provide life-sustaining alternatives. Concurrently, diverse ethnic/racial groups can also embrace this sense of specialness, that histories and experience once seen as worthy of only disdain can be looked upon with awe. (hooks, "Eating" 25–26)

In this passage hooks is talking, quite simply, about the power of play. For hooks, play is characterized by a subject's conscious choice to review his or her symbolic position (relative to the identities that dominate the prevailing social order), to reinspect an aspect of his or her identity which has negative connotations, and to reinscribe it with positive meaning. For example, play allows African American women poets like Clifton, Shange, and Lorde to review the tragic history of Black women's enslavement and reinterpret it as evidence of endurance, a characteristic which merits pride and celebration.

In "Selling Hot Pussy," bell hooks uses a scene from a late-twentieth-century African American film (1988) to capture the willfully audacious and revisionary spirit of literary and artistic play when it is employed as a vehicle through which to review (and to re-view—to evolve a new way of seeing) the Black body:

> A scene in Spike Lee's film *School Daze* depicts an all black party where everyone is attired in swimsuits dancing—doing the butt. It is one of the most compelling moments in the film. The black "butts" on display are unruly and outrageous. They are not the still bodies of the female slave made to appear as mannequin. They are not a silenced body. Displayed as playful cultural nationalist resistance, they challenge assumptions that the black body, its skin color and shape, is a mark of shame. (hooks, "Selling" 63)

Hooks believes that this scene challenges hegemonic constructions of Blackness and beauty and mainstream conceptions of worth that marginalize Black bodies. So too do Clifton's sister-friends and magical mothers, Shange's woman gods and spoken daughters, and Lorde's moonlight dancers. Each of these African American women manifests the transformative excess of the subject who is both woman and Black, as she challenges the institutions that would erase her from view. If Lee's "black 'butts'" are "unruly and outrageous," so too is Lorde's dancing, Black Colossa, Clifton's six-fingered hands, and Shange's woman god who bleeds but does not die. If Lee's *School Daze* answers the specter of the shackled, "still" bodies of female slaves with the spectacle of playful, unfettered Black bodies in motion, then Clifton meets and counters that same image with the exuberant spectacle of hair that can "jump up and dance" and hips that "need space to move around in." Shange's woman god, so unruly in her play that "the moon tugs the seas / to hold her," poses a similar challenge to the slave legacy of Black bodies in stasis. In "Scar," "homage to my hips," "homage to my hair," and other body portraits Shange, Clifton, Lorde, and their contemporaries invent the African American woman as transgressive, transformative subject. Articulated in the ancestral language of "to merle" and the procreative words of "Oh, I'm 10 Months Pregnant," marked and accentuated with the body rituals of "nappy edges" and "Sisters: To Elaine Philip on Her Birthday," and exemplified in the Black goddess Kali, the dancing Colossa, and Shange's unnamed woman god, the wicked excess of these Black bodies in motion flaunts each poet's recuperated power to define and invent subjectivities. The poems I have assembled for this chapter read the African American body through the lens of myth and magic in order to conduct the reader through an experience of the interaction between subjectivity, gender, and race that is rooted in each poet's perspective as a Black woman. Each of these poems creates a mythic landscape whose expression of the interests and pleasures of subjects who exist at the margins of Blackness and womanhood transforms the world beyond the text and urges readers toward a new awareness of the sociopolitical and economic origins of privilege, position, and meaning.

NOTES

INTRODUCTION: INVISIBLE BODIES, INVISIBLE WORK

1. See also Barbara Welter, "The Cult of True Womanhood"; Jeanne Boydston, *Home and Work*; Betsy Erkkila, *The Wicked Sisters*; Alicia Ostriker, *Stealing the Language;* Nancy Cott, *The Bonds of Womanhood.*

2. Mary Ryan finds that even as the middle class embraced the ideal of the True Woman within the home as a marker of prosperity, the emphasis upon woman as nurturer and caretaker within the household resulted in the reconceptualization of childhood as a period of education and development away from the public sphere, a transformation which contributed to the financial security of the household when male children began in increasing numbers to spend more years in school, thus entering the work force later, with more education, and better prepared to contribute to their families' upward mobility. See Mary Ryan, *The Cradle of the Middle Class*, esp. 185.

3. To universalize a particular experience of identity is to designate the concerns, behaviors, and circumstances of that identity as normal. For example, the Black nationalist movement of the late 1960s and early 1970s has been criticized for normalizing the experience of African American males in a way that positioned the concerns and perspectives peculiar to that identity category as the only "true" or "real" concerns and perspectives of Black people. The placement of the concerns of African American men at the center of Blackness designates them as normal in a way that marginalizes the interests and concerns specific to Black women as "special" or "unrepresentative" and thus abnormal. Jan Montefiore makes a link between the universalization of men's experience by male Romantic poets and the universalization of white middle-class women's experience in contemporary feminist poetry that is also applicable to works produced by white middle-class women poets of the nineteenth century:

   > [T]here are also certain political evasions which, if not actually inherent in the process of idealizing poetry as universal consciousness, are made very easy by it. The idea of his comprehensive identity enabled the bourgeois male Romantic poet to be far more humanly inclusive than his Augustan predecessors . . . but also, since "he" represented all humanity, to avoid engaging with the recalcitrant facts of class and gender. And similarly the tendency to privilege the notion of female experience, and to think of women's poetry as a magically

powerful collective consciousness, can make for a too easy and uncritical assumption of identity between all women. (Montefiore 12)

The universalization in both the contemporary period and the mid-nineteenth century of the experience of women of economic and ethnic privilege as representative of all women designates the concerns of such women as normal concerns. Interests and concerns specific to women whose interests call attention to race and class distinctions within the identity category of woman—most often poor women and women of color—are marginalized as abnormal. Thus, in universalizing white middle-class women's experience as a model for all women's experience, poets who advanced the ideal of True Womanhood avoided engaging with pressing contemporary issues related to race and class, particularly the issues of slavery and the exploitation of workers. See Jan Montefiore, *Feminism and Poetry*, esp. chapters 1–3.

4. In "Female Influence" the Reverend W. F. Strickland describes the origin and character of women's nature as the foundation of woman's influence within her sphere:

Nature's God has given [woman] a heart filled with all the refined and generous sympathies of our nature, added to a dignified and noble bearing, a winning and attractive demeanor, adapted to develop in man's nature all that is elevated in thought, pure in feeling, and magnanimous in action; and, from what her influence has accomplished in thus forming our character, we may justly infer what it is adequate to produce in all who have not recklessly gone beyond the limits of her sway. The elements of this great power are found in the heart of every virtuous woman. . . . Thus shall woman, endowed with this attribute of her greatness, go forth to bless our race; and by the exercise of a power thus attractive, and always irresistible, allure all, within the sphere of her influence, to brighter worlds, while, with smiles and sweetness, she leads the way. (Strickland 132)

5. For a detailed investigation of the social construction of the normal, see Michel Foucault, *The Order of Things* and *Madness and Civilization*.

6. Susan Coultrap-McQuin writes, "By 1860, only about 15 percent (up from 10 percent in the 1840s) of all women were wage earners outside the home, and those were predominantly young, poor, black, immigrants, or widows" (Coultrap-McQuin 24).

7. My references to signification draw on the post-structuralist notion that a signifier is invested with meaning relative to its context—the sign system in which it is deployed—at any given moment, especially the core post-structuralist notion of what Terry Eagleton calls the "open-ended play of signification," in which concepts—including racial, ethnic, and gender identities—are imbued with meaning by the interaction of cultural practices, traditions, beliefs, and other components that comprise the particular system of meaning that forms their context. See Terry Eagleton, *Literary Theory* (131). See also Michel Foucault, *The Order of Things*. I am particularly interested in the post-structuralist approach to signification for its rejection of the notion of a single, fixed meaning for any given concept. The term *woman* is one such signifier, whose meanings are wholly dependent on the hierarchies maintained within the sign system in which that term is being used. In the mid-nineteenth century, the meanings assigned to womanhood within a white, middle-class context are shaped by the ways in which that sign system privileges the cultural practices and gender roles associated with domesticity, white supremacy, and patriarchy.

8. William Empson's classic definition of the pastoral as tool for literary inversion—the simplification of complex ideas—applies well to the poet's use of the pastoral setting to distill and communicate an intricate system of cultural ideals and expectations. See William Empson, *Some Versions of Pastoral*.

9. In "Everywhere and Nowhere: The Making of a National Landscape" Angela Miller describes the relationship between the artist's representation of the American landscape and the development of a national identity. Miller calls "painters, writers, and critics" the "creators of the national landscape" (208) and suggests:

For Americans who positioned themselves at the vanguard of history, what was national was universal. The national landscape signaled a collective identity that was both unmistakably American and fit to be the heir of the ages. (Miller, "Everywhere and Nowhere" 208)

10. In *Nature and Culture: American Landscape and Painting, 1825–1875* Barbara Novak notes that during the first one hundred years of independence "[t]here was a widespread belief that America's natural riches were God's blessings on a chosen people" (Novak 16).

11. Angela Miller cites an anonymous commentator who explained in 1825,

"Grand natural scenery . . . tends permanently to affect the character of those cradled in its bosom, [and] is the nursery of patriotism most firm and eloquence the most thrilling." Drawing from the "elastic" air and "granite highlands," "free and joyous as the torrents that dash through their rural possessions," the hardy and enterprising character of Americans was the product of those "glorious regions of rugged adventure they loved to occupy." (Miller, *Empire of the Eye* 9)

Similarly, Barbara Novak remembers James Batchelder, who

[i]n 1848 . . . in a book called *The United States as a Missionary Field*, wrote that America's "sublime mountain ranges—its capacious valleys—its majestic rivers—its inland seas—its productiveness of soil, immense mineral resources, and salubrity of climate, render it a most desirable habitation for man, and are all worthy of the sublime destiny which awaits it, as the foster mother of future billions, who will be the *governing* race of man." (Novak 16)

12. In *The Empire of the Eye: Landscape, Representation, and American Cultural Politics, 1825–1875* Angela Miller defines the agrarian or "middle" landscape represented in the pastoral art and literature of the newly sovereign United States as "a rural Aracdia gently shaped by the hand of the farmer and aesthetically balanced between the extremes of wilderness and city" (Miller, *Empire of the Eye* 13).

13. The late-twentieth-century understanding of subjectivity is such that even when the subject is outside of the space with which he or she is most readily associated, the subject is still recognized as (and still signifies as) belonging to the same identity category as when her or she is located within that space. For example the African American male subject is still perceived as an African American male even when he leaves the urban space with which he is most commonly associated.

14. Linda Kerber writes that Welter and other women historians writing during the late 1960s and early 1970s were "all influenced to some degree by Betty Friedan and all [women] writing in the climate created by the popular success of *The Feminine Mystique*" (Kerber 13), arguably the defining text in feminism's second wave. See Linda Kerber, "Separate Spheres, Female Worlds, Woman's Place: The Rhetoric of Women's History," esp. 11.

15. Welter's second-wave feminist approach to the relationship between woman and her home continues to characterize much of the scholarship on American women's experience during the nineteenth century. This is especially true of those volumes of literary criticism and historical scholarship which rely heavily upon the prescriptive and creative literature of the period, writings in which the ideal of True Womanhood was ubiquitous. Susan Coultrap-McQuin explains the pervasiveness of the ideal of True Woman in the literature of the period as "what appears from a twentieth-century perspective to be an obsessive, almost ritualistic repetition of very narrow views of women" (Coultrap-McQuin 9–10). See Betsy Erkkila, *The Wicked Sisters*, esp. chapters 1 and 2; Alicia Ostriker, *Stealing the Language*, esp. chapters 1 and 2; Susan Coultrap-McQuin, *Doing Literary Business*; Sandra Gilbert and Susan Gubar, *The Madwoman in the Attic*; and Joanne Dobson, *Dickinson and the Strategies of Reticence*. Those late-twentieth-century historians whose writings on nineteenth-century women draw significantly on the prescriptive and creative literature

of the period include Nancy Cott, *The Bonds of Womanhood;* Jeanne Boydston, *Home and Work;* and Ann Douglas, *The Feminization of American Culture.*

16. See Jeanne Boydston, *Home and Work,* esp. chapters 1 and 2. See also Nancy Cott, *The Bonds of Womanhood.*

17. See Cathy N. Davidson, "No More Separate Spheres"; Martha Banta, *Imagining American Women: Ideas and Ideals in Cultural History;* and Lora Romero, *Home Fronts: Domesticity and Its Critics in the Antebellum United States.*

18. See Jacqueline Jones Royster, *Labor of Love, Labor of Sorrow: Black Women and the Family in Slavery and Freedom.*

1. A "SOLE AND EARNEST ENDEAVOR"

1. Given that I am conflating the terms *post-Reconstruction era* and *late nineteenth century,* my use of the latter assumes a "long" nineteenth century, lasting from 1800 to 1910, whose final decades correspond with the thirty-three-year period from the Compromise of 1877 to the passage of the Sixteenth Amendment, both of which fortified the central power of the U.S. federal government.

2. When, in 1883, *Godey's Magazine and Lady's Book* was purchased by J. H. Haulenbeck, it was already in serious decline. *Godey's* was absorbed by *Puritan* magazine in 1898. *The Ladies' Repository,* one of the most popular religious magazines of the mid-nineteenth century, folded in 1876. *The Ladies' Garland,* which marketed itself as an economical version of *Godey's* (the *Garland* had a considerably lower subscription price, which editors attributed to the absence of color illustrations and other extravagances found in "another magazine") folded in December of 1850.

3. In "A Woman's Kingdom" (1873) Mrs. H. W. Beecher describes the role of the True Woman:

> ". . . to every woman who has a home, Let home stand first, before all other things! No matter how high your ambition may transcend its duties, no matter how far your talents or your influence may reach beyond its doors, before everything else build up a true home! Be not its slave! Be its minister! Let it not be enough that it is swept and garnished, that its silver glistens, that its food is delicious. Feed the love in it. Feed the truth in it. Feed thought and aspiration, feed all charity and gentleness in it. Then from its walls shall come forth the true woman and the true man, who, together, shall rule and bless the land."
>
> Is this an overwrought picture? We think not. What honor can be greater than to found such a home? What dignity higher than to reign its undisputed, honored mistress.

4. For a discussion of the emergence of New Womanhood out of the long-entrenched ideal of True Womanhood, see Mary Louise Roberts's "True Womanhood Revisited."

5. Much of Carby's explication of the relationship between the Black woman's slave narrative and the Black woman's novel would also apply to the recently discovered *Bondwoman's Narrative* by Hannah Crafts. Written in the 1850s but never published, this full-length work of fiction by an escaped woman slave actually predates both Prince's and Jacobs's narratives. It was only discovered in 2001, however, fourteen years after *Reconstructing Womanhood* was first published.

6. While the poetry of True Womanhood idealized the blue-eyed male child, the art of True Womanhood (black and white and hand-colored domestic scenes and fashion plates in magazines like *Godey's* and the *Ladies' Repository*) showed a marked preference for pale white skin and long, dark hair—wavy or curled—in its women. See JoAnne Olian's *80 Godey's Full-Color Fashion Plates (1838–1880).* For a discussion of the origins and nature of Black female stereotypes, see Patricia Hill Collins, "Mammies, Matriarchs, and Other

Controlling Images," in *Black Feminist Thought: Knowledge, Consciousness, and the Politics of Empower*, esp. 67–90.

7. More specifically, these "Negro ladies" were crafted in the hope that their exemplary conduct and irreproachable modesty might challenge those deeply held beliefs about African American women and their bodies that had left them vulnerable to sexual brutality and exploitation under slavery.

8. Hazel Carby gives the example of virtuous, altruistic Iola Leroy, the title character of Frances E. W. Harper's landmark novel, who pines, "I wish I could do something more for our people than I am doing. . . . I would like to do something of lasting service for the race" (qtd. in Carby, *Reconstructing* 62).

9. African American women poets' rejection of mainstream notions of feminine comportment, the angel of the house, and the ideology of separate spheres preceded Black women novelists' abandonment of such constructs by roughly twenty years. In *Mythic Black Fiction: The Transformation of History*, Jane Campbell observes in the turn-of-the-century African American women's novel themes and trends that had already begun to appear in Black women's poetry as early as the mid-1870s. She writes:

> As the nineteenth century gave way to the twentieth, heroes and heroines began to reject the delimiting values white culture attempted to impose. Instead, messianic figures began to point to and act out the real values at work, at times embracing the beauty of black speech, of violent revolt (Campbell x).

During the last thirty years, the greater interest on the part of literature scholars in questions related to the development of the African American women's novel has resulted in a very limited and rather conservative reading of nineteenth-century literature. On those rare occasions when scholars in the field of African American women's literature have engaged with Black women's poetry of the nineteenth century, they have focused almost exclusively on the work of Frances Ellen Watkins Harper. In *Black Feminist Criticism*, Barbara Christian calls Harper "the most important of the nineteenth century Afro-American women writers" (Christian 120), a trend which has resulted in a conservative reading of the Black women's literature of the period similar to that which results from a novel-based study. This is largely because Harper, primarily an activist, brought to her prose (she penned arguably the most influential Black novel of the nineteenth century, *Iola Leroy*) and poetry the same primary interests—in disrupting stereotypes and calling attention to Black women's femininity—that informed and inspired her activism and community organizing. In *Black Feminist Criticism*, Christian explains that "Harper . . . [was] certainly aware of the images, primarily negative, of black people that predominated in the minds of white Americans. [She] constructed [her] heroines to refute those images, as their way of contributing to the struggle of black people for full citizenship in this country" (Christian, "Trajectories" 235). Sandi Russell suggests that Harper's written opposition to racist stereotypes which degraded Black women was a means to more integrationist and feminist ends: "Harper was in the vanguard of those who realised the full implications of white patriarchy, which included the making of a chasm between black and white women. She challenged the estrangement of southern white women from their black sisters" (Russell 15). For biographical information on Harper see Williams H. Robinson Jr., *Early Black American Poets: Selections with Biographical and Critical Introductions*; Barbara Christian, "Afro-American Women Poets: A Historical Introduction," esp. 120–21; and Hazel Carby, *Reconstructing Womanhood: The Emergence of the Afro-American Woman Novelist*, esp. 65–66.

10. Lizelia Augusta Jenkins Moorer published *Prejudice Unveiled, and Other Poems*, her only extant volume, in 1907.

11. Many of the nation's most prominent historically Black colleges and universities offered course work and programs of study in "domestic science" (later renamed "home economics") well into the second half of the twentieth century. Moorer refers to Claflin College, a historically Black college located in Orangeburg, South Carolina, founded in 1869.

12. Clara Ann Thompson (c. 1869–1940) was one of three poets born to former slaves living in Rossmoyne, Ohio. Clara Ann, her younger sister, and her brother Aaron Belford privately published seven volumes of verse between them during the years spanning 1899 to 1926. Clara spent her life in Rossmoyne, living with Priscilla and another brother, Garland Yancey Thompson (Sherman 122). All of Clara Thompson's poems that I discuss in this chapter were originally published in her 1908 volume, *Songs from the Wayside*.

13. Like her older sister Clara, Priscilla Jane Thompson (1869–1949) was born in Rossmoyne, Ohio. Priscilla's first volume of poetry, *Ethiope Lays*, was published in 1900. Her later book, *Gleanings of Quiet Hours*, was published in 1907. *The Feminist Companion to Literature in English* provides this additional autobiographical information:

> [Both were daughters] of the former slaves Clara Jane (Gray), who died young, and John Henry T[hompson]. They lived with an elder brother, who received dedications from both. Their educ[ation] at public school was supplemented by tutors: only CAT [Clara Ann] worked for a living (as a teacher), and only for a year. (Blain, Clements, and Grundy 1078)

14. Jacqueline Jones Royster describes the mid-nineteenth-century connotation of the term *lady*:

> To apply the term ladylike to a black woman was apparently the height of sarcasm; by socially prescribed definition, black women could never become "ladies," though they might display pretensions in that direction. The term itself had predictable racial and class connotations. White ladies remained cloistered at home, fulfilling their marriage vows as mothers in genteel domesticity. But black housewives appeared "most lazy"; they stayed "out of the fields, doing nothing," demanding that their husbands "support them in idleness." At the heart of the issue lay the whites' notion of productive labor; black women who eschewed work under the direct supervision of former masters did not really "work" at all, regardless of their family or household responsibilities. (Jones 59)

15. In this way the Thompson sisters' use of dialect resembles that of their male contemporaries in both poetry and prose. While white writers like the legendary Joel Chandler Harris used dialect to advocate their apologist views, Black writers like Paul Laurence Dunbar and Charles Chesnutt most often used dialect as a covert tool for subverting white supremacy, as they wrote against many of the racist stereotypes that white writers used dialect to reinforce. For a more detailed discussion of the uses of dialect by both African American and white writers of the post-Reconstruction period, see John Keeling's "Paul Dunbar and the Mask of Dialect."

16. Josephine D. (Henderson) Heard published *Morning Glories* (in which "Mother" first appeared) on March 17, 1890. She wrote with what she, in the preface, described as "a heart that desires to encourage and inspire the youth of the Race to pure and noble motives, to cheer" (Heard 1). Her volume includes a brief "Historical Sketch of the Life of the Authoress," which explains the origins of her birth and her development as a poet:

> Mrs. Josie D. (Henderson) Heard was born in Salisbury, North Carolina, October 11th, 1861. Her parents, Lafayette and Annie M. Henderson, though slaves, were nominally free, being permitted to hire their time and live in another city, Charlotte, North Carolina.
>
> At an early age, Josephine displayed her literary taste. . . . As early as five years of age she could read, and was a source of general comfort to the aged neighbors, delighting to read the Scriptures to them.
>
> She received her education in the schools at Charlotte . . . the Scotia Seminary at Concord, North Carolina[, and] . . . Bethany Institute [in] New York. . . . After her marriage [in 1882] she was encouraged by Rt. Rev. Benj. Tucker Tanner, Rt. Rev. B. W. Arnett, and many other friends to give more time to [her poetry]. At their solicitations she has ventured to bring to light these verses. (Heard 6–7)

In *African American Poetry of the Nineteenth Century* Joan R. Sherman explains that Josephine Delphine (Henderson) Heard took her paired surnames from her slave parents, Annie M. (Henderson) and Lafayette Heard (Sherman 124).

17. *Autobiography and Poems* is the only extant volume of poetry by Mrs. Henry Linden. Its date of publication is uncertain. In her autobiography Mrs. Linden describes the circumstances of her birth and early life:

> I was born September 22, 1859, under the British government in Canada, fourteen miles from London, and lived there to the age of eight, when my parents brought me to the states. We first went to Kentucky, Campbell county, where my grandfather lived at that time—my father's old home place.
> My father was born in slavery. He ran away before the war, when only a boy, and went to Canada, where of course he obtained his freedom.
> My mother was a Canadian. She had a good English education and taught school, and when my father went back to Kentucky it was a brand new thing to see a negro teacher. (Linden 3)

18. Effie Waller Smith was born in Pike County, Kentucky, on January 6, 1879. Smith began writing poetry at the age of sixteen and published three books of poems during her lifetime. Several of her poems were published in national magazines. Although Smith lived to the age of eighty-one, records indicate that she published no poems after the age of thirty-eight. "The 'Bachelor Girl'" was published in *Rhymes from the Cumberland* (1909), Smith's second collection of poetry.

19. The term *wicked excess,* coined by Betsy Erkkila, refers to women poets' willful transgression of the gender norms put in place to limit woman's role. The term *excess* refers to the willfulness of this transgression. See Betsy Erkkila, *The Wicked Sisters: Women Poets, Literary History, and Discord.*

20. In "The Darkened Eye Restored," Mary Helen Washington explains how representations of friendship aid in Black women writers' resistance of invisibility by adding depth, clarity, and detail to their depictions of African American womanhood:

> Women talk to other women in this tradition, and their friendships with other women [. . .] are vital to their growth and well-being. A common scene . . . is one in which women (usually two) gather together in a small room to share intimacies that can be trusted only to a kindred female spirit. That intimacy is a tool, allowing women writers to represent women more fully. (Washington, "Darkened Eye" 35)

21. U.S. Black writers often turn to signifying, a cornerstone of the African American oral tradition, when attempting to transfer the texture and tone of Black vernacular to the written page. For a detailed discussion of signification in African American literature and culture see Henry Louis Gates Jr., *The Signifying Monkey: A Theory of African American Literary Criticism,* and Geneva Smitherman, *Talkin' and Testifyin': The Language of Black America.*

22. In describing the collapse of public/private distinctions within post-Reconstruction Black communities, African American women's poetry of this period differs sharply from Black women's prose of this era, whose narrow obsession with sentimental tales of the tragically feminine, tragically pious, and—most often—tragically "mulatto" heroine threatened to limit the boundaries of Black womanhood almost as completely (and with effects as deleterious) as the ideal of True Womanhood.

23. One version of the lyrics for "City Called Heaven" reads as follows:

> I am a poor pilgrim of sorrow.
> I'm in this wide world alone.
> No hope in this world for tomorrow.
> I'm trying to make heaven my home.

Sometimes I am tossed and driven.
Sometimes I don't know where to roam.
I've heard of a city called heaven.
I've started to make it my home.

My mother's gone on to pure glory.
My father's still walkin' in sin.
My sisters and brothers won't own me
Because I'm trying to get in.

Sometimes I am tossed and driven.
Sometimes I don't know where to roam,
But I've heard of a city called heaven
And I've started to make it my home.

24. Little is known about the life of Mary Weston Fordham. It is likely that she was born in and/or spent part of her life in Charleston, South Carolina, where her only volume of poetry, *Magnolia Leaves*, was published in 1897.

2. THE BLACK WOMAN AS OBJECT AND SYMBOL

1. Also known as the Harlem Renaissance, the New Negro Renaissance is most often linked with the unprecedented artistic and social freedoms of the 1920s. A more precise approach to dating the movement would associate its beginning with the end of World War I and the Armistice of 1918.

2. Based upon post-Reconstruction poets' continued interest in antipastoral subjects and strategies well into the first decade of the twentieth century, I have placed the end of the post-Reconstruction period around 1910, only ten years before the beginning of the 1920s, the era most closely associated—in time, mood, and sheer volume of Black literature produced—with the New Negro or Harlem Renaissance era. In designating 1910 as the end of the post-Reconstruction period, I have also taken into consideration the impact of both the turn of the century and the First World War upon the significance of the Civil War and Reconstruction as defining moments in U.S. history.

3. Harriett Jacobs was forty-eight years old in 1861, when *Incidents in the Life of a Slave Girl* first appeared. Booker T. Washington was forty-five years old in 1901, when *Up from Slavery* was first published. On January 1, 1863, Abraham Lincoln's Emancipation Proclamation ended slavery in those Confederate states in active rebellion against the U.S. federal government. In 1865 Congress ratified the Thirteenth Amendment, ending slavery in all U.S. states and territories.

4. While Frederick Douglass's *Narrative* implicates white southern men and women in slavery's cruelty and dehumanization, Booker T. Washington's *Up from Slavery* presents a much more favorable picture. Washington's book is noted for its controversial portrayal of race relations under slavery as interactions structured by inequality but governed by mutual affection.

5. I use the term *parlor audience* to suggest the intimacy and small size of a reading audience whose first encounter with the writer's work might well have occurred at a private social gathering in her home. Black women poets of the post-Reconstruction era often used their introductions to address just such an audience. In the preface to *Virginia Dreams*, for example, Maggie Pogue Johnson explains the humble, local origins of her collection and expresses her equally modest aspirations: "At the solicitation of a few friends, I have selected several of my poems, and if the perusal of them brings pleasure to you, dear reader, the object of this volume will have been accomplished" (5). More important than the literal possibility that the audience for the poems of any Black woman writer might also be acquainted with her socially is the idea of a distinction between the small audience, whose preexisting familiarity with the writer is only enhanced by the readers' engage-

ment with her text, and the experience of the Harlem Renaissance poet, whose audience becomes familiar with the writer solely through the medium of her written work.

6. My understanding of the reading audience for Renaissance women's poetry is based on related scholarship on the composition of the audiences for *The Crisis, Opportunity, The Messenger*, and other periodicals that published the poetry of New Negro women. Sondra Kathryn Wilson describes James Weldon Johnson, W. E. B. Du Bois, Walter White, and other African American leaders' conviction that Negro magazines should be used, at least in part, as a vehicle for bringing African American literary talent to the attention of white readers. See Wilson's introduction to *The Crisis Reader*, esp. pages xxi–xxiv. Similarly, Arna Bontemps describes the crucial role of periodicals in connecting New Negro writers (especially poets) to the white intellectuals with access to mainstream publishing channels. See Bontemps's *The Harlem Renaissance Remembered*, esp. 272–73. I am also able to draw important conclusions about the constituencies from which white readers came by examining the background of those Euro-Americans who were most vocal and active in their support of and interest in New Negro literature. Such figures include heiress and publisher-activist Nancy Cunard, scholar Robert Thomas Kerlin, photographer Carl VanVechten, and critic Waldo Frank.

   Frequently hailing from middle- and upper middle-class northern families, Black women poets of the Renaissance era were often anomalies among their own people, most of whom were working-class domestics and laborers who either lived in the South or were recent migrants from South.

7. While many white readers of the Harlem Renaissance period did indeed employ Black maids, nannies, cooks, and other female servants, it is unlikely that such employers ever truly experienced their "Negro" employees as gendered subjects, largely because of the subjugated status and auxiliary function of these workers within the home. On the other hand, the African American woman poets' simultaneous manifestation of Blackness, intellectual development, and economic privilege had the potential to challenge the white reader's conception of the relationship between womanhood and Blackness in ways that firsthand interactions with working class and poor African American women might not.

8. The American Negro Academy was founded in 1897 to both foster and bring to light the cultural development of African Americans. During its earliest years of activity this almost all-male organization admitted only one woman, writer and educator Anna Julia Cooper. The fact that it was an almost exclusively male organization reflects a belief held by the broader community of Black artists and intellectuals of which it was a part that true artistic and intellectual excellence is the domain of men and that female brilliance and achievement are the exception rather than the rule.

9. In addition to welcoming the participation of heterosexual African American women, the Harlem Renaissance also tolerated and, in some cases, even encouraged the contributions of Black lesbians, gay men, and bisexual people. See Gloria T. Hull, *Color, Sex, and Poetry: The Women Writers of the Harlem Renaissance*; David Levering Lewis, *When Harlem Was in Vogue*; Lillian Faderman, *Odd Girls and Twilight Lovers: A History of Lesbian Life in Twentieth-Century America*, esp. 73–84; and Thomas Wirth, ed., *Gay Rebel of the Harlem Renaissance: Selections from the Work of Richard Bruce Nugent*.

10. Founded in 1897 by Alexander Crummell, the American Negro Academy was one of several Black cultural organizations established during the post-Reconstruction era to oppose what Ronald A. T. Judy describes as the increasing focus at U.S. research universities on "the scientific study of the inherent lack of civilization among Blacks" (Judy 127). Other similar organizations include the Negro American Society, founded in 1877; the Society for the Collection of Negro Folk Lore, founded in 1890; and the Negro Historical Society of Philadelphia, founded in 1897 by John Edward Bruce and Arthur Schomburg (who later established the Schomburg Center for Research in Black Culture).

   Negro Academy member James Weldon Johnson's *Book of American Negro Poetry* was received as a broadly inclusive collection by members of the literary and scholarly communities. In his foreword to *Caroling Dusk* Countee Cullen declares Johnson's anthology a "scholarly and painstaking survey, from both a historical and critical standpoint, of the entire range of verse by American Negroes" (Cullen, *Caroling Dusk* ix).

11. In the foreword to *Caroling Dusk* Cullen describes his motivation for compiling the volume:

    . . . there would be scant reason for the assembling and publication of another such collection were it not for the new voices that within the past three to five years have sung so significantly as to make imperative an anthology recording some snatches of their songs. (Cullen, *Caroling Dusk* ix)

12. Cullen includes Angelina Weld Grimké, Anne Spencer, Mary Effie Lee Newsome, Jessie Fauset, Alice Dunbar Nelson, Georgia Douglas Johnson, Blanche Taylor Dickinson, Clarissa Scott Delany, Gwendolyn B. Bennett, Gladys May Casely Hayford, Lucy Ariel Williams, Helene Johnson, and Lula Lowe Weeden.

13. For a discussion of the Harlem Renaissance and gender inclusiveness, see Sandi Russell's *Render Me My Song*, esp. chapter 2, "Words to a White World."

14. W. E. B. Du Bois lived from 1868 to 1963. James Weldon Johnson lived from 1871 to 1938.

15. Indeed, in his 1897 address, "Civilization, the Primal Need of the Race," academy founder Alexander Crummell makes explicit the link between racial uplift, racial equality, and immersion and achievement in the arts, emphasizing the organization's interest in " the civilization of the Negro race in the United States, by the scientific processes of literature, art, and philosophy, through the agency of the cultured men of this same Negro race" (Crummell 3). Crummell explains the organizing principle of the Academy, that "until we attain the role of civilization we cannot stand up and hold our place in the world of culture and enlightenment" (Crummell 3), an idea based on the concept that the "civilization" of a given "race" can be measured (or hastened) through its development of a fine arts tradition:

    Now gentle men, for the creation of a complete and rounded man, you need the impress and the moulding of the highest arts. But how much more so for the realizing of a true and lofty *race* of men. What is true of a man is deeply true of a people. The special need in such a case is the force and application of the highest arts; not mere mechanism; not mere machinery; not mere handicraft; not the mere grasp on material things; not mere temporal ambitions. (Crummell 3)

16. Here I am drawing on Carole Sheffield's explication of violence as a form of domination and social control. For a discussion of the use of violence to preserve power in hierarchical relationships between identity groups see Carole Sheffield's "Sexual Terrorism," in *Women: A Feminist Perspective*, edited by Jo Freeman.

17. I have already noted that Black residents of Jazz Age Harlem experienced unprecedented sexual freedom, including extraordinary tolerance for lesbians and gay men. Sexual freedom did not, however, mean a rejection of traditional, essentialist notions of gender and sexual difference. Postmodern notions of gender construction were still many decades away.

18. Consider Ralph Ellison's now famous characterization of the blues as "an impulse to keep the painful details and episodes of a brutal experience alive in one's aching consciousness, to finger its jagged grain, and to transcend it, not by the consolation of philosophy but by squeezing from it a near-tragic, near-comic lyricism" (Ellison 90). This often-cited description, from the essay "Richard Wright's Blues," is perhaps the definitive statement on the relationship between humor and song, sadness and loss, and African American strategies for survival. Decades earlier Paul Laurence Dunbar described the same trend in "We Wear the Mask":

    We wear the mask that grins and lies,
    It hides our cheeks and shades our eyes,—
    This debt we pay to human guile;
    With torn and bleeding hearts we smile,
    And mouth with myriad subtleties.

Why should the world be overwise,
In counting all our tears and sighs?
Nay, let them only see us, while
    We wear the mask.

We smile, but, O great Christ, our cries
To thee from tortured souls arise.
We sing, but oh the clay is vile
Beneath our feet, and long the mile;
But let the world dream otherwise,
    We wear the mask!

19. Used as a mask, Black manhood also helps the African American woman writer to overcome the anxiety of ladyhood and femininity that she experiences as that female figure whose Blackness automatically and perpetually calls her womanhood and her propriety into question. The mask of African American manhood allows the Black female poet to speak freely, with "masculine" authority and courage, but without jeopardizing the status of her womanhood.

20. For a detailed exploration of the racial and sexual politics of lynching in the U.S. see Sandra Gunning, *Race, Rape, and Lynching: The Red Record of American Literature*.

21. Between 1882 and 1933 Maryland whites lynched thirty African Americans. The last victim was George Armwood, a twenty-two-year-old mentally retarded Black male who was accused of assaulting an elderly white woman. Armwood was dragged through the streets, mutilated, hanged, and burned by a mob of three thousand men, women, and children, in Princess Anne, Maryland. The so-called Princess Anne Lynching and other similar Depression-era killings sparked a national outcry against racial violence and mob rule, eventually resulting in the introduction of the Costigan-Wagner Act in the House of Representatives. Defeated by the efforts of southern partisans in Congress, whose opposition was bolstered by President Franklin D. Roosevelt's refusal to speak out in support of the bill, Costigan-Wagner nonetheless galvanized a nationwide effort to end the practice of lynching.

22. The newspaper reports collected in Ralph Ginzburg's *100 Years of Lynchings* indicate that a substantial proportion of those lynchings carried out against African Americans were based on false accusations or cases of mistaken identity. For a perspective on the terroristic function of lynching as a tool for intimidation and social control, see Ida B. Wells-Barnett's "Southern Horrors: Lynch Law in All Its Phases," reprinted in *Southern Horrors and Other Writings: The Anti-Lynching Campaign of Ida B. Wells, 1892–1900*, edited by Jacqueline Jones Royster.

23. Consider the frequency with which necklaces made of teeth and other emblems associated with savagery and cannibalism appeared in whites' own stereotyped images of Black and brown tribal peoples. Such depictions were common in early cartoon shorts (like Warner Brothers' 1938 "Jungle Jitters") and on the packaging of common household products throughout the first half of the twentieth century (like the American Tobacco Company's Nigger Hair Tobacco). For a visual history of the evolution in European and North American advertising of the stereotype of the Black/African-as-savage, see Jan Nederveen Pieterse, *White on Black: Images of Africa and Blacks in Western Popular Culture*.

24. The same years that saw an unprecedented artistic and intellectual achievement by the writers and artists of the New Negro Movement were also marked by literally hundreds of racially motivated attacks against Black people. Beginning with the "red summer" of 1919, in which twenty-six race riots took place between April and October (at least seventy-six African Americans were lynched during that year), racial attacks continued throughout the Harlem Renaissance era, carried out by white attackers who were apparently unmoved by the eloquent protestations of the New Negro writers. Between 1920 and 1936 at least 429 African Americans were lynched. Along with race riots, like the Tulsa Riot of 1921, which is estimated to have resulted in the deaths of as many as two thousand Black people, these murders perpetuated a climate of fear in black communities throughout the nation.

25. Langston Hughes is a rare exception to this trend. His work features a number of colorful and outspoken Black women subjects who describe the impact of racism and poverty on their own lives, and in their own voices. Consider, for example, Hughes's "Mother to Son," in which the Black mother-as-speaker describes her own life of struggle using the now famous metaphor that casts her days as a slow climb up a long and winding staircase:

> Life for me ain't been no crystal stair.
> It's had tacks in it,
> And splinters,
> And boards torn up,
> And places with no carpet on the floor—
> Bare. (2–7)

Another unexpected source for poems depicting the daily lives of African American women is children's poetry of the Harlem Renaissance era, especially as featured in *Brownie's Book*. This magazine for Black children was founded by W. E. B. Du Bois, Augustus Dill, and Jessie Fauset, whose efforts to create a source of positive depictions of African Americans were a direct response to the immense popularity of D. W. Griffith's *The Birth of a Nation*. See David Levering Lewis, *W. E. B. Du Bois—Biography of a Race*.

26. The great irony of such poetry is its return to what is essentially a nineteenth-century "separate spheres"–based understanding of woman's interests, this in a time period (the Jazz Age of the 1920s) when the larger society was experiencing a general loosening of restrictions on women's public behavior and activities. For a detailed historical analysis of Jazz Age shifts in the image and role of white women, see Angela Latham, *Posing a Threat: Flappers, Chorus Girls, and Other Brazen Performers of the American 1920s*.

27. This is true of poems written by women and by men.

28. See G. F. Richings, *Evidences of Progress among Colored People*.

29. Despite the prosperity of the Harlem Renaissance era, most African American women of this period held full-time jobs as either domestic servants or agricultural laborers, and few lived in suburban communities. Jacqueline Jones Royster writes that "in 1920 fully 90 percent of black women in the city [of Pittsburgh] made their living as day workers, washerwomen, or live-in servants. The . . . servants and . . . laundresses not in commercial laundries totaled almost two-thirds of all gainfully employed black women in the North" (164). The circumstances in the South were not far different. Jones notes that the majority of black southern women employed between 1870 and 1930 found work as domestics (167). As late as 1930, a full 27 percent of Black women nationwide were employed in agriculture (201). See Jacqueline Jones Royster, *Labor of Love, Labor of Sorrow: Black Women, Work, and the Family from Slavery to the Present*.

30. During her seven-year confinement in the narrow coffinlike space of her grandmother's garret, Harriet Jacobs effectively dies away from her previous life as a slave girl, as her master's object of desire, and as the unwed mother of her white lover's children. Reborn through her escape to the North, Jacobs reassumes only her identity as mother, leaving behind those roles—as object of her owner's desire and as the lover of a local white bachelor—that formed a context for the perceived sexual transgressions of her earlier life.

31. See Robert Kerlin, *Negro Poets and Their Poems*.

32. See Carolivia Herron's introduction to the *Selected Works of Angelina Weld Grimké*.

33. I use "his" and other male pronouns in this and other similar poems (poems that make use of the Black woman as object and symbol) because, although Bennett's language in this poem is gender-neutral, the context of the poem itself—the desiring gaze of the speaker, offered against the backdrop of an early twentieth-century understanding of the intersection of gender and desire—does, in fact, identify the speaker as male, as conclusively as would an open declaration of his sex.

34. This fascination with the notion of Black kings and queens has spawned images from the dignified to the derisive, from Paul Robeson's legendary performance of the title character in the film *Emperor Jones* (1933) to *The Black King*, a biting satire of Garvey's own rise and fall (1932), to Warner Brothers' mocking vision of African self-rule in the animated short "The Isle of Pingo Pongo" (1938).

35. See William L. Van Deburg's *Modern Black Nationalism: From Marcus Garvey to Louis Farrakhan*.

36. See bell hooks, *Yearning: Race, Gender, and Cultural Politics*.

37. See Barbara Christian, "Afro-American Women Poets: A Historical Introduction."

38. In "Oriflamme" Fauset adheres to the convention of limiting the speaking subject to a male or nongendered persona and frames the struggle against racism using the masculinist language of battle (manifest here in the metaphorical "Pounding of our hearts on Freedom's bars" and the "fight with faces set").

39. In this poem, forced miscegenation is the only woman-specific form of racism that Johnson addresses. As was customary among Black writers of both the post-Reconstruction and New Negro Renaissance periods, however, Johnson's treatment of this issue revolves around the "tragic mulatto" figure and, as a result, is not perceived as a challenge to the male-centered definition of racism, since the tragic mulatto is an indirect expression of Black male disempowerment. In fact, many representations of sexual transgressions against Black women in slavery—from the representation of the tragic mulatto figure who results from such unions to the representation of Black women's experiences of sexual harassment and abuse (in *Incidents in the Life of a Slave Girl*, *The History of Mary Prince*, *Narrative of the Life of Frederick Douglass*, and other texts)—are, in fact, explorations of the relationship between manhood (Black or white) and the function of the Black female body either as contested space in the power struggle between Black and white men or as stage on which abolitionist writers play out the cruelty and aberration of white slave owners (like Dr. Flint in *Incidents* or Captain Anthony in Douglass's *Narrative*).

40. The lyrics of the African American spiritual "Shout All Over God's Heaven" imagine an afterlife abounding in material rewards:

> I got shoes, you got shoes, all of God's children got shoes.
> When I get to Heaven, gonna put on my shoes,
> I'm gonna walk all over God's Heaven, Heaven,
> I'm gonna walk all over God's Heaven.
> Everybody talkin' 'bout Heaven ain't-a goin' there Heaven, Heaven,
> I'm gonna walk all over God's Heaven.
>
> I've got a crown . . . wear it all over God's Heaven . . .
> I've got wings . . . fly all over God's Heaven . . .
> I've got a harp . . . play it all over God's Heaven . . .
> I've got a robe . . . shout all over God's Heaven . . .

41. In the period between 1922 and 1930 "The Palm Wine Seller" appeared in no less than three separate publications, including *Opportunity* (1930), *Journal of Negro Life* (1930), and Robert Kerlin's *Negro Poets and Their Poems* (1922), an anthology.

3. REVOLUTIONARY DREAMS

Portions of this chapter were originally published as an article in a special double issue of *Journal of African American Studies*, Summer–Fall 2004, volume 8, numbers 1–2. Copyright 2006 by Transaction Publishers, New Brunswick, New Jersey. This article was reprinted in *Free at Last? Black America in the Twenty-First Century*, edited by Juan Battle, Michael Bennett, and Anthony J. Lemelle Jr. Copyright 2006 by Transaction Publishers, New Brunswick, New Jersey.

1. See Barbara Christian, "The Race for Theory"; Alicia Ostriker, *Stealing the Language;* and Phillip Harper, "Nationalism and Social Division in Black Arts Poetry of the 1960s."

2. See "Black Women" by Imamu Amiri Baraka (LeRoi Jones), in *Raise, Race, Rays, Raze: Essays since 1965.*

3. For the writer-activists of the Black Arts Movement, the link between the prison system and the practice of lynching was clear. Both were deeply hierarchical forms of social control that exploited the demoralizing effects of what Black Arts writers would argue was the arbitrary removal of African American men as a way of controlling Black communities and limiting African American political power. For a more detailed discussion of prison as a tool for social control see Julia Sudbury, "Celling Black Bodies: Black Women in the Global Prison Industrial Complex," and Michel Foucault *Discipline and Punish.*

4. Just as the bold self-determination and confidence of Harlem Renaissance writers and artists caused Jazz Age observers to declare that period a New Negro Movement, so too did the audacious Afro-Centrism of the 1960s nationalist poets inspire scholars and editors to declare the work a "New Black Poetry." See *The New Black Poetry,* edited by Clarence Major (1969); and *Understanding the New Black Poetry* by Stephen Henderson (1973).

5. For the purposes of this chapter, the Black Arts Movement begins in 1965 with Imamu Amiri Baraka / LeRoi Jones's founding of Black Arts Repertory Theatre/School (BARTS) and ends in 1976 with the opening of Ntozake Shange's *For Colored Girls Who Have Considered Suicide When the Rainbow Is Enuf,* at Broadway's Booth Theatre. Although Larry Neale's noted essay "The Black Arts Movement" did not appear until 1968, these two developments in the staging of African American theatrical works functioned both practically and symbolically as an opening and an end, respectively, to the pioneering developments in the production of Black literature for a Black audience that Neale's essay eventually described. The founding of BARTS represents a deliberate choice to privilege the African American audience, while Shange's decision to bring *For Colored Girls* to Broadway signals a decisive movement away from that trend.

6. I deliberately use the anachronistic *helpmate* (from *help meet,* literally "suitable for him") to capture the neotraditionalism inherent in most Black Arts considerations of the relationship between the African American male and his legal or common-law wife. The earliest biblical use of the term (Genesis 2:18, KJV) suggests a limited role for woman as support and comfort for her male partner: "And the LORD God said, It is not good that the man should be alone; I will make him an help meet for him."

7. "Zubena" derives from the Arabic *al zubena,* meaning "purchase or redemption." *Al Zubena* is also the Arabic name for the constellation more commonly know in the West by its Latin name, Libra (the scales).

8. The term speaker-poet refers to the first-person voice in those poems in which the experiences and perspectives of the speaker—the "I" in the poem—seem indistinguishable from that of the poet (specifically those poems in which the poet is clearly using the medium to articulate his or her own specific experiences and beliefs).

9. See Baraka's "Beautiful Black Women," in *The Black Poets,* edited by Dudley Randall.

10. See Theophus Smith, *Conjuring Culture.*

11. One of the greatest challenges presented to the greater African American community by both the Black Arts Movement and the larger Black Power movement of which it was a part was their rejection of literally centuries of African American Protestant tradition and beliefs. The Black Power movement's rejection of the African American church both contributed to and grew out of the distance that many young African Americans undoubtedly felt from the church-led civil rights movement in the South. In particular, many young African Americans were disappointed by the skepticism with which organizations like the Southern Christian Leadership Conference (SCLC) initially greeted Stokely Carmichael and other young nationalists' calls for Black Power and Afro-centrism. Although relationships between the SCLC and Carmichael's Student Nonviolent Coordinating Committee

eventually warmed, the image of SCLC and its church affiliates as the dominion of an older, more moderate generation of Negro leaders remained in the minds of many young Blacks.

12. I refer to this as a reembrace because it represents a return to a strategy (the location of anti-racist resistance within experiences and spaces associated with the everyday life of Black people) originated by African American women poets of the post-Reconstruction era.

13. There is little recognition within the literature of the Black Arts and Black Power movements of the capacity for social change inherent in the expression of Black gay desire. For a detailed examination of the relationship between homophobia and sexual orientation and Black nationalist ideology, see Philip Harper, *Are We Not Men? Masculine Anxiety and the Problem of African-American Identity.*

14. For one of the classic critiques of what remains the widespread conception of Blackness as a male-gendered identity category (as a category that enters the sociopolitical discourse on gender and race based on the hyper visibility of its male constituents and the invisibility of its female ones) see *All the Women Are White, All the Blacks Are Men, But Some of Us Are Brave: Black Women's Studies,* edited by Gloria T. Hull, Patricia Bell Scott, and Barbara Smith. This text is, however, only one of the earliest to take up this issue, which in the last twenty years has become widely understood as a cornerstone of Black feminist thought.

15. In the psychoanalytic theory of Sigmund Freud, the pre-Oedipal phase is marked by the child's feeling of unity with the mother. In this earliest phase of development, the child is unaware that he/she and the mother are separate beings. Freud's pre-Oedipal stage corresponds with Jacques Lacan's Imaginary, the later stages of which are characterized by the child's emergence into language, by which process he or she comes to recognize him or herself as distinct from the mother. Thus language, and especially the capacity to articulate those interests and desires that distinguish the child from the mother, brings about the end of the Imaginary stage, along with its fleeting experience of perfect unity with the mother. Both the pre-Oedipal and the Imaginary phases are useful and interesting analogues for Black Arts women's complete adoption of the interests and goals of the African American male as their own.

16. Gwendolyn Brooks's *Annie Allen* (1949) stands out as one of the few mid-twentieth-century African American texts to address the life experiences of an African American woman. In 1950 Brooks was awarded a Pulitzer Prize for this collection of poems describing one Black woman's journey from girlhood to adulthood in a working-class urban setting. The theme of Black women's negotiation of the racist and sexist social landscape of urban America remained central in her work throughout her entire career. In *For My People* (1942) poet Margaret Walker integrates Black women's experiences into her consideration of the condition and needs of African American people of the World War II era. Passages like the following, from the title poem of this volume, illustrate the poet's understanding of "racial uplift" as the deliverance of Black women as well as Black men. She writes this poem of invocation:

> For my playmates in the clay and dust and sand of Alabama backyards playing baptizing and preaching and doctor and jail and soldier and school and mama and cooking and playhouse and concert and store and hair and Miss Choomby and company;
>
> . . . .
>
> For the boys and girls who grew in spite of these things to be man and woman, to laugh and dance and sing and play and drink their wine and religion and success, to marry their playmates and bear children and then die of consumption and anemia and lynching ("For My People").

17. In *The Sexual Mountain and Black Women Writers: Adventures in Sex, Literature, and Real Life,* Calvin Hernton explores African American women writers' attempts to overcome

prevailing notions within Black literary community about the particularity of African American women's experience.

18. See Ekaterini Georgoudaki, "Contemporary Black American Women Poets: Resisting Sexual Violence."

19. See Frantz Fanon, *Black Skin, White Masks*. Fanon refines his address of the hierarchical and binaristic positioning of Blackness as oppositional to whiteness in his later volume *The Wretched of the Earth*.

20. See Karen Jackson Ford, *Gender and the Poetics of Excess: Moments of Brocade*.

21. "Memorial: 3. rev pimps" and "to all brothers" appear in *Home Coming*, first published in 1969.

22. A number of Black Arts women poets—Nia Na Imani, Zubena (Cynthia Conley), Johari Amini, and others—continued to produce representations of the African American woman as lover-object throughout the entire Black nationalist period. For those writers who did eventually write beyond the limitations of this figure to create Black female subjects, such portrayals appear later in their Black Arts writings than their depictions of the Black woman as objects or as desiring subjects; the emergence in their work of emancipated female subjects represents an evolution in their engagements with questions of gender, power, and race. Carolyn Rodgers's "Yuh Lookin GOOD" (1968) precedes "U Name This One" (1969) by more than a year; Nikki Giovanni's "Beautiful Black Men" (1968) precedes the woman-centered excesses of "Ego Tripping" (1970) by roughly two years. The year 1969 stands as an important transition point in the poetry of Black Arts women, with few depictions of Black women subjects appearing in volumes published before that year.

4. LOCATING THE BLACK FEMALE SUBJECT

1. The growing influence during the late 1960s of the civil rights, feminist, and gay activist movements was reflected in increasing levels of political power, social acceptance, and national visibility for people of color, women, lesbians, and gay men during the 1970s, '80s, and '90s.

2. For a detailed analysis of the documentary evidence of federal counterintelligence programs directed against Black political organizations, see Ward Churchill and Jim Vander Wall, *The Cointelpro Papers: Documents from the FBI's Secret Wars against Domestic Dissent* (esp. 91–164). See also Frank Donner, *Protectors of Privilege: Red Squads and Police Repression in Urban America*.

The Civil Rights Act of 1964 was signed by President Lyndon B. Johnson and prohibited discrimination in voting, schools, education, and public facilities. Historic in the breadth of its vision, it failed to bring out the sort of rapid integration that African Americans and other antisegregationists had hoped for. Although it laid the legal foundation for full Black participation in all areas of public life, it stopped short of addressing residential segregation. The Civil Rights Act of 1968, also signed by President Johnson, had a more dramatic effect on the racial landscape of the nation. Its prohibition of racial discrimination in housing effected much more drastic changes in the ethnic landscape of the nation. Its effective release of more privileged, upwardly mobile African Americans to migrate to more affluent, often predominantly white, suburban neighborhoods, depleted the economic, intellectual, and artistic resources of Black urban communities across the United States. The resulting decrease in the economic diversity of many of the nation's largest African American communities left the burden of sustaining many of the artistic and literary programs and publications that had flourished during the height of the Black Arts Movement to those urban citizens and city governments on whom the impact of "Black middle-class flight" had taken its most damaging financial toll. For more on the impact of "Black flight" on urban African American communities, see bell hooks, *Salvation: Black People and Love* (esp. 42); Nelson Kofie, *Race, Class, and the Struggle for Neighborhood in Washington, D.C.* in the Studies in African American History and Culture series (esp. 41–62); and Miles Corwin, *And Still We Rise: The Trials and Triumphs of Twelve Gifted Inner-City Students* (esp. 176).

3. For a minority of Black Arts writers, their celebration of Blackness was manifested in their rejection of Protestant Christianity in favor of Islam. This was most often based on the link perceived by many revolutionary nationalists between the predominance of Islam in specific regions of Africa with their interest in recuperating the belief systems and practices of their West African ancestors. Sonia Sanchez joined the U.S.-based Nation of Islam in 1971. By the mid-1970s, however, she had abandoned the organization, due to her opposition to its repression of women.

4. Joyce A. Joyce proposes that Rodgers' embrace of Christianity "enhanced the depth of [her] works by reflecting personal growth as well as the political and cultural changes of the late 1970s and the 1980s." See Joyce A. Joyce, " The Aesthetic of E. Ethelbert Miller," first published in the essay collection *Warriors, Conjurers and Priests: Defining African-Centered Literary Criticism,* and reprinted in the online scholarly journal *Encontro.*

5. See Carolyn Rodgers, "The Black Heart as Ever Green" (11), in *The Heart as Ever Green.*

6. The "light of the world" metaphor occurs in John 8:12 (KJV): "Then spake Jesus again unto them, saying, I am the light of the world: he that followeth me shall not walk in darkness, but shall have the light of life." In the following passage Jesus extends this metaphor to include his followers as well: "Ye are the light of the world. A city that is set on an hill cannot be hid. Neither do men light a candle, and put it under a bushel, but on a candlestick; and it giveth light unto all that are in the house" (Matthew 5:14–15, KJV).

7. Rodgers's reembrace, in this and subsequent volumes, of the faith of her childhood is foreshadowed in "It Is Deep," from her 1969 collection *Songs of a Blackbird* (and reprinted in the 1975 volume *How I Got Ovah*), which depicts the poet's reassessment of her mother's Christian faith (she is described as a "religious Negro" [43]) in the context of that figure's survival, with dignity intact (her mother is "proud of / having waded through a storm" [43–44]), of the challenges and indignities of segregated America. Having abandoned the narrowly circumscribed vision of liberation and social change advocated in the Black Arts Movement, Rodgers displays a new appreciation for her mother's struggles and triumphs and their role in shaping her own political consciousness; and the poem ends with this tribute: "My mother . . . / . . . is very obviously, / a sturdy Black bridge that I / crossed over, on." (43–46)

8. Phillis Wheatley is most widely known for her status as the first African American known to have published a book, *Poems on Various Subjects, Religious and Moral,* first printed in London, in 1773.

9. In 1991 Anita Hill, at the time a law professor at the University of Oklahoma, came forward with allegations of sexual harassment against then Supreme Court nominee Clarence Thomas. The United States Senate Judiciary Committee conducted hearings on the matter, which were broadcast nationally on American television from October 11 through October 13 of the same year. The hearings exposed deep divisions in the national consciousness with regard to gender and sexual accountability.

10. See Kobena Mercer, *Welcome to the Jungle: New Positions in Black Cultural Studies,* esp. chapter 5, "Black Masculinity and the Sexual Politics of Race."

11. For examples of this trend, see June Jordan, "Poem about My Rights" and "A Poem for the Women of South Africa," in *Passion: New Poems;* Elizabeth Alexander, "The Venus Hottentot" and "Boston Year," in *The Venus Hottentot;* and Alice Walker, "Revolutionary Petunias" and "Burial," in *Revolutionary Petunias & Other Poems.*

12. See Sharon Olds, *The Dead and the Living* (esp. "The Taking"), *The Gold Cell* (esp. "Saturn" and "Late Poem to My Father"), and *The Father* (esp. "Beyond Harm" and "Waste Sonata"); Louise Glück, *Ararat* (esp. "Widows") and *Descending Figure* ("Dedication to Hunger"); and Marge Piercy, *What Are Big Girls Made Of?* and *My Mother's Body* (esp. "What Remains" and "Why Marry at All?").

13. For a detailed discussion of the marginalization of Black women within mainstream (white), bourgeois feminism, see Audre Lorde, "An Open Letter to Mary Daly," in *Sister Outsider: Essays and Speeches* (66–71); and bell hooks, *Feminist Theory: From Margin to Center.*

14. Although Clifton published her first book in 1969, at the height of the Black Arts Movement, it is not until her third book of poetry, *An Ordinary Woman*, published in 1974, that we begin to see poems that focus upon the African American woman's body as metaphor for the position of the Black female subject within the larger society.

15. See Patricia Hill Collins, *Black Feminist Thought: Knowledge, Consciousness and the Politics of Empowerment*, for a further exploration of experience as a framework for developing an antiessentialist vision of African American women's subjectivity.

16. See Collins, *Black Feminist Thought*, for a more detailed exploration of the cognitive gap between dominant systems of meaning based on "either/or dichotomous thinking" and Black feminist systems of meaning based upon the paradigm of simultaneity.

17. I use the term *magical* based on my understanding of the meaning and function of *magical realism*, first coined in the 1920s by German art critic Franz Roh (Roh is recognized by most literary and art historians as the originator of this term), but most frequently associated with Latin American literature of the twentieth century. In particular, I am interested in the propensity of magical realist writers for using images of the unreal (impossible actions, objects, settings, and circumstances) to depict or describe real, material circumstances—most often those of the marginalized or the oppressed—that the dominant discourse fails to account for, i.e., those whose experiences outside of the descriptive capacity of the dominant language and meaning systems occur as a side effect of their existence in discursive spaces far outside of the sociopolitical and economic mainstream.

18. This poem is printed in the lower righthand corner of the title page of the book.

19. Indeed, such forms have traditionally served to reinforce the established social order of a specific culture, nation, or region.

20. Published one year before *Two-Headed Woman* appeared, *An Ordinary Woman* was Clifton's first volume to write womanhood beyond the constraints imposed by the Black Arts Movement.

21. Lucille Clifton was born with six fingers on each hand, a trait passed down through the women of her maternal line. Part allegory and part autobiography, "i was born with twelve fingers" crafts from the circumstances of her own birth and ancestral legacy a celebration of the power inherent in African American women's perceived deviance as women who are not white.

22. See Theophus Smith, *Conjuring Culture* for an exploration of this and other "Africanisms" that have made their way into African American cultural and religious practices.

23. See Lucille Clifton's *Generations* for a more detailed account of the poet's known ancestors.

24. In her review of Clifton's *Quilting* Leslie Ullman praises "to my last period" as a reflection of a new "presence" in the poet's work, one that "speaks from new depths" (Ullman 178), and she applauds the candor with which the poet describes the bodily and emotional transformations of midlife, noting that

> Clifton speaks from the freedom of an individual who acknowledges her full female self, including the losses suffered by heart and body. Like the menstrual blood she describes in "poem in praise of menstruation," her poems are both dark and nourishing, painful and life-giving, a "wild river" that "flows also / through animals / beautiful and faithful and ancient / and female and brave." (Ullman 180)

25. Even in "poem to my uterus," which initially appears to address the specifics of Clifton's own thoughts in the face of her coming surgery—memories of the role that her uterus has played in her life and her own apprehensions about life without that "estrogen kitchen

/ [her] black bag of desire" (15–16)—the speaker considers only those functions of the uterus that are common to most women. She considers its role in conception, gestation, and hormone production. Similarly, her questions reveal only the most general misgivings: she asks, "where can I go [. . .] without you / where can you go without me" (17–21).

26. Like "daughters," this poem refers to the poet's own ancestry, which she is able to trace, via her great-grandmother, back to the Dahomey people. Also known as the Fon, Dahomeans make up the largest ethnic group in the West African nation of Benin, a former French colony that gained independence in 1960 as the Republic of Dahomey. For a discussion of the relations between the legend of the amazons and the military culture of Dahomey, see Stanley B. Alpern, *Amazons of Black Sparta: The Women Warriors of Dahomey.*

27. Although this poem portrays the myth of the amazons as African in origin, this aspect of the legend appears to have its roots in classical Greek mythology. See Jessica Amanda Salmonson, *The Encyclopedia of Amazons: Women Warriors from Antiquity to the Modern Era.*

28. Genesis 2:21–22 (KJV) describes the creation of woman as follows: "And the LORD God caused a deep sleep to fall upon Adam, and he slept: and he took one of his ribs, and closed up the flesh instead thereof; And the rib, which the LORD God had taken from man, made he a woman, and brought her unto the man."

29. In "Above the Wind," an interview with *Callaloo* editor and founder Charles Rowell, Lorde describes herself as "a Black, Lesbian, Feminist, warrior, poet, mother doing my work" (61). Her explanation, that "I underline these things, but they are just some of the ingredients of who I am" and that "I pluck these out because, for various reasons, they are aspects of myself about which a lot of people have had a lot to say, one way or another" (61), suggests that she claimed those identities most publicly and most vehemently whose coexistence posed the greatest challenge to widely accepted and conventional notions of the meaning of each of those categories individually. In "Audre Lorde: Textual Authority and the Embodied Self," Margaret Kissam Morris explains this practice in slightly more specific terms: "When Lorde names herself by identifying her multiple subject positions, she customarily begins with race; thus, she privileges the term that has been the source of her earliest experiences with prejudice" (Morris 169).

30. In the introduction to *Chosen Poems* Lorde explains that she did not include any poems from *The Black Unicorn* "because the wholeness of that sequence/conversation cannot yet be breached."

31. See Robert Farris Thompson, *Flash of the Spirit: African and Afro-American Art and Philosophy* (esp. 17–97).

32. See Audre Lorde, "Uses of the Erotic: The Erotic as Power," in *Sister Outsider: Essays and Speeches.* This collection was published in 1984, six years after *The Black Unicorn.*

33. Ekaterini Georgoudaki writes:

> Lorde's search for a non-Western matrilineal tradition embracing the lesbian experience and affirming female power . . . leads her to Africa, the Afro-Americans' original home. From the history and mythology of Africa she borrows images of female goddesses (Seboulisa, Yemanja, Oshun, Oya, etc.), queens, warriors (Amazons), witches and other women to reconstitute her image of the black female self and to project her vision of a future woman-centered world. Through identifying with witches and invoking goddesses to give her strength and artistic inspiration Lorde re-enacts the role of the black woman conjurer appearing in Anglo- and Afro-American literary texts. In this role she rejects the religious values and ethos of an oppressive white Western culture and she affirms and appropriates the spiritual knowledge and sacred powers of her Grenadian mother, her African and her Afro-American slave ancestresses. Like them, the poet transcends Eurocentric divisions of consciousness, feels part of the natural order of things, attains a deeper understanding of life, and communes with the divine, with the spirits of the ancestors, and with other living beings. (Georgoudaki, *Race* 87)

34. In addition, the juxtaposition of sun and moon also suggests the means by which Black womanhood has endured as a marginal identity group. Sun and moon, like the menstrual cycle, the changing of seasons, and other images of nature's regular patterns of diminishment and renewal point to Black woman's endurance even through and despite periods of reduced visibility and power.

35. Georgoudaki describes how Lorde constructs the figure of the mythic Black Amazon-goddess to use as a vehicle to transgress sociopolitical boundaries:

> [I]n [Lorde's] process of constructing this identity and transforming the world her consciousness operates on the personal, historical, and mythical levels, and crosses boundaries of space, time, and culture. (Georgoudaki, *Race* 90)

36. Patricia Yaeger writes, "As women play with old texts, the burden on the tradition is lightened and shifted; it has the potential for being remade" (Yaeger 18). The same can be said of poems that invent mythologies to highlight and explain elements of women's daily lives. Such poems elevate the ordinary and thus expand notions of the sacred and the holy beyond their traditional and more limited association with institutionalized Euro-patriarchal dominance.

BIBLIOGRAPHY

Adams, Jeanette. "Black Cultural Confrontation (During)." *Journal of Black Poetry* 1.11 (Spring 1969): 34.

Alexander, Elizabeth. *The Venus Hottentot.* Charlottesville: UP of Virginia, 1990.

Alpern, Stanley B. *Amazons of Black Sparta: The Women Warriors of Dahomey.* New York: New York UP, 1998.

Allin, Abby. "Little Emily." *Godey's Magazine and Lady's Book* 43 (1851): 56.

Amini, Johari. "About Man." *Journal of Black Poetry* 1.11 (Spring 1969): 24.

Annie. "The Peasant's Song." *Godey's Magazine and Lady's Book* 45 (1853): 473.

Atherton, Jessie. "A Mother's Influence." *Godey's Magazine and Lady's Book* 56 (1858): 159.

Banta, Martha. *Imagining American Women: Ideas and Ideals in Cultural History.* New York: Columbia UP, 1987.

Baraka, Imamu Amiri (Leroi Jones). "Black Dada Nihilismus." *The Dead Lecturer.* New York: Grove, 1964. 61–64.

———. "Beautiful Black Women." *Transbluesency: Selected Poems (1961–1995).* New York: Marsilio, 1995. 97–101.

———. "Black Women." *Raise, Race, Rays, Raze.* New York: Random House, 1971. 148–52.

———. "From an Almanac." *Preface to a Twenty-Volume Suicide Note.* New York: Totem, 1961. 43–44.

———. "To a Publisher." *Preface to a Twenty-Volume Suicide Note.* New York: Totem, 1961. 18–20.

Beecher, Mrs. H. W. "Woman's Kingdom." *Motherly Talks with Young Housekeepers.* New York: J. B. Ford, 1873.

Bennett, Gwendolyn B. "To a Dark Girl." Cullen, *Caroling Dusk* 157.

Birch, Eva Lennox. *Black American Women's Writing: A Quilt of Many Colors.* New York: Harvester Wheatsheaf, 1994.

Birtha, Becky. *The Forbidden Poems.* Seattle: Seal, 1991.

Blain, Virginia, Patricia Clements, and Isobel Grundy, eds. *The Feminist Companion to Literature in English: Women Writers from the Middle Ages to the Present.* New Haven: Yale UP, 1990.

Bontemps, Arna. *The Harlem Renaissance Remembered.* New York: Dodd, Mead, 1972.

Boydston, Jeanne. *Home and Work: Housework, Wages, and the Ideology of Labor in the Early Republic.* New York: Oxford UP, 1990.

Bragg, Linda Brown. "On My First Trip to Mississippi." *A Love Song to Black Men.* Detroit: Broadside, 1974. 22–23.

Brooks, Gwendolyn. *Annie Allen.* New York: Harper, 1949.

Buell, Lawrence. *New England Literary Culture from Revolution through Renaissance.* Cambridge: Cambridge UP, 1986.

Butler, Judith. *Gender Trouble: Feminism and the Subversion of Identity.* New York: Routledge, 1990.

Campbell, Jane. *Mythic Black Fiction: The Transformation of History.* Knoxville: U of Tennessee P, 1986.

Carby, Hazel V. *Reconstructing Womanhood: The Emergence of the Afro-American Woman Novelist.* New York: Oxford UP, 1987.

———. "'On the Threshold of Woman's Era': Lynching, Empire, and Sexuality in Black Feminist Theory." *Dangerous Liaisons: Gender, Nation, and Postcolonial Perspectives.* Ed. Anne McClintock, Aamir Mufti, and Ella Shohat. Minneapolis: U of Minnesota P, 1997. 330–43.

Carlson, Robert G. "Banana Beer, Reciprocity, and Ancestor Propitiation among the Haya of Bukoba Tanzania." *Ethnology* 29 (1990): 297–311.

Carrington, Joyce Sims. "An Old Slave Woman." *Opportunity* 4 (March 1926): 84.

"Childhood." *Ladies' Repository, and Gatherings of the West* 5 (1842): 223.

Christian, Barbara. *Black Feminist Criticism: Perspectives on Black Women Writers.* New York: Pergamon, 1985.

———. "The Race for Theory." *Cultural Critique* 6 (Spring 1987): 51–63.

Churchill, Ward, and Jim Vander Wall. *The Cointelpro Papers: Documents from the FBI's Secret Wars against Domestic Dissent.* Boston: South End Press, 2002

Clare, Marie J. "I've Been Forth into the World Mother." *Godey's Magazine and Lady's Book* 45 (1852): 86.

Clifton, Lucille. "amazons." Clifton, *The Terrible Stories* 21.

———. "Calming Kali." Clifton, *An Ordinary Woman* 57.

———. "The Coming of Kali." Clifton, *An Ordinary Woman* 47.

———. "daughters." Clifton, *Next: New Poems* 30.

———. "female." Clifton, *Next: New Poems* 33.

———. *Generations: A Memoir.* New York: Random House, 1976.

———. "homage to my hair." Clifton, *Two-Headed Woman* 5.

———. "homage to my hips." Clifton, *Two-Headed Woman* 6.

———. "I. at creation." Clifton, *Next: New Poems* 22.

———. "i was born with twelve fingers." Clifton, *Two-Headed Woman* 4.

———. "Kali." Clifton, *An Ordinary Woman* 37.

———. "lumpectomy eve." Clifton, *The Terrible Stories* 22.

———. "my dream of being white." *Blessing the Boats: New and Selected Poems, 1988–2000.* Brockport, NY: BOA, 2000. 41.

———. *Next: New Poems.* Brockport, NY: BOA, 1993.

———. "1994." *The Terrible Stories* 24.

———. *An Ordinary Woman.* New York: Random House, 1974.

———. "poem in praise of menstruation." Clifton, *Quilting: Poems, 1987–1990* 36.

———. "poem to my uterus." Clifton, *Quilting: Poems, 1987–1990* 58.

———. *Quilting: Poems, 1987–1990.* NY: BOA, 1991.

———. "Sisters: For Elaine Philip on Her Birthday." Clifton, *An Ordinary Woman* 5.

———. "song at midnight." *The Book of Light.* Port Townsend, WA: Copper Canyon, 1993. 24.

———. *The Terrible Stories.* Brockport, NY: BOA, 1996.

———. "to merle." Clifton, *Two-Headed Woman* 9.

———. "to my last period." Clifton, *Quilting: Poems, 1987–1990* 59.

———. *Two-Headed Woman.* Amherst: U of Massachusetts P, 1980.

———. "won't you celebrate with me." *The Book of Light.* Port Townsend, WA: Copper Canyon, 1993. 25.

Coleman, Wanda. "An Ex Carbon Copy of White Women Speaks." *Journal of Black Poetry* 1.13 (Winter–Spring 1970): 95.

Collins, Patricia Hill. *Black Feminist Thought: Knowledge, Consciousness, and the Politics of Empowerment.* New York: Routledge, 1990.

Combahee River Collective. "A Black Feminist Statement." Hull, Scott, and Smith, 13–22.

Cook, Mrs. "The Old Arm-Chair." *Godey's Magazine and Lady's Book* 50 (1855): 273.

Corwin, Miles. *And Still We Rise: The Trials and Triumphs of Twelve Gifted Inner City Students.* New York: Harper Perennial, 2001.

Cott, Nancy F. *The Bonds of Womanhood: "Woman's Sphere" in New England, 1780–1835.* New Haven: Yale UP. 1977.

Coultrap-McQuin, Susan M. *Doing Literary Business: American Women Writers in the Nineteenth Century.* Chapel Hill: U of North Carolina P, 1990.

Crummell, Alexander. "Civilization, the Primal Need of the Race." *The American Negro Academy Occasional Papers* 2 (1897): 3–7.

Cullen, Countee, ed. *Caroling Dusk: An Anthology of Verse by Negro Poets.* 1927. Rpt. as *Caroling Dusk: An Anthology of Verse by Black Poets of the Twenties.* Secaucus, NJ: Carol, 1993.

———. "Yet Do I Marvel." Cullen, *Caroling Dusk* 182.

Cuney, Waring. "No Images." Cullen, *Caroling Dusk* 212.

Davidson, Cathy N. "No More Separate Spheres!" *American Literature* 70.3 (1998): 443–63.

Davies, Carole Boyce. *Black Women, Writing, and Identity: Migrations of the Subject.* New York: Routledge, 1994.

Davis, Angela Y. *Women, Race, and Class.* New York: Random, 1981.

Delany, Clarissa Scott. "Solace." Cullen, *Caroling Dusk* 141.

Derricotte, Toi. *Captivity.* Pittsburgh: U of Pittsburgh P, 1989.

De Weever, Jacqueline. *Mythmaking and Metaphor in Black Women's Fiction.* New York: St. Martin's, 1992.

Dickinson, Emily. *The Poems of Emily Dickinson.* Ed. Thomas H. Johnson. 3 vols. Cambridge: Belknap, 1955.

Dobson, Joanne. *Dickinson and the Strategies of Reticence: The Woman Writer in Nineteenth-Century America.* Bloomington: Indiana UP, 1989.

Donner, Frank. *Protectors of Privilege: Red Squads and Police Repression.* Berkeley: U of California P, 1990.

Douglas, Ann. *The Feminization of American Culture.* New York: Knopf, 1977.

Dove, Rita. *Thomas and Beulah.* Pittsburgh: Carnegie-Mellon UP, 1986.

Doward, Cornelia M. "Old." *Godey's Magazine and Lady's Book* 50 (1855): 348.

Dunbar, Paul Laurence. "We Wear the Mask." *The Collected Poems of Paul Laurence Dunbar.* Ed. Joanne M. Braxton. Charlottesville: U of Virginia P, 1993. 71.

Eagleton, Terry. *Literary Theory: An Introduction.* Minneapolis: U of Minnesota P, 1983.

Edith. "The Homeward Bound." *Ladies' Companion and Literary Expositor* 9 (1838): 72.

Ellison, Ralph. " Richard Wright's Blues." *Shadow and Act.* New York: Random, 1964. 77–94.

Empson, William. *Some Versions of Pastoral.* Norfolk, CT: New Directions, 1950.

Erkkila, Betsy. *The Wicked Sisters: Women Poets, Literary History, and Discord.* New York: Oxford UP, 1992.

Faderman, Lillian. *Odd Girls and Twilight Lovers: A History of Lesbian Life in Twentieth-Century America.* New York: Columbia UP, 1991.

Fanon, Frantz. *The Wretched of the Earth.* New York: Grove P, 1965.

Fauset, Jessie. "La Vie C'est La Vie." *Crisis* 24 (July 1922): 124.

———. "Oriflamme." *Crisis* 19 (January 1920): 128.

Finley, Ruth. *The Lady of Godey's, Sarah Josepha Hale.* Philadelphia: Lippincott, 1931.

Ford, Karen Jackson. *Gender and the Poetics of Excess: Moments of Brocade.* Jackson: UP of Mississippi, 1997.

Fordham, Mary Weston. "The Dying Girl." *Magnolia Leaves.* Charleston, S.C.: Walker, Evans & Cogswell, 1897. New York: AMS, 1973. 53–55.

Forsyth, Pauline. "The Water-Lily." *Godey's Magazine and Lady's Book* 50 (1855): 254.

Foucault, Michel. *Discipline and Punish.* New York: Pantheon Books, 1977.

———. *Madness and Civilization: A History of Insanity in the Age of Reason.* Trans. Richard Howard. New York: Pantheon, 1965.

——. *The Order of Things: An Archaeology of the Human Sciences.* Trans. Alan Sheridan. New York: Pantheon, 1970.

Gardiner, Mrs. H. C. "Rural Life." *Ladies' Repository, and Gatherings of the West* 7 (1842): 264.

Gates, Henry Louis. *The Signifying Monkey: A Theory of Afro-American Literary Criticism.* New York: Oxford UP, 1988.

Georgoudaki, Ekaterini. *Race, Gender, and Class Perspectives in the Works of Maya Angelou, Gwendolyn Brooks, Rita Dove, Nikki Giovanni, and Audre Lorde.* Thessaloniki, Greece: Aristotle University of the Thessaloniki, 1991.

——. "Contemporary Black American Women Poets: Resisting Sexual Violence." *Journal of American Studies of Turkey* 3 (1996): 107–24.

Gilbert, Sandra M., and Susan Gubar. *The Madwoman in the Attic: The Woman Writer and the Nineteenth-Century Literary Imagination.* New Haven: Yale UP, 1979.

Gilman, Caroline. "The Fortieth Wedding-Day." *Boston Weekly Magazine* 1 (1838): 130.

Ginzburg, Ralph, ed. *100 Years of Lynchings.* New York: Lancer Books, 1962. Baltimore: Black Classic, 1988.

Giovanni, Nikki. "Beautiful Black Men." Randall 320.

——. "Ego Tripping (there may be a reason why)." *The Women and the Men.* New York: Morrow, 1975. 28–29.

——. "Linkage (for Phillis Wheatley)." *Those Who Ride the Night Winds.* New York: Morrow, 1983. 25.

——. *Re:Creation.* Detroit: Broadside, 1970.

——. "Revolutionary Dreams." *The Women and the Men.* New York: Morrow, 1975. 19.

Glazier, Jack. "Mbeere Ancestors and the Domestication of Death." *Man* 19 (1984): 133–48.

Glück, Louise. *Ararat.* New York: Ecco, 1990.

——. *Descending Figure.* New York: Ecco, 1980.

Goodwin, E. Marvin. *Black Migration in American from 1915 to 1960: An Uneasy Exodus.* Lewiston, NY: Mellon, 1990.

Graves, A. J. *Woman in America: Being an Examination into the Moral and Intellectual Condition of American Female Society.* New York: Harper, 1843.

Gray, Janet. "Passing as Fact: Mollie E. Lambert and Mary Eliza Tucker Lambert Meet as Racial Modernity Dawns." *Representations* 64 (November 1998): 99–133.

Grimké, Angelina Weld. "Beware Lest He Awakes." *Selected Works of Angelina Weld Grimké.* Ed. Carolivia Herron. New York: Oxford UP, 1991. 118–20.

——. "Greenness." Cullen, *Caroling Dusk* 36–37.

Gunning, Sandra. *Race, Rape, and Lynching: The Red Record of American Literature.* New York: Oxford UP, 1996.

Harper, Frances Ellen Watkins. *Iola Leroy; or, Shadows Uplifted.* Philadelphia: Garrigues, 1893.

Harper, Michael S. *Images of Kin: New and Selected Poems.* Urbana: U of Illinois P, 1977.

Harper, Philip. *Are We Not Men? Masculinity, Anxiety, and the Problem of African-American Identity.* New York: Oxford UP, 1996.

Hayford, Gladys Casely. "The Palm Wine Seller." Kerlin 288–89.

——. "A Poem." *Opportunity* 7 (July 1929): 220.

Heard, Josephine D. (Henderson). "Mother." *Morning Glories.* Philadelphia, 1890. 25. Rpt. in Sherman, vol. 4.

Henderson, Mae Gwendolyn. "Speaking in Tongues: Dialogics, Dialectics, and the Black Woman Writer's Literary Tradition." *Reading Black, Reading Feminist: A Critical Anthology.* Ed. Henry Louis Gates Jr. New York: Meridian, 1990. 116–42.

Henderson, Stephen. *Understanding the New Black Poetry: Black Speech and Music as Poetic References.* New York: William Morrow, 1973.

Hermione. "How Do You Like the City?" *Ladies' Repository, and Gatherings of the West* 7.2 (1842): 53.

——. "My Heart Is in My Forest Home." *Ladies' Repository, and Gatherings of the West* 7 (1842): 78.

Hernton, Calvin C. *The Sexual Mountain and Black Women Writers: Adventures in Sex, Literature, and Real Life.* New York: Anchor, 1987.

Herrmann, Emily. "Dusk." *Godey's Magazine and Lady's Book* 44 (1850): 12.

Hoagland, Everett. "love Child—a black aesthetic." Randall 312.

Holloway, Karla F. C. *Moorings & Metaphors: Figures of Culture and Gender in Black Women's Literature*. New Brunswick: Rutgers UP, 1992.

hooks, bell. "Eating the Other." *Black Looks: Race and Representation*. Boston: South End, 1992. 21–39.

———. *Feminist Theory: From Margin to Center*. Boston: South End, 1984.

———. "Loving Blackness as Political Resistance." hooks, *Yearning*.

———. "Selling Hot Pussy." *Black Looks: Race and Representation*. Boston: South End, 1992. 61–77.

———. *Salvation: Black People and Love*. New York: Harper Perennial, 2001.

———. *Sisters of the Yam: Black Women and Self-Discovery*. Boston: South End, 1993.

———. *Yearning: Race, Gender, and Cultural Politics*. Toronto: Between-the-Lines, 1990. Boston: South End.

Houston, Virginia. "Query." *Opportunity* 8 (September 1930): 264.

Howat, John K. *American Paradise: The World of the Hudson River School*. New York: Metropolitan Museum of Art, 1987.

Hughes, Langston. "Mother to Son." *Selected Poems of Langston Hughes*. New York: Knopf, 1990. 187.

Hull, Gloria T. *Color, Sex, and Poetry: The Women Writers of the Harlem Renaissance*. Bloomington: Indiana UP, 1987.

Hull, Gloria T., Patricia Bell Scott, and Barbara Smith, eds. *All the Women Are White, All the Blacks Are Men, but Some of Us Are Brave: Black Women's Studies*. Old Westbury, NY: Feminist, 1982.

Imani, Nia Na. "My Man." *Journal of Black Poetry* 1.16 (Summer 1972): 80.

Ione. "The Sailor Boy." *Ladies' Companion and Literary Expositor* 15 (1841): 230.

Irigaray, Luce. *Sexes and Genealogy*. Trans. Gillian C. Gill. New York: Columbia UP, 1993.

Irving, Isabel. "To My Little Edward." *Godey's Magazine and Lady's Book* 46 (1853): 63.

J.J.A. "A Mother's Pride." *Ladies' Companion and Literary Expositor* 4–6 (1836): 134.

J.T.P. "The Homebound Ship." *Ladies' Companion and Literary Expositor* 9 (1838): 72.

Jacobs, Harriet. *Incidents in the Life of a Slave Girl. Told by Herself*. Ed. Lydia Marie Child. Boston. 1861.

Jefferson, Thomas. *Notes on the State of Virginia*. Chapel Hill: U of North Carolina P, 1955.

Johnson, Georgia Douglas. "The Heart of a Woman." *The Heart of a Woman*. Boston: Cornhill, 1918. 13.

———. "Ivy." *The Selected Works of Georgia Douglas Johnson*. Ed. Claudia Tate. New York: Macmillan, 1997. 223.

———. "Love's Tendril." *The Selected Works of Georgia Douglas Johnson*. Ed. Claudia Tate. New York: Macmillan, 1997. 73.

———. "My Son." *Crisis* 29 (November 1924): 28.

———. "Peace." Kerlin 61.

———. "Question." *Bronze: A Book of Verse*. Boston: Brimmer, 1922. 151

———. "Shall I Say, 'My Son, You're Branded'?" *Bronze: A Book of Verse*. Boston: Brimmer, 1922. 121.

Johnson, James Weldon. "O Black and Unknown Bards." Randall 42.

———. *The Book of American Negro Poetry: Chosen and Edited with an Essay on the Negro's Creative Genius*. New York: Harcourt, Brace, 1922.

Johnson, Mae Smith. "To My Grandmother." Kerlin 305–6.

Johnson, Maggie Pogue. "De Men Folks ob Today." *Virginia Dreams: Lyrics for the Idle Hour, Tales of the Time Told in Rhyme*. N.p.: n.p., 1910. 43–44. Sherman, vol. 4.

———. "Old Maid's Soliloquy." *Virginia Dreams: Lyrics for the Idle Hour, Tales of the Time Told in Rhyme*. N.p.: n.p., 1910. 9–11. Sherman, vol. 4.

———. Preface. *Virginia Dreams: Lyrics for the Idle Hour, Tales of the Time Told in Rhyme*. N.p.: n.p., 1910. 5.

———. "What's Mo' Temptin' to the Palate." *Virginia Dreams: Lyrics for the Idle Hour, Tales of the Time Told in Rhyme*. N.p.: n.p., 1910. 29–30. Sherman, vol. 4.

———. "When Daddy Cums from Wuk." *Virginia Dreams: Lyrics for the Idle Hour, Tales of the Time Told in Rhyme*. N.p.: n.p., 1910. 7–8. Sherman, vol. 4.

Jordan, June. "The Difficult Miracle of Black Poetry in America; Or, Something Like a Sonnet for Phillis Wheatley." Massachusetts Review. 27.2 (Summer 1986): 252–62.

———. *Naming Our Destiny: New and Selected Poems.* New York: Thunder's Mouth, 1989.

———. *Passion: New Poems 1977–1980.* Boston: Beacon, 1980.

Joyce, Joyce Ann. "The Aesthetic of E. Ethelbert Miller." *Warriors, Conjurers and Priests: Defining African-Centered Literary Criticism.* Encontro 1:1 (1996): 18 pars. Latin American Studies Center. <http://www.lasc.umd.edu/publications/encontro/lit/em05E.htm>. Accessed September 25, 2006.

Judy, Ronald A. T. "Untimely Intellectuals and the University." *boundary 2* 27.1 (2000): 121–33.

Keeling, John. "Paul Dunbar and the Mask of Dialect." Southern Literary Journal 25.2 (Spring 1993): 24–38.

Kerber, Linda. "Separate Spheres, Female Worlds, Woman's Place: The Rhetoric of Women's History." *Journal of American History* 75.1 (1988): 9–39.

Kerlin, Robert Thomas. *Negro Poets and Their Poems.* Washington, DC: Associated Publishers, 1935.

Knight, Etheridge. "Cell Song." *The Essential Etheridge Knight.* Pittsburgh: U of Pittsburgh P, 1986. 9.

———. "Hard Rock Returns to Prison from the Hospital for the Criminal Insane." *The Essential Etheridge Knight.* Pittsburgh: U of Pittsburgh P, 1986. 7.

———. "Rehabilitation & Treatment in the Prisons of America." *The Essential Etheridge Knight.* Pittsburgh: U of Pittsburgh P, 1986. 114.

———. "The Warden Said to Me the Other Day." *The Essential Etheridge Knight.* Pittsburgh: U of Pittsburgh P, 1986. 20.

Kofie, Nelson F. *Race, Class, and the Struggle for Neighborhood in Washington, D.C.* New York: Garland, 1999.

Larrington, Carol, ed. *The Feminist Companion to Mythology.* London: Pandora, 1992.

Latham, Angela. *Posing a Threat: Flappers, Chorus Girls, and Other Brazen Performers of the American 1920s.* Hanover, NH: Wesleyan UP, 2000.

Lewis, David Levering. *W. E. B. Du Bois—Biography of a Race, 1868–1919.* New York: Holt, 1993.

———. *When Harlem Was in Vogue.* New York: Vintage, 1981.

Linden, Mrs. Henry. "I Am as Happy as a Queen on Her Throne." *Autobiography and Poems.* Springfield, OH: n.p., n.d. 23. Sherman, vol. 4.

Lorde, Audre. *The Black Unicorn.* New York: Norton, 1978.

———. "From the House of Yemanja." Lorde, *The Black Unicorn* 6–7.

———. "An Open Letter to Mary Daly." Lorde, *Sister Outsider* 66–71.

———. "Poetry Is Not a Luxury." Lorde, *Sister Outsider* 36–39.

———. "Scar." Lorde, *The Black Unicorn* 48–50.

———. *Sister Outsider: Essays and Speeches.* Trumansburg, NY: Crossing, 1984.

———. "Seasoning." Lorde, *The Black Unicorn* 35.

———. "Uses of the Erotic: The Erotic as Power." Lorde, *Sister Outsider* 53–59.

———. "A Woman Speaks." Lorde, *The Black Unicorn* 4.

Loud, Marguerite St. Leon. "The Deserted Homestead." May 193–95.

Major, Clarence. *The New Black Poetry.* New York: International Publishers, 1969.

Malva. "The Wife to Her Soldier Husband." *Godey's Magazine and Lady's Book* 70 (1865): 45.

May, Caroline, ed. *The American Female Poets: With Biographical and Critical Notices.* Philadelphia: Lindsay and Blakiston, 1853.

McDowell, Deborah E. *"The Changing Same": Black Women's Literature, Criticism, and Theory.* Bloomington: Indiana UP, 1975.

M'Donald, Mary N. "To Lizzie." May 376.

Mercer, Kobena. *Welcome to the Jungle: New Positions in Black Cultural Studies.* New York: Routledge, 1994.

Miller, Angela. *The Empire of the Eye: Landscape Representation and American Cultural Politics, 1825–1875.* Ithaca: Cornell UP, 1993.

———. "Everywhere and Nowhere: The Making of the National Landscape." *American Literary History* 22 (1992): 207–27.

Montefiore, Jan. *Feminism and Poetry: Language, Experience, Identity in Women's Writing.* New York: Pandora, 1987.

Moorer, Lizelia Augusta Jenkins. "What We Teach at Claflin." *Prejudice Unveiled, and Other Poems.* Boston: Roxburgh, 1907. 124–26. Sherman, vol. 3.

Morris, Margaret Kissam. "Audre Lorde: Textual Authority and the Embodied Self." *Frontiers: A Journal of Women Studies* 23:1 (2002). 168–88.

Mortimer, Lelia. "Anna's Cottage." *Godey's Magazine and Lady's Book* 45 (1852): 285.

Moss, Thylias. *Small Congregations.* Hopewell, NJ: Ecco, 1993.

Neal, Alice B. "My Own Fireside." *Godey's Magazine and Lady's Book* 42 (1851): 75.

Neal, Mary. "My Lost Darling—A Song." *Godey's Magazine and Lady's Book* 46 (1853): 26.

Nederveen Pieterse, Jan. *White on Black: Images of Africa and Blacks in Western Popular Culture.* New Haven: Yale UP, 1992.

Nelson, Alice Dunbar. "I Sit and Sew." Kerlin 145–46.

———. "Violets." Kerlin 55.

Nelson, Claudia. *Boys Will Be Girls: The Feminine Ethic and British Children's Fiction, 1857–1917.* New Brunswick: Rutgers UP, 1991.

Newsome, Marry Effie Lee. "Pansy." Cullen, *Caroling Dusk* 56.

Novak, Barbara. *Nature and Culture: American Landscape and Painting, 1825–1875.* New York: Oxford UP, 1980.

Olian, JoAnne, ed. *80 Godey's Full-Color Fashion Plates (1838–1880).* Mineola, NY: Dover, 1998.

Olds, Sharon. *The Dead and the Living.* New York: Knopf, 1984.

———. *The Father.* New York: Knopf, 1992.

———. *The Gold Cell.* New York: Knopf, 1987.

Osgood, Frances S. "Happiness Lost and Found." *Ladies' Companion and Literary Expositor* 14 (1841): 226.

Ostriker, Alicia. *Stealing the Language: The Emergence of Women's Poetry in America.* Boston: Beacon, 1986.

Parke, H. Merran. "My Home." *Godey's Magazine and Lady's Book* 46 (1853): 42.

Parkinson, M. Y. "The Mariner of Life." *Ladies' Repository, and Gatherings of the West* 10.11 (November 1850):376.

Perrault, Jeanne. "'That the pain be not wasted': Audre Lorde and the Written Self." *Auto/ Biography Studies* 3.2 (1988): 1.

Piercy, Marge. *My Mother's Body.* New York: Knopf, 1985.

———. *What Are Big Girls Made Of?* New York: Knopf, 1997.

Popel, Esther. "Blasphemy—American Style." *Opportunity* 12 (December 1931): 368.

———. "Flag Salute." *Crisis* 41 (August 1932): 231.

Porter, Ann E. "Going to School." *Godey's Magazine and Lady's Book* 46 (1853): 67.

———. "The First Born." *Godey's Magazine and Lady's Book* 44 (1850): 356.

R.H. "Lines on an Infant Sleeping." *Ladies' Companion and Literary Expositor* 14 (1841): 4.

Randall, Dudley, ed. *Black Poetry: A Supplement to Anthologies Which Exclude Black Poets.* Detroit: Broadside, 1969.

Razafkeriefo, Andrea. "The Negro Woman." Kerlin 301–2.

Richings, G. F. *Evidences of Progress among Colored People.* Philadelphia: Ferguson, 1902.

Roberts, Mary Louise. "True Womanhood Revisited." *Journal of Women's History* 14.1 (2002): 150–55.

Robinson, Sandy. "I Had to Be Told." *Journal of Black Poetry* 1.13 (Winter–Spring 1970): 34.

Robinson, William Henry. *Early Black American Poets: Selections with Biographical and Critical Introductions.* Dubuque, IA: Brown, 1969.

Rodgers, Carolyn. "I Have Been Hungry." *How I Got Ovah: New and Selected Poems.* Garden City, NY: Anchor Press/ Doubleday, 1975. 49.

———. "It is Deep." *Songs of a Blackbird.* Chicago: Third World, 1969. 12–13.

———. *The Black Heart as Ever Green.* New York: Anchor Press/Doubleday, 1978.

———. "The Last M.F." *Songs of a Black Bird.* Chicago: Third World, 1969. 37–38.

———. *Morning Glory.* Chicago: Eden, 1989.

———. "Some Me of Beauty." *How I Got Ovah: New and Selected Poems.* Garden City, NY: Anchor Press/Doubleday, 1975.

———. *A Train Called Judah.* Chicago: Eden, 1996.

———. "U Name This One." *Songs of a Blackbird.* Chicago: Third World, 1969. 23.

———. "Yuh Lookin GOOD." Randall 266.

Romaine, Anna L. "Home in the Rain." *Godey's Magazine and Lady's Book* 60 (1860): 349.

Romero, Lora. *Home Fronts: Domesticity and Its Critics in the Antebellum United States.* Durham: Duke UP, 1997.

Rowell, Charles H. "Above the Wind: An Interview with Audre Lorde." *Callaloo* 23.1 (2000): 52–63.

Royster, Jacqueline Jones. *Labor of Love, Labor of Sorrow: Black Women, Work, and the Family from Slavery to the Present.* New York: Basic Books, 1985.

Russell, Sandi. *Render Me My Song: African-American Women Writers from Slavery to the Present.* New York: St. Martin's, 1990.

Ryan, Mary P. *The Cradle of the Middle Class: The Family in Oneida County, New York, 1790–1865.* New York: Cambridge UP, 1981.

Salmonson, Jessica A. *The Encyclopedia of Amazons: Women Warriors from Antiquity to the Modern Era.* New York: Anchor Books, 1992.

Sanchez, Sonia. "black magic." Sanchez, *Home Coming* 12.

———. *A Blues Book for Blue Black Magical Women.* Detroit: Broadside, 1973.

———. *Home Coming.* Detroit: Broadside, 1969

———. "Introduction of Toni Morrison, and Others, on the Occasion of the Publication of Her Book *Race-ing Justice, En-Gendering Power: Essays on Anita Hill, Clarence Thomas, and the Construction of Social Reality.*" *Wounded in the House of a Friend.* Boston: Beacon, 1995. 54.

———. "Memorial: 3. rev pimps." Sanchez, *Home Coming* 31.

———. "to all brothers." Sanchez, *Home Coming* 10.

———. "to all sisters." Sanchez, *Home Coming* 27.

Sapphire. *American Dreams.* New York: High Risk Books, 1994.

Sawicki, Jane. *Disciplining Foucault: Feminism, Power, and the Body.* New York: Routledge, 1991.

Scruggs, Charles. "'All Dressed Up but No Place to Go': The Black Writer and His Audience during the Harlem Renaissance." *American Literature* 48 (1977): 543–63.

Shange, Ntozake. *For Colored Girls Who Have Considered Suicide When the Rainbow Is Enuf.* New York: Macmillan, 1976.

———. *The Love Space Demands.* New York: St. Martin's, 1991.

———. "nappy edges." *Nappy Edges.* New York: St. Martin's, 1978. 3.

———. "Oh, I'm 10 Months Pregnant." *A Daughter's Geography.* New York: St. Martin's, 1983. 31–32.

———. "resurrection of the daughter." *Nappy Edges.* New York: St. Martin's, 1978. 90–92.

———. *Ridin' the Moon in Texas: Word Paintings.* New York: St. Martin's, 1987.

———. "We Need a God Who Bleeds Now." *A Daughter's Geography.* New York: St. Martin's, 1983. 51.

Sheffield, Carole. "Sexual Terrorism." *Women: A Feminist Perspective.* Ed. Jo Freeman. New York: McGraw-Hill, 1994. 1–21.

Sherman, Joan R., ed. *Collected Black Women's Poetry.* 4 vols. New York: Oxford UP, 1988.

Sigourney, Lydia H. "Death of an Infant." *Selected Poems.* 11th ed. Philadelphia: Parry and McMillan, 1856. 30–31.

———. "Evening at Home: Written in Early Youth." *Selected Poems.* 11th ed. Philadelphia: Parry and McMillan, 1856. 39–41.

———. "Recollections of an Aged Pastor." *Ladies' Companion and Literary Expositor* 5 (1836): 103.

———. "Sleeping Child." *Ladies' Repository, and Gatherings of the West* 5 (1842): 283.

———. "The Sleeping Infant." *Ladies' Companion and Literary Expositor* 15 (1841): 171.

Sinclair, John. "Breakthrough." *The New Black Poetry.* Ed. Clarence Major. New York: International Publishers, 1969. 114.

Smith, Barbara. "Toward a Black Feminist Criticism." *The Truth That Never Hurts: Writings on Race, Gender, and Freedom.* New Brunswick: Rutgers UP, 1889. 3–21.

Smith, Effie Waller. "The Bachelor Girl." *Collected Works of Effie Waller Smith*. Ed. Henry Louis Gates. New York: Oxford UP, 1991. 233.

Smith, Elizabeth Oakes (Seba). "The Ministry of Childhood" *Ladies' Companion and Literary Expositor* 10 (1839): 163.

Smith, Theophus H. *Conjuring Culture: Biblical Formations of Black Culture*. New York: Oxford UP, 1974.

Smitherman, Geneva. *Talkin' and Testifyin': The Language of Black America*. Boston: Houghton Mifflin, 1977. Detroit: Wayne State UP, 1986.

"Song of the Spirit of Life." *Godey's Magazine and Lady's Book* 46 (1853): 165.

Spencer, Anne. "Creed." Cullen, *Caroling Dusk* 51.

St. Armand, Barton Levi. *Emily Dickinson and Her Culture: The Soul's Society*. Cambridge: Cambridge UP, 1984.

Strickland, W. F. "Female Influence." *Ladies' Repository, and Gatherings of the West* 6 (1846): 132–33.

Sudbury, Julia. "Celling Black Bodies: Black Women in the Global Prison Industrial Complex." *Feminist Review* 80 (2005): 162–79.

Thompson, Clara Ann. "The Easter Bonnet." Clara Thompson, *Songs from the Wayside* 91. Sherman, vol. 2.

———. "Johnny's Pet Superstition." Clara Thompson, *Songs from the Wayside* 7. Sherman, vol. 2.

———. "A Lullaby." Clara Thompson, *Songs from the Wayside* 63. Sherman, vol. 2.

———. "Mrs. Johnson Objects." Clara Thompson, *Songs from the Wayside* 17. Sherman, vol. 2.

———. *Songs from the Wayside*. Rossmoyne, OH, 1908. 63.

Thompson, Priscilla Jane. "An Afternoon Gossip." Priscilla Jane Thompson, *Gleanings of Quiet Hours* 39–44. Sherman, vol. 2.

———. "The Favorite Slave's Story." Priscilla Jane Thompson, *Gleanings of Quiet Hours* 49–64. Sherman, vol. 2.

———. "Freedom at McNealy's." Priscilla Jane Thompson, *Gleanings of Quiet Hours* 65–69. Sherman, vol. 2.

———. *Gleanings of Quiet Hours*. Rossmoyne, OH, 1907.

———. "The Husband's Return." Priscilla Jane Thompson, *Gleanings of Quiet Hours* 13–16. Sherman, vol. 2.

———. "Insulted." Priscilla Jane Thompson, *Gleanings of Quiet Hours* 75. Sherman, vol. 2.

———. "The Old Freedman." Priscilla Jane Thompson, *Gleanings of Quiet Hours* 97–99. Sherman, vol. 2.

Thompson, Robert Farris. *Flash of the Spirit: African and Afro-American Art and Philosophy*. New York: Vintage, 1984.

Ullman, Leslie. Rev. of *Quilting: Poems, 1987–1990*, by Lucille Clifton. *Kenyon Review* 14.3 (Summer 1992): 178–80.

Van Deburg, William L., ed. *Modern Black Nationalism: From Marcus Garvey to Louis Farrakhan*. New York: New York UP, 1997.

Walker, Alice. *In Search of Our Mothers' Gardens: Womanist Prose*. San Diego: Harcourt Brace Jovanovich, 1983.

———. *Revolutionary Petunias & Other Poems*. New York: Harcourt, Brace, 1973.

Walker, Margaret. *For My People*. New Haven: Yale UP, 1942.

Washington, Mary Helen. Introduction. *Black-Eyed Susans: Classic Stories by and about Black Women*. Ed. Mary Helen Washington. Garden City, NY: Anchor, 1975. xxxii.

———. "'The Darkened Eye Restored': Notes Toward a Literary History of Black Women." *Reading Black, Reading Feminist: A Critical Anthology*. Ed. Henry Louise Gates, Jr. New York: Penguin, 1990. 30–43.

Watkins, Lucian B. "Ebon Maid and Girl of Mine." Kerlin 271–72.

Weakley, Sarah A. "To My Sleeping Babe." *Ladies' Repository, and Gatherings of the West* 7 (1842): 373.

Wells, Ida B. "Southern Horrors: Lynch Law in All Its Phases." *Southern Horrors and Other Writings: The Anti-Lynching Campaign of Ida B. Wells, 1892–1900*. Ed. Jacqueline Jones Royster. Boston: Bedford Books, 1997.

Welter, Barbara. "The Cult of True Womanhood, 1820–1860." *American Quarterly* 18 (1966): 151–75.

Wentworth, Mrs. M. E. "Storm in the Harbor." *Ladies' Repository, and Gatherings of the West* 7 (1842): 58.

Weston, Amanda. "The Summer Shower." *Ladies' Repository, and Gatherings of the West* 7 (1842): 313.

White, Newman Ivey, and Walter Clinton Jackson, eds. *An Anthology of Verse by American Negroes.* Durham, NC: Trinity College P, 1924.

Wilson, Mrs. C. B. "The Three Gifts." *Godey's Magazine and Lady's Book* 18 (1839): 158.

Wilson, Sondra K., ed. *The Crisis Reader: Stories, Poetry, and Essays from the N.A.A.C.P.'s Crisis Magazine.* New York: Modern Library, 1999.

Wirth, Thomas, ed. *Gay Rebel of the Harlem Renaissance: Selections from the Work of Richard Bruce Nugent.* Durham: Duke UP, 2002.

Withers, Martha G. "My Flower." *Godey's Magazine and Lady's Book* 43 (1851): 116.

Yaeger, Patricia. *Honey-Mad Women: Emancipatory Strategies in Women's Writing.* New York: Columbia UP, 1988.

Zubena (Cynthia M. Conley). "To My Mate (Wherever He May Be)." *Journal of Black Poetry* 1.13 (Winter–Spring 1970): 55.

INDEX

New Negro Movement. *See* Harlem Renaissance

New Womanhood, 24–25, 168n4

Newsome, Mary Effie Lee, 77, 174n12; "Pansy," 75

Novak, Barbara, *Nature and Culture: American Landscape and Painting, 1825–1875,* 167n10, 167n11

novel, Black women's 3, 25–26, 168n5, 169n8, 169n9

O

Olds, Sharon, 126; *The Dead and the Living,* 181n12; *The Gold Cell,* 181n12; *The Father,* 181n12

Orishas. *See* Dahomey; Lorde, Audre: "From the House of Yemanja"

Ostriker, Alicia, *Stealing the Language,* 121, 165n1, 167n15, 178n1

P

pastoral tradition, 4, 166n8; in classical literature, 4; and True Womanhood, 5–18, 47–49, 51, 126, 127, 154; in the United States, 4, 167n12

Piercy, Marge, 126; *What Are Big Girls Made Of?,* 181n12; *My Mother's Body,* 181n12

Play and playfulness, as transgression, 161–63, 184n36

Popel, Esther, 65; "Flag Salute," 65–68; "Blasphemy—American Style," 65, 68–69

Porter, Anne E., "The First Born," 12

Prince, Mary, 168n5, *The History of Mary Prince: A West Indian Slave,* 25, 168n5, 177n39

R

R. H., "Lines on an Infant Sleeping," 12

Razafkeriefo, Andrea, "The Negro Woman," 84–86, 87, 88

reconstruction, 19, 23, 24, 54, 97, and post-Reconstruction, 19, 21, 23–52, 54–56, 60, 77, 96, 98, 110, 168n1, 170n15, 171n22, 172n2, 172–73n5, 173n10, 177n39, 179n12

Richardson, Samuel, *Clarissa,* 78

Robinson, Sandy, "I Had to Be Told," 101, 102

Rodgers, Carolyn, 115, 118, 122, 123, 125, 181n4; "The Black Heart as Ever Green," 123–24, 181n5; and Christianity; *The Heart as Ever Green,* 123, 181n5; *How I Got Ovah,* 181n7; "I Have Been Hungry," 113; "It Is Deep," 181n7; "The Last M.F.,"

106, 110, 112; *Morning Glory,* 123; "Some Me of Beauty," 95; *Songs of a Blackbird,* 181n7; *A Train Called Judah,* 123–24; "U Name This One," 116–17, 118; "Yuh Lookin GOOD," 106–8, 180n22

Rowell, Charles, "Above the Wind," 155, 183n29

S

Sanchez, Sonia, 114, 118, 122, 123, 125, 149, 181n3; "black magic," 101–3; *A Blues Book for Blue Black Magical Women,* 123, 124; "Introduction of Toni Morrison, and Others, on the Occasion of the Publication of Her Book *Race-ing Justice, En-Gendering Power: Essays on Anita Hill, Clarence Thomas, and the Construction of Social Reality,*" 124–25; "Memorial: 3 rev pimps," 110, 111–12, 115, 117–18, 180n21; "to all sisters," 112, 114–15; "to all brothers," 114, 115, 180n21; "Poem at Thirty," 149–50, 51; *Homecoming,* 180n21

Sapphire, *American Dreams,* 126

Schomburg Center for Research in Black Culture, 173n10

Schomburg, Arthur, 173n10

Science, discourse of, 145, 155, 161

Scott, Patricia Bell. *See* Hull, Gloria T., *All The Women Are White, All the Blacks Are Men, But Some of Us Are Brace: Black Women's Studies*

separate spheres, ideology of, 9, 19, 31, 44, 56, 169n9, 176n26; public/private split, 9, 18, 31, 40, 41, 43, 44–51, 56, 73, 129, 171n22

sex and sexuality, 174n17, 175n20, 179n13, 181n9. *See also* woman, Black, representation of: as desiring subject

sexism, 106, 124

Shange, Ntozake, 120, 127–29, 160, 161–62, 163; *A Daughter's Geography,* 120, 130, 134; *For Colored Girls Who Have Considered Suicide When the Rainbow is Enuf,* 129–30, 178n5; *The Love Space Demands,* 130; *Nappy Edges,* 130–31, 163; "Oh, I'm 10 Months Pregnant," 134, 135–36; "resurrection of the daughter," 131–34, 135; *Ridin' the Moon in Texas,* 130; "We Need a God Who Bleeds Now," 134–35

"Shout All Over God's Heaven," 90, 177n40. *See also* spirituals

Sigourney, Lydia H., "Recollections of an Aged Pastor," 17

simultaneity, paradigm of, 129, 156

Inventing Black Women was designed and typeset on a Macintosh computer system using InDesign software. The body text is set in 9.75/14 Warnock Pro and display type is set in Lithos Pro. This book was designed and typeset by Kelly Gray and manufactured by Thomson-Shore, Inc.